The Dakota War

The Dakota War

The United States Army Versus the Sioux, 1862–1865

by
Micheal Clodfelter

McFarland & Company, Inc., Publishers
Jefferson, North Carolina, and London

British Library Cataloguing-in-Publication data are available

Library of Congress Cataloguing-in-Publication Data

Clodfelter, Micheal, 1946–
    The Dakota war : the United States Army versus the Sioux,
1862–1865 / by Micheal Clodfelter.
      p. cm.
    Includes bibliographical references and index.
    ISBN 0-7864-0419-1 (library binding : 50# alkaline paper)
    1. Dakota Indians—Wars, 1862–1865. I. Title.
    E83.86.C56   1998
    973.7—dc21
                                      97-39147
                                       CIP

Manufactured in the United States of America

*McFarland & Company, Inc., Publishers
  Box 611, Jefferson, North Carolina 28640*

To all the forgotten warriors on both sides
of the Dakota War

and

To my wife, Rena Katherine,
who makes all things possible.

Acknowledgments

Though this narrative is based largely on original sources—particularly on the indispensable official records of *The War of the Rebellion*—I was greatly aided in my overall understanding of the big picture of the Indian wars in the upper Great Plains by Robert Hahn Jones's *The Civil War in the Northwest*. His groundbreaking study is invaluable in its military, political, and administrative detail of both the Santee uprising in Minnesota and the Sibley-Sully campaigns in the Dakotas. I also appreciate greatly his permission to reprint the three superb maps from his book.

My research for this book would have been impossible without the help of the staff and the resources of the state historical societies of Minnesota, South Dakota, and North Dakota. Most particularly, I would like to thank Todd Strand, photo archivist, and James A. Davis, reference specialist, of the State Historical Society of North Dakota, as well as Donna Koepp, librarian at the Government Documents and Map Library of the University of Kansas.

Finally, my heartfelt thanks to my mother, Betty, and my wife, Rena, for their careful reading and correcting of the manuscript, and to my son, Thomas, for his help with the index. This book was truly a family effort.

Also, thanks to my friend and native South Dakotan, Curt Just, for being the first to point me along the path of "Sam Brown's Ride."

Table of Contents

"The white men are like locusts when they fly so thick that the whole sky is a snowstorm."
Chief Little Crow of the Santee Dakota
August 18, 1862

"Those fellows can whip the devil and all his angels."
Brigadier General Alfred Sully
August 8, 1864

Introduction

Whitestone Hill and Killdeer Mountain: These names should have the same familiar ring as Fetterman, Wagon Box, Washita, Rosebud, and even Little Bighorn. Sibley and Sully, the commanders in blue who fought the Dakota battles, should be no less remembered than Crook, Miles, Mackenzie, and even Custer. The name of Wahpekute Sioux renegade leader Inkpaduta should be no less synonymous with frenzied brutality and implacable resistance to the encroachment of the white race than that of Geronimo. Yet these battles and the men who fought them are lost in the fog of history. Why?

The obscurity of the violent events in North Dakota in the early 1860s may be partly explained by our national tendency to forget, bury, or ignore much of our history. Generally, an event is widely remembered only if it is encrusted with legend, enshrined as a metaphor for our national virtue (or, for the revisionists, our national shame), or either so unequivocally fabulous or ripely scandalous that it helps satiate our passion for either the sacred or the profane.

Another reason the Dakota battles are lost to national memory lies in their timing and location. In 1863 and 1864, the eyes of America were riveted on the Southeast, where the Civil War was playing out to its bloody end. A fracas on the faraway frontier hardly seemed worth a glance. The battles of Whitestone Hill and Killdeer Mountain, which engaged thousands of combatants on both sides and laid low hundreds of warriors, red and white, were greater in scope, intensity, and bloodshed than almost all Indian battles fought in the West (the exceptions being the Little Bighorn and a few encounters, such as Sand Creek and Wounded Knee, that were more massacres of Indian noncombatants than pitched battles). But the Dakota battles were mere skirmishes compared to the great contemporary bloodlettings on the fields of Pennsylvania and Virginia. With tens of thousands dying at Chancellorsville and Gettysburg, Chickamauga, the Wilderness, and Cold Harbor, the deaths of a few hundred Sioux and a few score frontier volunteers were hardly noticed.

By contrast, the ghastly events in Minnesota in the year before the Dakota Campaigns began received a great deal of horrified attention, and those events became part of the nation's historical memory. But the wholesale massacre of up to eight hundred white civilians in a matter of a few weeks by bands of "red savages" would naturally evoke the rage and scrutiny of a nation whose deepest fear, since colonial days, had always been the possibility of Indian attacks. Even in the midst of the country's greatest crisis and conflict, a red uprising of such scope and barbarity—it was probably the bloodiest short-term massacre of white settlers by American Indians since the founding of the republic—demanded recognition, retribution, and remembrance. Even with Second Manassas, Antietam, and the Emancipation Proclamation, the nation was very much aware of the Minnesota Massacre. Today, historians, students of Western history and Indian warfare, and citizens of Minnesota, retain the memory of that awful August of 1862, when an American state came close to destruction at the hands of its original inhabitants. But the campaigns against the Sioux in the Dakota Territory from 1863 to 1865, which were a direct consequence of the Minnesota Massacre, were neither horrifying enough nor decisive enough to hold the attention of a nation absorbed in its greatest internal struggle. As a result, they are little remembered today.

With the conclusion of the Civil War, the West once again drew the nation's attention, as well as its adventurers, into its vast, inviting, but always dangerous spaces. And the inevitable conflict between red and white, between "the progressive and the primitive," became part of this almost mythic lore, enlarged upon by sensation-seeking journalists, dime novels, Wild West shows, and later by Hollywood. Thus, Crook and Custer, Crazy Horse and Cochise, the Seventh Cavalry and the Ogalala Sioux, the Little Bighorn and Adobe Walls became as much a part of America's myth as of its history. But not Sibley and Sully, Inkpaduta and Little Crow; not the Santee Sioux and the Sixth Iowa Cavalry; not Whitestone Hill and Killdeer Mountain. This volume is an attempt to recover some of that western history and to remind readers of those forgotten battles on the Dakota prairies.

Prologue

Major Albert E. House's command was surrounded and in distinct danger of annihilation. Nearly choking on the heat and dust of a searing September day in the Dakota Territory, the three hundred men from four companies of the Sixth Iowa Cavalry Regiment were ringed by as many as fifteen hundred howling Sioux warriors in the brush and bramble at the foot of Whitestone Hill. The unbloodied Iowa cavalrymen stood firm and resisted the pull of panic, but most of them expected this first battle of their battalion to be their last.

This vanguard of Brigadier General Alfred Sully's 1863 expedition had been dispatched into Dakota to punish the Sioux for their massacre of hundreds of settlers in Minnesota the year before, and House's green battalion had followed the scent of their Indian scouts into this encampment in the southeastern part of present-day North Dakota to encounter far more hostiles than they had anticipated. For weeks the soldiers of Sully's column had searched the dry, brown Dakota prairies without success for the warriors of the Sioux confederacy. Now there were hundreds of Indians on every side of Sully's point battalion, more Indians than any of the Iowa pony soldiers had ever seen before. Some four hundred miles east of and thirteen years prior to the Battle of the Little Bighorn, the men of a volunteer Iowa horse regiment were on the precipice of a catastrophe every bit as overwhelming as that which would strike the Seventh Cavalry Regiment troopers on America's most famous battleground.

House's cavalrymen, dismounted and stitched in a thin blue hem across the dusty robe of the prairie, squinted down the sights of their muskets and carbines and prepared for the rush of fifteen hundred Dakota warriors who would almost certainly swamp their pitiful perimeter. But then instead of the expected twang of arrows catapulting from bows and the sporadic shouts of musketry, an ominous quiet settled over the battlefield. A moment of silence before the storm? The prelude to the final passion of an all-out attack?

Facing eternity one moment, granted a reprieve the next, the men of

3

the Sixth Iowa were startled by a sudden proposal for a parley shouted from
the warrior ranks. Talk, it seemed, would momentarily interrupt the cavalry troopers' countdown to calamity. House accepted the offer of negotiations and walked out from his perimeter to briefly confer with several Dakota
leaders. The major, rather brazenly in view of his command's circumstances,
demanded the Indians' surrender. The Sioux professed only peaceful intentions and insisted that the village hugging the hill called Whitestone housed
no tribesmen hostile to the United States government. The major, however,
put little faith in this protestation of peaceableness, particularly when he
spotted extensive movement behind the Indian lines. Convinced that the
parley was only a diversion to cover preparations for a grand assault, House
broke off the negotiations and returned to his battalion.

Indian participants in the battle would later claim that the activity House
spotted was just women drying meat for the winter, or perhaps preparations
to evacuate the village of women and children in case of a resumption of hostilities. The surrounded soldiers believed otherwise. White veterans of the
Battle of Whitestone Hill later testified that the parley and respite from
combat was a ploy by the Santee Sioux war chief Inkpaduta to give his warriors time to paint and preen themselves for the great victory that was in the
offing—and to allow the women time to prepare a grand feast in celebration.
Just a short time before, House's men had launched a surprise attack on the
Indian village, forcing the natives to defend themselves without benefit of
their ritual preparations. Now they had seen that the attacking battalion was
small in numbers and ripe for annihilation, and so they wanted the opportunity to complete what might become the greatest Sioux victory ever in as
flamboyant and resplendent a fashion as possible. But the adornment of
plumage and paint, the gathering of sacred symbols and lucky charms, the
chanting of a warrior's songs and the pumping of pride, all took time. Thus
the deceit of the parley was needed to give the Indians time to prepare for
victory; the cavalrymen were given time to survive.

Major House had made good use of the lull in the battle. Without
thoroughly scouting the village to determine the size of his target, he had
advanced against the encampment and nearly delivered his men into disaster. But now, granted a second chance by Inkpaduta's decision to allow
vanity to delay victory, the battalion commander took advantage of these
precious minutes and escaped the fate (and, ironically, the immortality) of
Fetterman and Custer by dispatching the battalion guide to Sully's main
column ten miles to the north. Just as the Santee Sioux and their Teton allies,
in all their martial finery, were ready to carry out the rush that would overwhelm House's men, the rest of Sully's brigade arrived on the darkening
scene to deliver a true "cavalry-to-the-rescue" charge that saved the trapped
advance battalion and changed the terms of the ensuing slaughter.

The Battle of Whitestone Hill culminated in a major victory for Sully's command. Though counts vary considerably, between 150 and 300 Santee, Yanktonai and Teton Sioux, including some women and children, were killed. If the larger figure is correct the Indians who died on that North Dakota hill outnumbered the U.S. cavalrymen killed at the Little Bighorn thirteen years later. Although Army casualties were substantial—as many as twenty-two killed and fifty wounded—they were insignificant compared to what they might have been had Sully's main force not reached the battlefield in time to rescue House's beleaguered battalion. Had Inkpaduta not paused to parade his vanity and puff up the prowess of his warriors, the Little Bighorn might today be regarded as the lesser battle, and the name of Inkpaduta and Major Albert House could have been as famous (or infamous) as those of Crazy Horse, Sitting Bull, and George Armstrong Custer. Instead, Whitestone Hill and the men who fought there are largely forgotten.[1]

Minnesota and vicinity, 1862. (From *The Civil War in the Northwest* by Robert H. Jones. Courtesy of Robert H. Jones.)

Part One

The Minnesota War, 1862

1. The Frontier Army

Life on the western frontier was, at best, difficult for all but a very fortunate few. In particular, life was difficult for the men whose duty it was to protect and police that frontier. For eleven dollars a month if he was an infantryman or twelve dollars a month if he was a cavalryman, the enlisted man of the frontier army of the early 1860s lived a life of drudgery and danger, with a raise to seventeen dollars a month the only thing to look forward to, if he lived long enough.[1]

The men who collected this pay and the slightly higher pay of the officer corps numbered only 16,367 at the outbreak of the Civil War. Though this was the authorized strength, because of furloughs, sick leave, detached duty, and, above all, desertion, it was rarely if ever attained. Of the 13,000 or so actually present for duty early in 1861, about two-thirds were assigned to garrisons in the West. Thus about 8,000 men were guarding an area that amounted to half a continent inhabited by about one million potentially hostile natives.[2]

Fortunately for the white settlement of the American West, but unfortunately for the indigenous defense of that vast arena, the Indians there never produced a leader of the stature of Tecumseh, Pontiac, or even Little Turtle to unite the red nations against the invader. At best, factions of two or more tribes might unite to oppose the white man, as with the Sioux, Arapaho, and Northern Cheyenne on the northern plains and the Kiowa, Comanche, and Southern Cheyenne on the southern plains during the wars of the 1860s and 1870s. Sometimes simultaneous, but quite separate, wars might break out in various regions of the West, such as the Plains Indian wars and the Apache wars of the 1860s and 1870s. But more often than not, the regulars and volunteers of the frontier army had to face only isolated and scattered outbreaks by a single tribe or, as was even more often the case, only a part of a tribe, while the majority remained peaceful or even took the side of the white man. The odds were further narrowed because the American soldiers were often aided in their campaigns against hostile concentrations by Indian allies from tribes that were traditional enemies of the hostiles and had never engaged in warfare with the U.S. Army—such as the Crows, Pawnees, and Arikaras of the Plains.

Though Indian fighting was the most exciting of duties assigned to the soldiers of the frontier army, it was certainly not the most common nor even the most hazardous. Life at a frontier post was often very hard and very short. Guard duty, picket duty, and fatigue duty were the norms rather than Indian fighting. Poor pay, poor rations, and poor prospects were the common experiences of the soldier in the West. And a quick death on the battlefield was a far less common end for the blue troopers of the frontier army than a lingering and loathsome death from disease.

Though chroniclers of the Civil War are quick to call attention to the deaths from diseases accounting for two-thirds of the fatal toll of that war and are just as conscientious in compiling deaths by microbes as by bullets in other conflicts, historians of the Indian Wars are strangely reticent in mentioning the awful toll inflicted by sickness on the frontier. It is as if the deaths caused by arrowhead or musket ball were the only deaths that really counted in the campaigns of the army fighting the Indians. But the soldiers who served on the boundary line between red and white cultures knew that their chances of dying from dysentery or consumption were greater than those of succumbing to the thrust of a warrior's lance.

Cholera, dysentery, scurvy from a lack of fresh vegetables, venereal diseases, and respiratory ailments annually inflicted far more casualties than did red warriors. Medical records before, during, and after the Civil War bear out this sad fact. In the first five years after the Mexican War the Medical Department recorded 134,708 cases in an army that averaged 10,000 men and lost 1,835 to the grave. Before the Civil War each soldier took an average of three trips to the hospital each year and one of every thirty-three men died of disease annually. The medical situation improved little after Appomattox. For each 1,000 men in uniform the medical staff, always shorthanded and often assisted by barely competent civilian contract doctors, treated 1,800 cases per year—1,550 were for disease, 250 for wounds or accidental injuries. From each 1,000 treated about thirteen died—eight from disease and five from all other causes, including combat. Sexually transmitted diseases topped the list, with malaria and diseases of the respiratory and digestive tracts close behind.[3]

In this respect, the Dakota campaigns were no different from those of Civil War and other Indian operations. Commanders' reports constantly referred to numerous troopers down with disease and to columns slowed and staggered by sickness. But those commanders, though always concerned with the impact of illness on their ranks, were less than precise in their record keeping. Thus we have only rough estimates of the numbers felled by germs and infections in the course of the prairie campaigns of 1863–65.

The combat branch of the U.S. Army primarily responsible for the defense of the Western frontier was the cavalry. Prior to the Black Hawk Indian War of 1832, the army was almost exclusively an infantry force. Developing a significant cavalry branch was considered by the leaders of the new democratic nation both too expensive and, with its historical echoes of feudal knights and seventeenth–century cavaliers, too aristocratic. That attitude was changed by the failures of the Black Hawk War. This first prairie war witnessed foot soldiers fruitlessly chasing pony-mounted Indians for months until the Sauk and Fox band of Black Hawk was finally caught on the banks of the Bad Axe River. In March 1833 a regiment of dragoons was authorized and ordered to be formed.

For the next two decades dragoon units were parceled out to isolated posts on the Great Plains. In the first years only 500 dragoons were assigned to guard hundreds of thousands of square miles of frontier against Indian nations that could muster as many as 25,000 braves. On long patrols, sometimes as much as 3,000 miles in a summer, the dragoons had to endure a killing heat and meager meals cooked over fires fueled by dried buffalo chips whose smoke either ruined appetites or added flavor to the salt pork or beef jerky, depending on individual tolerances or experience with this frontier cuisine.

In the course of a five-year enlistment, the typical dragoon saw combat only once. Their Plains Indian foes rarely made war in the sense of the white man's view of martial conflict; rather than conduct war in the formal sense, they raided. Although the combined tribes could boast big numbers, they more often fought one another than joined forces against the army. Thus their numbers were almost always far too small to even contemplate fighting in the white man's style of combat—standing in open formation to discharge volleys at one another in a mutual slaughter, a method of battle the Indians considered madness.

The Plains Indians have often been called the finest light cavalry in the world, but their martial limitations were almost as numerous as their capabilities. They were superb horsemen, highly mobile, and able to live off the land like no others. Their endurance was unequaled, they were skilled bowmen, bold and daring, who knew intimately the terrain and took every advantage of it. But they were far more accomplished as raiders than as soldiers, lacked almost all discipline, fought as individuals instead of as units, and had no precepts of command and control. The Plains tribesmen were effective only against relatively small units or poorly trained and armed formations. They were truly the Cossacks of the plains, terrifying for individuals, but no match for properly trained, highly disciplined cavalry troops.

Their greatest liability, the failing that led to their greatest defeats, was that their camps were easily taken by surprise, once they were found, because the Indians consistently neglected such cavalry basics as picket duty and reconnaissance. Time and again the Indians would pay dearly for their failure to carry out the boring but essential duties of posting guards and sending out scouts. Villages were surprised and heavy losses were suffered at Ash Hollow, Whitestone Hill, the Washita River, and Palo Duro Canyon. (Even the Little Bighorn was a tactical case of a large Indian village being the target of a surprise attack, although there Indian numbers and Custer mistakes drastically reversed the usual outcome.)

The occasional surprise attack on an Indian camp aside, most of the time the army was frustrated in its campaigns against the Plains tribes. Usually ten soldiers had to be deployed against each Indian brave for a campaign to enjoy any success (a ratio comparable to that of the guerrilla conflicts of the twentieth century). The infrequent incidents of combat in the course of a typical Indian campaign were usually accidental meeting engagements following months of fruitless patrolling. Then, once battle was joined, the firefight would usually be over in only a few minutes as the Indians, willing to fight only on their terms, broke away from close combat as soon as possible.

On the rare occasions when soldier and brave did clash, the soldier usually had an overwhelming advantage in firepower. Besides their muskets, carbines, and rifles, the frontier soldiers were often supported by light artillery, the decisive weapon in so many battles of the western frontier. The most commonly employed artillery pieces were the Models 1840 and 1841, twelve-pounder mountain howitzers mounted on a "prairie carriage." So often did the mountain howitzer make the vital difference in frontier battles that it could legitimately claim the title of "the gun that won the West."[4]

Despite relatively infrequent combat, many future generals of the Civil War learned their trade in the Indian fighting army of the 1850s. Men who opposed each other in that war, had very often fought earlier beside each other against raiding tribesmen. The army was more of a clan than a major institution in those days, so small that a soldier in a single enlistment might meet or serve under sixty officers and NCOs destined to be generals in the great internal conflict ahead. The pre–Civil War army probably had a higher proportion of well-educated and talented men than any other in American history. Many of them were educated immigrants, seeking a fresh start.

Officially, the army trained each recruit thoroughly before his regular assignment, but the demands of the western frontier, where at least half of the army was stationed, often short-circuited this training cycle and required a rapid transfer of the recruit to the front where he learned his craft on the job. The manpower shortage for officers was just as keen. West Pointers, fresh from four years of schooling in the refinements of Napoleonic warfare, were more than likely to find themselves assigned to some dusty, forlorn prairie or desert post, where they would learn the dirty details of Indian fighting the hard way.

Discipline in this frontier army was rigid and unforgiving. The brutally enforced discipline encouraged desertion, which, in turn, increased the ferocity of the discipline. In a typical year a quarter of the enlisted men tried to desert. Punishment for such an attempt (and also for many lesser infractions) was a flogging with a rawhide whip, which, unlike the British cat-of-nine-tails, could cut a man to ribbons with a few lashes. The modern-day prohibition against officers striking enlisted men was ignored in that era, with officers flailing away with impunity to assert their authority and demonstrate their toughness.

Regardless of, and in part because of, the harsh conditions and discipline they endured, the dragoons carried themselves with a superior air and considered themselves the elite combat arm. Among them were many soldiers who had served as French curiassiers under Napoleon, Hungarian hussars, and Irish veterans of the British army. They also carried their culture with them to the raw-edged West, bringing to remote posts such symbols of eastern civilization as books, musical instruments, newspapers, and theatrical and debate clubs.

Even with these reminders of a more refined life, many soldiers found their existence unendurable in these extended Plains assignments. Alcoholism was epidemic and suicide a way out often taken. Officers and men also had to deal with the same corruption of the civilian government that enraged so many Indians. Scandals involving army rations were nearly as common as those involving Indian annuities. Containers marked "bacon" might prove to be filled with rocks; moldy rations were so common that soldiers resignedly broke off the greener sections and consumed the rest. Men sometimes deliberately committed infractions that they knew would land them in a military prison because conditions in the prisons were thought to be better than those in some frontier posts. Troopers often referred to their barracks, usually only a collection of crude huts erected and filled with men suffering from V.D., cholera, dysentery, and scurvy, as "the government workhouse."[5] Many military posts matched the nearby Indian reservations in squalor and despair.

Indians and soldiers both suffered from swindling traders. While crooked settlers sold shoddy goods at vastly inflated prices to soldiers, other white traders latched upon the money and goods to be distributed to the Indians as annuities in claim for the whiskey and cheap trinkets that the Indians had purchased from them on credit. Many military men blamed the Indian outbreaks on crooks and incompetents in the Indian Bureau, as well as on the intransigence of the government bureaucracy and the stinginess of Congress. The soldiers could well understand and sympathize with the Indians in their dealings with white civilian authority. They were used to months going by, sometimes even more than a year, before their pay arrived, to short or totally missing rations, to bureaucratic bungling and arbitrary authority increasing their suffering. But when the food or money promised in return for the cession of their land did not arrive the Indians, rather than resigning themselves to these injustices as the soldiers had to do, often reacted with indignation that sometimes evolved into warfare.

Although forced to fight the Indians, for whom they often had a certain sympathy since they were both being cheated by and despised by the white civilian community, soldiers also carried on a considerable physical and emotional commerce with the native inhabitants of the Great Plains. Each year the army staged treaty-signing festivals at various posts on the prairie. Chiefs in ornate costumes were awarded fancy medals and good conduct certificates, goods were distributed, and then great feasts, horse races, and even sham battles were staged. And, of course, more territory was signed away. At these festivals and in the normal course of events, there was considerable sexual interplay between soldiers and native women. Fort Stevenson, for example, was considered the best post on the Missouri River because it was overrun with willing squaws, with "plenty of time to make love."[6] Venereal disease was one of the more common ailments afflicting frontier soldiers.

Despite all this peaceful and sometimes passionate interaction between soldiers and Indians, a more common condition between the two was hostility. Central to the culture of the Plains tribes and ingrained in their history and philosophy was the warrior ethos. Boundaries between tribes had rarely been negotiated without prior recourse to war. The introduction of the white settlers to the Plains amounted to, in effect, a new tribe entering the arena of an ancient war. The white intruders, in turn, were used to a history of fighting for land. The two cultures were ultimately irreconcilable. Even though there were individuals on both sides who argued for reason rather than violence, theirs were minority voices. Even if those voices had belonged to people in power, the individuality and democracy of both societies guaranteed that the young men of both cultures, reared on tales of the glory of war, would ignore the concerns of their elders and seek their idea of justice in battle. Young braves were enraged as they witnessed their weary old chiefs sell their birthrights for beads and booze. Young officers and frontier commanders were infuriated by a government policy of sanctuary, whereby Indian marauders could return to government-protected reservations after they had tired of a season of raiding and scalping. The series of minor conflicts on the frontier in the 1850s was only a harbinger: a greater clash between the cultures was inevitable.

Indian Scouts and Allies

One aspect of the American Indian wars often given little attention is the fact that the struggles for North America were frequently as much extensions of intertribal warfare as they were armed conflicts between the indigenous race and the European invaders. In many cases the struggles were even intratribal conflicts—in effect, Indian civil wars—when kinsmen fought kinsmen for the sake of the white man. For example, Oglalas made up most of the force that arrested and killed Crazy Horse in September 1877; Teton Indian police fought the Ghost Dancers and killed Sitting Bull at Standing Rock in 1890, and Geronimo was finally tracked down and forced to surrender in Skeleton Canyon in 1886 by Apache scouts in the service of the U.S. Cavalry.

Tribal conflicts dating back decades, and in some cases centuries, proved more intractable and more decisive to thousands of warriors than did any fear or resentment of the white strangers from the east. Certainly, white rule was inevitable and the European conquest of the continent was written in the same stars that flickered out for the tribesmen while at the same time shining so brightly for the intruders. But that conquest would have been far more difficult and would have taken many more years had not intertribal rivalry proved to be a stronger influence than any innate resistance to the white invaders. The Indians of the West formed into no great confederacies. In most cases the separate tribes fought separate and thus hopeless conflicts, unable to unify as many of the eastern tribes had in order to face this greatest threat to their freedom and way of life.

The Native Americans of the West fought for their old ways, and their old ways included constant warfare with one another. The tribes that did fight the white man for the most part fought in isolation. Inevitably they lost and often then joined the white soldiers in the war against other tribes. In nearly every major battle and campaign of the western wars significant contingents of Native Americans served as scouts or outright combatant units alongside the soldiers of the American government. The Sibley-Sully campaigns were no different in that respect. Winnebagos, Chippewas, Arikaras, and Assiniboines served as the eyes and ears of the American columns, continuing those tribes' long tradition of hostility to the Dakota nation.

Though the various alliances of the eastern tribes, from that of King Philip in New England in 1675–76 through Little Turtle's coalition in 1790–95 and Tecumseh's league during the War of 1812, all eventually collapsed before the power of the technologically more advanced invaders, the eastern resistance lasted far longer and required a far greater military effort to defeat than did that of the western tribes. The eastern warriors held out, in effect, from the first Powhatan uprising against the Jamestown settlements in 1622 until the removal of most (but certainly not all) of the Seminole combatants from the Florida swamps in 1842. Compared to this 220-year resistance, the western tribes were conquered in less than four decades from the first serious clashes in the early 1850s to Wounded Knee in 1890. Though the American army and militia forces were greatly aided by native allies in the campaigns in the eastern forests, the majority of the eastern Indian nations had to be battled and defeated in open warfare at one time or another in the course of two centuries. This was certainly not true of the West, which, ironically and erroneously enough, the vast majority of our popular cultural images associate with Indian warfare. Only a minority of the western tribes resisted the American conquest (though the resistance in the Southwest to the Spaniards and Mexicans was much more widespread and longer lasting). And of the minority who did fight only a handful of tribes fought for decades before a final surrender—the Apache, the Kiowa, the Comanche, the Cheyenne, and the Sioux. The fighting men of far more tribes enlisted as scouts or auxiliaries in aid of the army that was stealing their country. The braves who fought for the U.S. Army—Pawnee, Osage, Shoshone, Crow, Ute, Hopi, and many members of even the most combative of the tribes—may have numbered, all told, as many as the warriors who resisted the destruction of Indian America.

The Dakota War was no exception to this extensive employment of Indian auxiliaries. Mixed-blood Sioux Gabriel Renville recruited a contingent of half-breed and full-blood Indian scouts for Sibley's brigade. Yankton agent Dr. W. A. Burleigh enlisted a platoon of Yankton scouts to reconnoiter for Sully in southeastern Dakota during his 1863 campaign. Sully provided the scouts with old uniforms and rations and promised them pay (although it took the scouts twenty years to collect it). Joining Sully in his 1864 thrust into western Dakota was a fifty-man reconnaissance corps called the "Nebraska Scouts," which included Burleigh's Yanktons as well as a few whites and several Winnebagos recently deported to Nebraska from Minnesota. They proved more than usually valuable. Following the Battle of Killdeer Mountain, Sully plunged into the Badlands in pursuit of the hostiles and soon found his command lost and short of water. One of his young Indian scouts led the expedition by the hand, so to speak, to guide it to the Little Missouri River and the resupply steamboats.[7]

In recognition of this service Dakota governor Newton Edmunds successfully recommended that the scouting contingent be expanded to one hundred Yanktons and fifty Poncas. The patrolling scouts did yeoman service that late summer, killing several hostiles and undoubtedly preventing many attacks on settlers. In Edmunds's view Indian scouts were typically more effective than twice their number of white solders.[8]

2. The Sioux Nation

A confusion of terms and titles swirls around the warriors who fought at Whitestone Hill and Killdeer Mountain—Sioux, Siouan; Dakota, Lakota; Teton, Santee. Those warriors were members of the Dakota nation, speaking a dialect of the Siouan tongue, the largest of the linguistic families, except for the Algonquin stock. The Dakota, of which the term Lakota, in the western Sioux dialect, is a variation (and Nakota was the variation used by the Yankton tribe), did not have a chief executive heading a centralized nation-state apparatus but were a loose confederation of many closely related Siouan-speaking bands whose alliance was first forged in the lake country from which the upper Mississippi River in northern Minnesota was fed.

The ethnological origin of the Dakota Indians is in dispute. The most likely theory describes an Asiatic migration that moved by slow steps in a more or less southeastward march to the Minnesota lakes. A less likely explanation postulates an indirect route from the common Amerindian source of Siberia over the land bridge and ultimately to Minnesota via Virginia and the Carolinas. According to the latter theory, based largely on the Siouan dialect of the Carolina Catawbas, the ancestors of the Dakotas followed the buffalo along this circuitous route through the Cumberland Gap and then, under the pressure of the Iroquois and the Algonquin confederacies, were forced ever westward toward the prairies and the northern forests.[1]

Whatever their pathway to the northern lakes and woods, these Siouan peoples shared similar dialects and similar stories that eventually led to alliances. "Dakota" is derived from the Santee word "koda" and the Teton term "kola," meaning "friend." Thus Dakota came to mean an alliance of friends.[2]

Ironically, though the name they gave themselves was appropriated by two American states, the moniker the white race affixed to the Dakota Indians was—to the everlasting indignation of the Dakotas—a corruption of the name their most implacable enemies, the Chippewa, used for them, namely,

17

Naduwessi (meaning "snakes" or "enemies"). The Dakotas were referred to as the Naduwessioux (or Nadoues-sioux)—a pluralization of the Chippewa term—by the French explorers, led by Peter Esprit Radisson, who first came into contact with the Dakota during a series of expeditions from 1654 to 1659.[3]

As the Dakotas began to form and reform into tribes and confederacies of separate identities, the names by which they became known reflected largely geographical distinctions. The Teton confederacy derived its name from "Tetonwanis," meaning "people who live on the prairie." The name Santee came from "Isantee," meaning "Knife Lake." The four tribes of the Santee confederacy (considered the eastern division of the Sioux nation) became known as the Mdewakanton, the people of the sacred or spirit lake; Wahpekute, the people who shoot in the leaves (or hunt in the timber); Wahpeton, the people of the leaf (or people who live in the timber); and Sisseton, people who live in the swamp. All four Santee tribes brought their names from their original north woods homeland north of the Mississippi River. So too, in all likelihood, did the two tribes making up the branch of the Sioux between the eastern Santees and the western Tetons—the Yankton and the Yanktonai. (The latter divided into the Upper Yanktonai and the Lower Yanktonai, also called the Hunkpatina.) Yankton derived from "E-hank-ton-wan," meaning "people of the further end." Yanktonai came from "E-hank-ton-wan-na," meaning "little people of the further end." This "further end" refers either to the place these bands occupied in tribal councils or related to the site of their homes in the forest, which were located at the further end of the Mille Lacs (although at least one prominent Indian ethnologist claims Yanktonais simply means "Little Yankton Band").[4]

The Dakotas' original northern Mississippi River homeland was not a peaceful territory. Possession of these woods and lakes was in constant dispute with the Chippewa, an enemy the Dakota fought for two centuries, far longer than they fought the white man. Pressing from the northeast, the Chippewa had the military advantage—but also the cultural corruption—of first contact and much more frequent communication with the French. This military advantage was purely in the shape of the musket, and it was the gunpowder-equipped Chippewa who ultimately prevailed over the largely bow-and-arrow Dakota.

With further expansion into the north woods blocked by the Chippewa, the Dakota looked westward toward the plains. The prime appeal of the prairie was its great herds of humpbacked bison. In fact, the Dakota always claimed that this buffalo bounty prompted their migration to the northern plains, rather than admitting that the Chippewa in the Great Lakes woods had been superior to them. The first to migrate from their forested lakes home were the Tetons, who eventually settled into seven bands: the Oglala ("scatters their own"), Brule ("burned thighs"), Hunkpapa ("campers at the opening of the circle"), Miniconjou ("planters by water"), Sans Arcs ("without bows"), Oohenonpa ("two kettle"), and Sihasapa ("Blackfeet," a Teton tribe separate and distinct from the Algonquian-speaking Blackfeet tribe of Montana). The Tetons settled west of the Missouri River and numbered some 18,000 by 1850, making them the largest of the three Sioux divisions. Next out of the woods were the Yanktons and Yanktonais, who settled between the Red River of the north and the Missouri River. And finally, the four tribes of the Santee migrated, though they moved the shortest distance, just south and west of the Mississippi River to the edge of the forests and the prairies of southern Minnesota.[5]

The First Sioux War, 1854–55

The first significant clash between the Sioux and white America took place not in the Minnesota forest and lake country of the eastern Sioux but in the Wyoming prairies of the western Sioux. Fort Laramie, where Lakota and soldier first fought, had been established as a trading post and way station for emigrant wagon trains. Years of trade and wary coexistence at the post ended and thirty-six years of ebbing and flowing hostility between the Sioux and the U.S. Army began in the summer of 1854 when one of those emigrants claimed that a Miniconjou Sioux had shanghaied and butchered his stray cow.

In response, a green lieutenant anxious for the affirmation that combat would bring, trooped thirty soldiers and two twelve-pounder howitzers out of Fort Laramie on August 19 and route-stepped to a camp of Brules who had gathered near the post to trade. The lieutenant, John L. Grattan, was met by Chief Conquering Bear, who tried to talk but encountered only arrogance. Someone fired a shot—both sides claimed the other fired the first musket ball—and the battle began. Conquering Bear was the only Indian to die, but Grattan and all thirty of his men fell.[6]

The battle was called the Grattan Massacre, even though not a single noncombatant was killed. Retaliation was swift by the standards of the time. An expedition of six hundred bluecoats were deployed from Fort Kearny, Nebraska, the following spring. Led by Colonel William S. Harney, a hard-charging veteran of the Black Hawk and Seminole wars, the column looked for a suitably large Sioux village to punish for the crime of winning a battle against a detachment of the U.S. Army. On September 3, 1855, the Brule band of Little Thunder, tepeed at Ash Hollow on Blue Water Creek near Nebraska's Platte River, was assaulted by Harney's command. Though the Indians there, except for a handful of braves, had not participated in the annihilation of Grattan's detachment and did not consider themselves at war with the United States, they nonetheless paid the price for the Fort Laramie debacle. Dividing his force to attack the camp from two directions, a tactic used successfully many times in the Indian Wars until it failed disastrously at the Little Bighorn, Harney pounded the Sioux village with his howitzers and charged. The camp was destroyed, the 250 inhabitants put to flight and pursued for eight miles. Eighty-five Sioux men, women, and children were killed. Another seventy, all women and children, were taken prisoner. Harney reported four killed, seven wounded, and one missing at Ash Hollow, which he, of course, termed a battle even though as many unarmed as armed Indians were killed. The ruthlessness of the assault earned Harney the sobriquet, given by the Sioux, of "Mad Bear."[7]

Little Crow

The man who brought down the greatest calamity upon the American frontier in the nineteenth century and who ultimately made necessary the punitive marches into the Dakota Territory was an individual rife with contradictions and torn by cultural confusion. Called by his people Taoyateduta (His Red Nation), Little Crow was born around 1810 and thus was about fifty years old at the time of the outbreak.[8] Though forceful, vain, and proud, Little Crow throughout his life often seemed to lack an inner guiding star as he vacillated between the "long-hair" blanket Indians who insisted on retaining their original lifestyle and the "cut-hair" farming Indians who were adapting to the white man's ways. And just as he gravitated to one pole or the other according to the pull of the times, so too had his power and prestige risen and fallen among his Mdewakanton Sioux.

Little Crow understood that the onrush of European civilization could not be stopped. He tried to adapt, taking on many of the invaders' ways in his personal life and negotiating treaties of cession and accommodation with the whites in 1851 and 1858 while outfitted in a velvet-collared black frock coat in his public persona. Having twice traveled to Washington, Little Crow was fully cognizant of the power of the American republic and was determined to bargain for the best terms possible both for his people and for himself.

Little Crow was not blind to the fact that any amount of power he accumulated among the Sioux would have to accommodate itself to the greater power of the United States. Thus he was assiduous in talking terms with the federal government—so assiduous that less accommodating Mdewakantons accused him of accepting bribes from the white man in return for signing away the Indians' heritage and even threatened to kill him for his

Little Crow (courtesy of the State Historical Society of North Dakota).

betrayal. By the summer of 1862, Little Crow was living in a two-story wood house built for him by the Indian agent, Major Thomas Galbraith. He had cut his hair to shoulder length and wore the clothes of the white man. He even started attending church services. It seems that his conversion was nearly complete and that Little Crow was destined for the life of a gentleman farmer.[9]

But Little Crow could never entirely abandon his Indian inner being. He had struggled too hard to achieve the respect of his people. In his youth, Little Crow had been a boozing, gambling, womanizing debauchee with six wives and twenty-two children, so dissolute that his father, Big Thunder, head chief of the Mdewakanton, despaired of him. In October 1845 Big Thunder—whose father had signed the first Sioux treaty with the U.S. government in 1805, but had allied himself with the British in the War of 1812—lay on his deathbed after accidentally shooting himself. Though Little Crow was his first-born son, Big Thunder chose a half-brother to succeed him as leader of the tribe. Little Crow, who had been trying to clean up his act after marrying four sisters and acquiring the manners and oratorical powers of a leader, felt betrayed. The elders of the tribe supported the old chief's decision, however, pointing to Little Crow's reputation for laziness and his reluctance to join the war parties against the Chippewa as evidence of a lack of the qualities necessary for tribal leadership.

Little Crow was determined to claim what he considered to be his inheritance. Canoeing to the main Mdewakanton camp, he stormed ashore to demand his birthright, regardless of threats to his life by his half-brothers. Folding his arms across his chest, Little Crow dared his brothers to shoot him, and someone took up the dare. The bones of both wrists were shattered by the bullet, and the army surgeon at Fort Snelling, to which he was carried, insisted that only amputation of both hands could save his life. Little Crow refused, preferring to take his chances with the ministrations of the tribal medicine men. With no hands, his dreams of becoming a chief would be forever dead, and he had no desire to continue life without that dream.

The healing process took weeks, but eventually Little Crow recovered, although his hands and fingers were deformed and crippled for the rest of his life. His courage and his recovery convinced the tribal elders that he had both the character and the confirmation of the Great Spirit to lead his people. The designated chief and another half-brother who had supported him were killed and Little Crow became a chief.[10]

Later, when the time came to choose, when four blanket Indians precipitated a war, Little Crow had only to recall the pain he had endured and glance at his scarred wrists to give up his white furniture, his white apparel, and his white ways. He had tried to straddle two cultures, accepting the best of the new and retaining the best of the old, but when the props were so suddenly and so violently kicked out from under him he had no doubt as to which way he would fall. He had been chief of his people in peace for seventeen years; now, in the last year of his life, he would be their chief in war.

3. Inkpaduta and the Spirit Lake Massacre

Though Little Crow was, in a sense, the titular leader of the Santee Sioux Uprising in Minnesota, the true champion of chaos on the Minnesota and Dakota frontier in the 1850s and 1860s was the smallpox-scarred, Wahpekute renegade Inkpaduta (meaning "Red Cap" or "Red End," supposedly from the effusive bleeding that resulted when the baby Inkpaduta's enlarged foreskin was circumcised). It is impossible to lay the blame for all the violence of a decade at the feet of this hard and haughty warrior, though given his reputation and record, he would undoubtedly have reveled in such recognition. The Sioux, like all Plains Indians, possessed too sovereign a soul and was too flamboyant in his individuality to accept fully the discipline and domination of a military commander. War chiefs were chief warriors—warriors of the first rank who led by example and inspiration, not by order and regimentation. A war leader could suggest and convince, but he could not command. Where, when, and how the Lakota and Dakota tribes staged their attacks, fought their battles, and decided their strategy was decided by consensus, not by command. And a consensus by the majority by no means obligated the individual who wished to fight on another day, on another field, in another manner, to conform to the decisions of his peers. No one chieftain or warrior decided the course and shape of the resistance to white America in Minnesota and the Dakotas.

On the other hand, if command did not compel, character and conviction could sway loyalties and even subvert common sense. If there was an Indian aristocracy, it was an aristocracy of strength—physical strength, strength of will, strength of purpose. Whatever less admirable qualities Inkpaduta may have possessed, and he had a wealth of them, this cunning catalyst of the Spirit Lake and Minnesota massacres projected an unswerving strength of will in his life-long opposition to white America. From Spirit Lake to the last battles in the Badlands, Inkpaduta was present, in spirit if not always in body, instigating, inflaming, and, in his own dark and almost

demented way, inspiring the warriors of the Sioux nation to both coura-
geous resistance and appalling cruelty.

The source of Inkpaduta's hatred and hostility toward the fair-haired,
fair-eyed interlopers from the east rests more in his genes than in his experiences. He was no more a victim of the white man's deceit and avarice than
other Dakotas—both those who accepted the inevitable and sought accommodation with a power that could not be denied and those who tried to
stem the tide for a season or two but ultimately submitted to the flood.
What drove and sustained Inkpaduta's wrath and rage, if it is to be explained
at all, was an inheritance of character, not a chain of cause and effect. That
doleful inheritance was a legacy bequeathed by his father, Wamdesapa, a
Wahpekute chief of violent temper and villainous character, who in 1828,
thirteen years after his son's birth, had killed Tascaye, the main chief of the
Wahpekutes, undoubtedly while in the grip of his famous and fiendish rage,
and was declared an outcast from the tribe.[1]

The son inherited the father's exile, his resentment, and his explosive
disposition. On the death of Wamdesapa in 1848 (some say at the hands of
his own son), Inkpaduta inherited his father's place at the head of the outlaw band. The very next year Inkpaduta exacted a measure of revenge for
the twenty-year exile by sneaking his renegades into the sleeping camp of
a hunting party of Wahpekutes near the headwaters of the Des Moines
River in Minnesota and stabbing to death eighteen of his fellow tribesmen.

Over the next decade Inkpaduta remained an exile, mostly in the Missouri River valley, leading with the force of his personality a small band of
twenty or fewer like-minded rebels who refused to accept the authority of
the tribal council. Only during a period of warfare with the Sioux nation's
long-time nemesis, the Chippewa, did Inkpaduta join in an uneasy alliance
with his former fellow tribesmen. His bravery and skill in battle was recognized in every corner of the tribal realm, but so too were his impetuous
temper and independent manner.

Ironically, Inkpaduta's relationship with the new race on the Minnesota
frontier was often better than that with his kinsmen. He had frequent contact with the white settlers in the areas he roamed, and he even established
a close friendship with Curtis Lamb, one of the first farmers to stake a claim
in Woodbury County, Iowa. Lamb learned the Siouxan dialect from the man
who in a few years was to bear the most hated name on the northern prairie
frontier. In the early 1850s there was nothing in Inkpaduta's background or
bearing toward the whites that pointed to infamy a few years down the road.

If Inkpaduta was not a particular thorn in the side of the white settlement early in the decade, he remained an outlaw to the elders of the Santee. He was not summoned to the Traverse des Sioux council in 1851, nor
was he given a voice in any of the other negotiations that dispossessed the

Santee of most of their Minnesota lands and laid out the narrow limits of the reservation along the Minnesota River. All this notwithstanding, his palm was ever outstretched when the time came each year for the Santee to receive the compensation for the loss of their forests, lakes, and prairies. From the first disbursement of the annuity through 1856, Inkpaduta appeared at the agency to claim a share. Each time, at the insistence of the tribal elders, the agent refused to grant Inkpaduta a share of the goods and money that were distributed to placate the Sioux for the loss of their heritage, but the renegade never went away empty-handed. By threatening the annuity Indians themselves and the peace upon which their annuities depended, Inkpaduta was able to extort a tribute from his more passive tribesmen at least equal to the size of their individual annuities.[2]

It is, of course, with the Spirit Lake Massacre that Inkpaduta's infamy will forever be linked, but the man who carried out Iowa's bloodiest incident in its history remained embroiled in, if not at the head of, the Sioux resistance to Anglo-America, not just in the Minnesota Massacre and the Dakota campaigns, but throughout the battles of two decades.

Following the atrocities in Iowa in March 1857, Inkpaduta's band became a refuge for renegades from all bands of the Dakota nation. After Spirit Lake, Inkpaduta moved his main camp from the lakes near Madison, Minnesota, and made his mobile headquarters mostly among the Yanktonai, who roamed along the James River. It has been speculated that in the weeks prior to the August 1862 outbreak Little Crow, sensing trouble, sent for the man who had a talent for trouble, and that the two—the respected, renowned chief of the Santees, a pillar of the uneasy peace in Minnesota, and the outcast outlaw and perpetrator of the deadliest deed ever done in Iowa's history—plotted together to ignite an uprising that was Spirit Lake writ large. This seems unlikely, however. The uprising, though brewing for years atop the simmering coals of resentment and injustice, was largely a spontaneous outburst, not an intricately planned conspiracy. Little Crow undoubtedly realized that once the uprising was in full flare, he needed the warrior skills and inciting spirit of Inkpaduta, but it is less likely that the reluctant warrior Little Crow, swept into war by circumstance, would seek the advice and alliance of a man geared and trained for conflict all his life.

If Inkpaduta did not stand on the right hand of Little Crow during the worst days in Minnesota's history, he was, without doubt, in the thick of things. How much blood was on his hands during those demon days is impossible to say. Blood flowed too freely to do an accounting, but Inkpaduta and his followers certainly shed much of it. As for the battles of the August Uprising, witnesses reported seeing Inkpaduta at Wood Lake; he was certainly present at Fort Abercrombie.[3]

Heading a war party of Yanktonais, Inkpaduta was held responsible for many of the depredations that threatened renewed panic on the Minnesota frontier in the spring of 1863. Ranging wide, his band murdered a white civilian near New Ulm and another near Yankton, South Dakota, in May and butchered a farming family in Nebraska in July. That same month Inkpaduta assumed for the first time a position of leadership in combat rather than in mass murder. Taking charge at Big Mound, Dead Buffalo Lake, and Stony Lake, Inkpaduta demonstrated dexterity at evacuating the Dakota women and children in the thick of combat and at covering the retreat of the Sioux warriors in the face of Sibley's soldiers.

Through these encounters, Inkpaduta earned the admiration of the Sioux people as a war chief and not just a raider. This so recently won reputation suffered some damage a few months later at Whitestone Hill, when Inkpaduta had shouted, "They are but a few; let us wait," and committed the vainglorious mistake of delaying the final attack on the almost entrapped column of Major House in order to give his warriors time to paint their faces and bodies for what was to be an overwhelming victory. As described in the prologue, this gave Sully time to force-march reinforcements to the rescue of House and turn the tide of battle. But Inkpaduta partially redeemed himself by skillfully evacuating 2,000 Dakota noncombatants from a ravine where they were trapped.

Early in the summer of 1864 Inkpaduta's raiding instincts again pulled him down into the settlements along the frontier to loot and steal horses, but the Yanktonais, who had by now pretty much adopted Inkpaduta as their war leader, summoned him back to help them confront Sully's second Dakota expedition. He fought the invaders at both Killdeer Mountain and in the Badlands, though evidently not in a role of superior leadership. Ironically, the men of Sibley's and Sully's expeditions never realized that Inkpaduta was a leader in the Dakota battles or was even present. On the other hand, his bad reputation guaranteed that he was assigned the blame for nearly every act of murder and mayhem committed on the northern prairies in 1863 and 1864. Even a few of his own tribesmen blamed him for killings he did not commit, covering up their own crimes and protecting themselves from retaliation by the whites.

The culmination of the Dakota campaigns in 1865 did not end Inkpaduta's resentment or his raids. Fleeing to Canada in 1865, he raided frequently across the border and in 1866 joined the Tetons in the Red Cloud War. After the 1868 treaty Inkpaduta continued to roam among the recalcitrants, never accepting peace with white America, never surrendering the way of the raid. Though eclipsed by leaders such as Crazy Horse and Sitting Bull, old Inkpaduta was very much a presence in the Sioux War of 1876–77 and led a contingent of the Sioux-Cheyenne confederacy that battered Reno's command at the Little Bighorn.

In 1877, when Sioux defeat followed rapidly on the heels of the Sioux's greatest victory, Inkpaduta returned once again to Canada. Refusing to the end to follow the path to peace by way of surrender that most of the Sioux nation accepted, Inkpaduta remained a raider to his dying day, which occurred in Canada in 1879 when he was sixty-four. Though clearly a military leader with considerable talent, Inkpaduta is remembered by history, and justly so, as an incorrigible killer without equal in the long story of the Sioux people.[4]

Spirit Lake

Inkpaduta's rage did not crash down upon the Spirit Lake settlements arbitrarily. Massacre did not fall on the settlement simply because it was sited at the wrong place at the wrong time, a settlement caught in the path of a force of nature as feral and unpredictable as a tornado. Provocation existed in abundance. The massacre was at least as much the result of grudges gratified, grief repaid with greater grief, as it was a spontaneous moment of madness.

Iowa had seemed so secure from the red menace following the cession treaties of 1851 that effectively removed the tribes from the Iowa prairies that Fort Dodge, the northernmost military post in the state, had been abandoned in March 1853 and its small garrison transferred north to Fort Ridgely, Minnesota. But Iowa, an Indian name that means "here is the place," was still the home for a great many Indians regardless of any words on any treaty paper. Indians who resented that their right to roam the Iowa grasslands had been bartered away in treaty councils that they had neither attended nor endorsed remained in the northern and western regions of the state. These areas were beyond the line of concentrated white settlement, for most whites recognized the danger in pushing too hard too soon against the natives. However, a few hardier and haughtier souls chose to venture beyond this frontier and clashes became inevitable.

By far the worst of these occurred in 1854. Following a spate of minor Indian disturbances, a whiskey seller and horse thief named Henry Lott and his equally low-life son descended upon the isolated hunting lodge of Wahpekute chief Sintomniduta, overlooking a stream—thereafter called Bloody Run—in Humbolt County, twenty-five miles north of abandoned Fort Dodge. Sintomniduta was, according to some reports, the blood brother of Inkpaduta.[5] The chief, his wife, mother, and children—in all, nearly a dozen mostly unarmed people—were slaughtered. Though the Wahpekutes demanded that the local military authorities bring the murderers to justice, the army made only a half-hearted attempt at pursuit and the Lotts easily escaped.

The abiding bitterness that followed Bloody Run was hardly dissipated in the fall of 1856 by the coerced confiscation of arms from some of the local Wahpekutes by settlers, perhaps fearful of Indian intentions following rumors of discontent among the tribesmen at the steady increase of the admittedly still sparse population of whites in the region. The winter of 1856–57 was one of the worst on record in Iowa history. The bitter cold and blinding blizzards, combined with a shortage of firearms (due to the confiscation) to hunt what little game was available meant a hard, hungry winter for the Sioux in Iowa, and a number of Indians died as a direct result of these conditions. Among them was one of Inkpaduta's sons.[6]

In the fall of 1856 Inkpaduta and his renegade band of ten men, including four of his sons or sons-in-law and their families, had ranged through eastern Dakota and northwestern Iowa down to the lower valley of the Little Sioux River. There had been several clashes with settlers, but the winter had put a frozen calm on the region. When the weather eased up somewhat in late February, Inkpaduta got the raiding itch once again and rode toward Iowa's Clay County, fifty miles south of Lake Okoboji.

The Indians appeared near the site of the future town of Peterson, where a few settlers had staked their claims. A young girl named Jane Bicknell later recorded in her diary the panic she felt as the Sioux loudly demanded food and then took all the flour and cornmeal they could find in the family's cabin. Then, before departing, they released their pent-up hostilities and their winter-restrained wildness by slitting open the family's comforters and pillows to scatter the feathers on the ground. The outburst was frightening to little Jane's family but relatively benign compared to what the renegades would very soon be slitting open.

The frenzy that had seized the Indians quickly escalated as they rode to a second cabin, where they rampaged around the house as its inhabitants stood by helplessly. This time the raiders did more than tomahawk quilts and stab pillows. A boy was kicked into a fireplace, where he suffered serious burns, and two young women were abducted. The girls were taken to the Indians' camp and, in the argot of the time, "subjected to every indignity," but were apparently not raped. After releasing the women in the morning, the raiders moved on north. Thus far, the depredations had been serious but not unusual in terms of the long history of violent incidents perpetrated by both sides on the other over the past decade. No blood had been shed, though a boy had been burned; no lives had been lost. But that was soon to change.[7]

That Inkpaduta's men were caught up in a raiding frenzy is undeniable. But the fuel that drove their frenzy from one of pilferage and destruction to one of bloodlust and butchery was probably provided by a sight that offended their deepest senses and concentrated their rage when they reached the Okoboji lakes on the evening of March 7. The three lakes there were holy to the pantheistic Santees, and for a long time they had been set aside as a place to revere the spirits that united man to nature. The largest of the lakes, Minne-Wauken (meaning "Spirit Waters"), was so sacred that no Santee would ever fish or canoe in its waters. Now, on those sacred shores, white men had built their log cabins and erected their split rail fences to lay claim to land and lakes that no one but the spirits were to ever possess. The breaking point had been breached. The raiders now became killers.

On the morning of March 8 Inkpaduta's band appeared at Rowland Gardner's house near the shore of Lake Okoboji. The Santees asked for and received breakfast from the apprehensive Gardners and then became more menacing in tone and demeanor as they demanded ammunition. When offered half of the family's ammo supply, the Sioux insisted on all of it, then left the house. Two men present at the Gardner residence, including Gardner's son-in-law, Harvey Luce, departed soon after the Indians left to spread the alarm and warn their neighbors of the Santees' hostile attitude. It was too late.

As the Iowa evening settled in, the Indians returned. This time they asked for nothing and demanded only blood. The entire family, with the exception of thirteen-year-old Abbie, was slaughtered—Mr. and Mrs. Gardner, their son Rowland, their daughter Mrs. Luce, and her two children. Carrying Abbie away as a captive, Inkpaduta and his blood-crazed band spread death throughout the Spirit Lake settlement, killing another twenty-six whites and abducting Mrs. Noble, Mrs. Marble, and Mrs. Thatcher. Morris Markham, who had been elsewhere during the day of death, returned that night to discover the massacre. He then fled to the nearest settlement, Springfield, Minnesota, thirty miles to the north.[8]

The renegades, after plundering and torching all, leisurely made their way up the Des Moines River to Springfield, which they reached on March 26, more than two weeks after the Spirit Lake Massacre. Along the way Inkpaduta was joined by a band of Sissetons, possibly led by their chief Sleepyeyes (though he later denied any involvement). Alerted by Markham, twenty-one settlers of Springfield barricaded themselves in a stout log house and fought off the ensuing Indian attack with the loss of one boy killed and two men and a woman wounded. The hostiles withdrew from the settlement at nightfall, after murdering a family of four who had unwisely not sought shelter with the others. The raiders also killed three more whites at the settlement store before they departed.[9]

As soon as Markham had reached them with his frightful news of Spirit Lake, the Springfield settlers had dispatched two of their number toward Fort Ridgely, sixty miles away. This being the winter of the "deep snow,"

Top: Gardner family cabin at Lake Okoboji. Abbie Gardner was abducted from this cabin after her family was killed by Inkpaduta's raiders during the Spirit Lake Massacre of 1857. *Bottom:* Gardner family cemetery.

the messengers made slow progress, reaching the fort only on March 18. Company A of the Tenth Infantry Regiment, led by Captain Barnard E. Bee, was mustered out and marched toward Springfield. The company was guided by the half-breed scout Joseph LaFramboise. Arriving the day after Inkpaduta's attack, the snow-stepping soldiers of Company A trailed the attackers through deep powder. Inkpaduta's scouts reported the soldiers' movements from observation posts in the treetops. Though the soldiers got close enough for Inkpaduta to detail one brave for the mission of murdering the captives should the soldiers storm their camp, the pursuers were ultimately unable to locate the hostiles and had to break off the hunt.[10]

The Santee raiders rode northwest, employing their captive women as slaves. In the most desperate straits among the abductees was Mrs. Thatcher. In the midst of the madness at Spirit Lake, she had had her three-week old son torn from her arms and killed before her eyes. A broken arm suffered in the melee was not only ignored by her captives but made much worse by their insistence that she carry heavy loads, cut firewood, and complete the other tasks assigned to their white slaves. The woman's steady deterioration slowed the Indians' movement and wore down their already minimal patience with their captives.

As the group crossed the Big Sioux River near present-day Flandreau, South Dakota, balancing on a tree that had fallen across the stream swollen by spring floods, a warrior pulled a heavy pack from Mrs. Thatcher's back. The captive realized that this was no act of compassion, but rather signaled that she was about to die. Mrs. Thatcher turned to Abbie Gardner and asked her to give her husband (who had been away from the settlement at the time of the massacre) a last message of love should Abbie herself manage to survive this ordeal. Halfway across the tree bridge, the Indian behind her pushed Mrs. Thatcher into the icy stream. Miraculously, the weakened woman had enough strength to swim one-armed to the shore, only to be clubbed back in. But Mrs. Thatcher did not die easily. Somehow she thrashed her way to the opposite shore, where a warrior again bludgeoned her into the water. Swept downstream with Indians whooping and hurling clubs at her, Mrs. Thatcher reached out and clung to a fallen tree, where her misery was finally ended by a bullet.[11]

Inkpaduta rode on to Lake Herman where he camped for ten days. Two Christianized Indians from Lac qui Parle, Minnesota, arrived in camp to talk Inkpaduta into releasing one of his captives. Mrs. Noble was picked to go free, but the rattled woman suspected the motives of her would-be liberators and made the fatal miscalculation of electing to remain with the devils she knew. In her place, Mrs. Marble was freed. The Christian Indians took her to Judge Charles Flandrau, who rewarded the Indians with $1,000 for the captive's freedom. The judge and agency missionaries then organized a rescue party of Christian Indians to negotiate with Inkpaduta for the freedom of the remaining captives.

Inkpaduta had moved on to the James River. The two remaining captives had been purchased from the rest of the band by a Yankton who had perhaps heard of Judge Flandrau's generosity and decided to cash in doubly. One night on the James, a warrior named Roaring Cloud burst into the Yankton's tent where he was hiding the two women and ordered Mrs. Noble to follow him. What he intended to do with her will never be known. When the twenty-year-old woman refused to leave the tent, Roaring Cloud seized her by the arm, dragged her from the tent, and struck her three heavy blows with a length of firewood that Mrs. Noble had just cut. After the woman died, the Yankton complained loudly about the treatment of his property, but he had not attempted to defend her from Roaring Cloud nor did he retaliate for her loss. The next morning Inkpaduta's Indians used Mrs. Noble's corpse as a target for their arrows and then scalped her. Three days later Flandrau's rescue team, after carefully concealing the goods they carried to purchase the abductees' freedom, approached Inkpaduta's camp and managed to negotiate Abbie Gardner's release. Her liberation marked the end of the ordeal for the last of the Spirit Lake victims. A total of forty-two whites had been slain (including those killed at Springfield), from the first moments of the massacre to the blows that ended Mrs. Noble's life.[12]

Though rescue of the few survivors had been accomplished, retribution had not. A short time after Abbie Gardner had been freed, word reached Judge Flandrau that Inkpaduta was encamped at the Yellow Medicine River in order to be present for the annuity distribution. The perpetrator of the Spirit Lake Massacre had apparently decided that a mere massacre should not prevent him from extorting his share of the annuity goodies. The judge recruited twenty mounted volunteers armed with revolvers and double-barrelled shotguns and a detachment of fifteen musket-bearing soldiers transported in wagons from Fort Ridgely and headed to the Upper Agency. Flandrau met an Indian informant at Butte, midway between the Upper and Lower Agencies, who guided the armed party to six tepees four miles from the Yellow Medicine Agency.

With a detached squad detailed to cut off a retreat by the Indians, Flandrau's force crept upon the Santees under the cover of darkness. They got to within 200 yards of the camp by daybreak when the Indians, who had rolled up the skirts of their tepees during the hot night, spotted the approaching gunmen. Roaring Cloud, the man responsible for the last victim of Spirit Lake, raced with his squaw from his tepee in a mad dash for the river bluffs. The first volley of shotgun blasts from the volunteers missed the fleeing renegade, who reached the brush at the bluffs' edge and fired four shots at his pursuers; one bullet struck a soldier's cartridge box but otherwise did no damage. The soldiers returned fire and killed him.

The corpse of Roaring Cloud along with his howling squaw was placed in a wagon and escorted through 8,000 Indians waiting for the annuity, many of whom raised threatening voices but did not translate their anger into violence. The soldiers and volunteers walked this gauntlet to reach the agency, where they fortified themselves in an old log building to await reinforcements. Help arrived in the form of the Buena Vista Battery, a veteran unit of the Mexican War. The appearance of the battery's howitzers was enough to disperse the threatening Indians and the crisis passed.[13]

Roaring Cloud had been, after all, the only one of Inkpaduta's gang present at the agency or at least the only one apprehended. His death had not been enough to satisfy either the government or local citizens that vengeance had been exacted. Knowing that Indians had a far better chance of catching fellow Indians, federal agents demanded that the reservation tribesmen bring Inkpaduta to justice before they were allowed to collect another annuity. On July 22 Little Crow led 106 Upper and Lower Agency Sioux, mostly Sissetons and Wahpetons, westward in hunt of Inkpaduta.

The agency Indians rode to Lake Herman, where they picked up the trail of the renegades and tracked them down to Lake Thompson. A brief firefight with Inkpaduta's band resulted in the deaths of three of the renegades, but Inkpaduta himself escaped. Hopeful that this was enough to satisfy the whites, Little Crow led his men back to Yellow Medicine to ask for the distribution of the annuities.

Major Pritchette, who had been sent by the Department of the Interior to oversee the operation, was not placated. He insisted that only the total extermination of Inkpaduta's gang could satisfy the souls of the dead of Spirit Lake. The impasse reached crisis proportions as the Upper Agency bands organized a soldiers' lodge and placed their camps on a war footing. On August 10 Major Pritchette met in council with the Santees. The Indians insisted that they should no longer bear the onus of the massacre and that they had striven mightily, if with limited success, to bring Inkpaduta to justice. The major stood his ground, demanding Inkpaduta's scalp before handing out a single shell or bag of flour. The council meeting broke up on the shoals of hard feelings, but a few days later Major William Cullen, the Superintendent of Indian Affairs based at St. Paul, overruled Pritchette's intransigent stand and ordered the annuities to be disbursed.[14]

The threat that the Spirit Lake Massacre might set the whole Minnesota frontier aflame was dissipated for now, but the resolution (or rather, irresolution) of the episode sowed the seeds of the conflict that would erupt five years later. The Santees, or at least the more belligerent among them, interpreted Cullen's decision to accept the evasion of Inkpaduta's band from retaliation as evidence of white weakness. The whites seemed afraid to press the matter further for fear that a handful of hostiles would grow into a Sioux army. Indians already surly and rebellious against the white invasion grew more insolent in the wake of Inkpaduta's demonstration that the Anglo-Americans could be bloodily and successfully opposed. Indians who had been resigned to the inevitability of white domination now began to have second thoughts about the futility of resistance. And Little Crow, who had accommodated himself to a white man's Minnesota, now saw a chance for Santee renewal and accepted the seemingly unalterable fact that a major red-white confrontation in Minnesota could not be avoided. Probably from the moment Major Cullen conceded Inkpaduta's escape from justice, Little Crow dedicated himself to the work of reconquest of what had all been Santee soil at one time.

Many whites were surprised and enraged that the pursuit of Inkpaduta had been ended after relatively little effort. They claimed that converging columns from forts Randall and Ridgely, guided by a few friendly Indians, could have cornered and caught Inkpaduta with ease. Whether the wily renegade could indeed have been snared by the cumbersome columns of white soldiers when his own kinsmen had failed to catch him is open to question. But there is no doubt that the slight military effort made could have been and should have been greatly increased, not only because Inkpaduta might then have been captured but, more important, because a major military expedition would have signaled to the rest of the Dakota nation that atrocity on the frontier was sure to bring down upon them the wrath of the American republic. Because this message was not sent, Spirit Lake led ultimately to the August horror of 1862 and to the necessity of mounting some of the most massive military campaigns ever conducted by the U.S. Army against the western Indian tribes.

4. Little Crow and the Minnesota Massacre

They catch the eye in a way that the other aged, often toppling tombstones do not. In old cemeteries in a wedge of twenty-three southwest Minnesota counties, one can discover in staggered, straggling lines of chipped and time-calloused stone markers a common theme and refrain, a similar syntax and a lingering litany inscribed in weathered words on the gravestones. Invariably etched on the stones after the deceased's name are the words "Killed by Indians on August 18, 1862" or "August 19" or a succession of late August and early September days in that second year of America's Civil War. They are a mute and mottled testament to Minnesota's summer of blood and its day of judgment that ultimately rendered a broad swath of the state temporarily depopulated of white people and permanently stripped of its Santee Sioux heritage. The simple inscription "Killed by Indians," repeated on stone after stone, becomes a mantra for the dead and reminds the living that history passes by swiftly, but calamity can pause to linger at least for awhile and leave its mark, if only in the form of these solemn, silent stones.

An argument over eggs provoked the bloodiest massacre of civilians in American history.

Four young Mdewakantons, two of them dressed in Indian apparel and two dressed like white men—all in their twenties and all from Rice Creek village in the Lower Sioux Agency—were hunting outside the boundaries of the reservation, forty miles northeast of their village, on Sunday, August 17, 1862. Unsuccessful in their search for game and hungry, the four—Brown Wing, Breaking Up, Killing Ghost, and Run Against Someone When Crawling—headed for home. Near Acton Township the Santees found eggs in a hen's nest near the split-rail fence marking the property of Robinson Jones, who operated a combination grocery store and post office. When one of the Sioux warned another not to take the eggs and risk the white man's retribution, a surly exchange of taunts, boasts, and dares ensued. The posturing of young bucks soon escalated to proclamations of murderous intentions. The eggs were hurled down and war splattered from the broken shells.

Some of the braves' bravado faded when they actually confronted Jones and briefly argued with him over their demands for food. Jones shrugged off the hint of menace in the air and walked with a friend named Webster off toward the nearby farmstead of Howard Baker, where Jones's wife was visiting. The four Santees, now seemingly mollified, followed. At Baker's the Indians suggested a round of target shooting. Taking turns blasting at a block of wood mounted atop a tree stump, the Indians reloaded immediately after each round while the white men, demonstrating the dangerous complacency that local whites had developed toward a Santee tribe they felt was cowed and subdued, waited to reload until their turn to shoot came again. Thus the settlers' rifles were empty when all four of the Mdewakantons turned their weapons on Jones and shot him down.

When the Indians took aim at the women watching from the homestead's doorway, Baker jumped in front of his wife and took the bullet fired in her direction. Webster and Mrs. Jones were also gunned down, but the Indians then fled the scene without bothering to dispose of Mrs. Baker and Mrs. Webster. Passing back by Jones's store, one of the Indians paused to take aim and fire a fatal bullet into Jones's fifteen-year-old adopted daughter.[1]

As they fled south, the killers stole a pair of horses and a wagon from another homestead and raced on to their village, which they reached at sunset. Their tale of murder excited the young men of Rice Creek, one of the most militant of the Santee camps. Rice Creek was also the location of the tribe's Soldiers' Lodge meetings. Chief Red Middle Voice was all for expanding the incident into an uprising, but he needed allies. Traveling eight miles further south to Shakopee's camp, some 100 Sioux warriors, their blood rising and their spirits surging for the first time in months, recruited Shakopee and then proceeded on to seek the approval of the one man whose leadership they felt was vital for a successful uprising against the Americans— Little Crow.[2]

The most important chief of the Santee Sioux faced a monumental decision as he listened to and mediated the varying voices calling for peace or war on the night of August 17. Almost a whole lifetime of accommodation to the white man had helped entrench his power with his people while also having undermined it. Little Crow was prosperous as well as powerful, in large part because of the arrangement by which the white Minnesotans and he worked together to advance each others' interests. But rising white greed and recent incidents had so angered many Santees that Little Crow's continued acquiescence to the white takeover of the tribal territory threatened to erode his authority completely as the Eastern Sioux increasingly listened to more militant voices.

Little Crow realized the ultimate futility of his position. If he chose war, the Santee would lose everything. If he hung back while others seized the reins of warfare, his standing, his status, his place in the historical memory of his people would be lost forever. The weight of the knowledge that war could result only in Santee defeat lifted and floated free from hard reality on the balloon of vanity, honor, and the need for a place in Dakota legend.

Before committing himself, Little Crow clearly pointed out to the young braves eager for action the ultimate futility of a war against the United States. "You are full of the white man's devil water. You are like dogs in the hot moon when they run mad and snap at their own shadows. We are only a little herd of buffalo left scattered.... The white men are like the locust when they fly so thick the whole sky is a snowstorm.... Kill one, two, ten, and ten times ten will come to kill you."

To emphasize the disaster sure to come if the clamor of combat would seduce the Santee, Little Crow painted his face black and draped a blanket over his head. Angered by this display of reluctance, Red Middle Voice called Little Crow a coward. In response Little Crow cast off the blanket, cast off his reticence, and leapt to his feet to slap his accuser's headdress off his skull and onto the floor.

"Braves!" he proclaimed. "You are little children.... You are fools. You cannot see the face of your chief; your eyes are full of smoke. You cannot hear his voice; your ears are full of roaring waters. You will die like the rabbits when the hungry wolves hunt them in the Hard Moon. Taoyateduta [Little Crow] is not a coward; he will die with you!"[3]

The bane of his blessing given, Little Crow on the following day led his people to weeks of mass murder and mayhem and to the ultimate disaster he had so presciently described.

The killings at Acton were unprovoked that day, but the deaths of those white settlers and all the hundreds who died in the days following did not come out of the blue. The once vast Santee tribal lands in Minnesota had been slowly absorbed by the white wave breaking over the prairie for decades and had then been eroded more rapidly by the cession Treaty of Travois de Sioux in 1851 (which promised the Sioux three million dollars in cash and annuities over a fifteen-year period) and by a second land sale treaty in 1858. By 1862 the sweep of the Santee domain had been reduced to a sliver, 10 miles wide and 150 miles long, in a northwest to southeast finger tracing the flow of the Minnesota River on its south bank from Big Stone Lake near the Dakota border to the German-Scandinavian settlement of New Ulm.[4]

About 6,600 Santee Sioux lived on the reservation, with the Mde-wakanton and Wahpekute bands concentrated below the junction of the Yellow Medicine River with the Minnesota River and the Sisseton and Wahpeton bands living above the Yellow Medicine River. The Redwood Agency, located about fourteen miles northwest of Fort Ridgely, served the Mdewakanton Lower Reservation, and the Yellow Medicine Agency, at the mouth of the Yellow Medicine River, serviced the Sisseton Upper Reservation. About 3,000 to 4,000 Yanktonai Sioux lived in eastern Dakota Territory, directly west of the Santee Reservation. On the Santee Reservation itself, eighty acres were allotted to each Sioux family and annuities were disbursed annually in payment for the millions of acres ceded to the white race.[5]

Sioux Indian agent Thomas J. Galbraith enunciated the government's policy in trying to transform the Santee. "The theory, in substance, was to break up the communal system among the Sioux; weaken and destroy their tribal religion; individualize them by giving each a separate home, and having them subsist by industry—the sweat of their brows; till the soil; make labor honorable and idleness dishonorable; or, as it was expressed in short, 'make white men of them.'"[6]

Few of the annuity Sioux, however, became real farmers. Those that did were scorned by both races as imitation whites and called "cut-hair and breeches Indians" or "Dutchmen" and sometimes "scalp-lock Indians." The small number of Santee farmers had about 30,000 acres under cultivation by 1862.[7]

Chief Big Eagle later provided a long litany of reasons for the 1862 outbreak. Foremost among them were the scurrilous traders appropriating many of the Indians' annuity goods as payment for debts owed them. The Sioux got along little better with the agents than they did with the traders. Big Eagle derided the new agents appointed in 1861 and in particular the new superintendent of the Northern District, Clark Thompson, whose innovations in his dealings with the Sioux, such as substituting goods for money during the annuity payments, were not appreciated by the Indians. A particularly grating misunderstanding occurred when Thompson encouraged the Santees to expect "a further bounty" without informing them that this was simply an advance on the 1862 annuity. When the Santee negligently skipped the annual hunt in lazy anticipation of this "great gift," they became "greatly exasperated" when they realized the truth.[8]

The Dakota Sioux to a large extent were the agents of their own destruction, accepting the white man's annuities and many of the white man's ways in return for the loss of the land of their ancestors. But they were often cheated of the paltry sums awarded them in the form of annuities for so many magnificent acres, swindled by both corrupt Indian agents and con artists posing as traders. The payment for half of their remaining land in the 1858 treaty (all of it on the north bank of the Minnesota) went directly into the hands of traders to pay off old debts. The Sioux never saw a penny of it. The cheating, the deceit, and the corruption had reached alarming proportions by the second year of the white man's Civil War.

The annuity payments were made in both gold and provisions. When the money supply dried up because of the costs of the Civil War, the Indian agent, Major Galbraith, decided to delay as well disbursement of the food supplies that the Santees had grown dependent on, even though the provision stocks were full. Complaints by the Indians of empty stomachs met with little more than indifference and the scornful comment of a man named Andrew Myrick, one of the local tradesmen who handled the food allotments, "Let them eat grass."[9]

There were festering cultural differences as well as economic disputes that fed the Indians' resentment. The superior attitude exhibited by so many whites irritated the Sioux because, according to Big Eagle, "the Dakotas did not believe there were better men in the world than they." The Sioux males also greatly resented the white man's frequent abuse of Indian women.[10]

The Sioux also saw the whites as suddenly vulnerable in the early 1860s, where before they had seemed invincible. When Galbraith enlisted a volunteer company of half-bloods at the agencies, many Sioux became convinced that the Northern whites must be in desperate straits in their struggle with their Southern brethren. It seemed that an opportunity had arisen for the Sioux to retake the land they had so thoughtlessly bartered away. A war against the whites might prove to be a galvanizing event, uniting the Sioux and possibly even forging alliances with their ancient enemies, the Chippewas and the Winnebagos, in common cause against the white interlopers.

The news of the outbreak of the Civil War did have a stimulating effect on the northern Indians. According to Congressional testimony, "The war of the Union, has been a fruitful source for trouble among the Sioux, exciting inquiry, restlessness, and uneasiness. The effect ... upon the savage and superstitious minds of the Indians can be easily imagined." Another white observer claimed that "if there had been no Southern war, there would have been no Dakota Uprising and no Minnesota Massacre!"[11]

There were numerous rumors of both Confederate agents and British agitators from Canada visiting the Indians in order to foment unrest. There was never any proof presented of these phantom agents, though it is a fact that in 1863 and 1864 the Sioux received some supplies and support from Canada, but whether this was for particular purposes or just to prevent the Sioux from carrying their hostility across the border is open to question.[12]

There were also rumors of Chippewa and Winnebago collusion with the Sioux. Again, no evidence exists of a Sioux-Chippewa conspiracy (a highly unlikely alliance given the fact that the two tribes had fought one another far longer than they had fought the white man). Some of the 4,000 Chippewas were restive, and a simultaneous, although not allied, uprising by the Chippewa tribe was only narrowly averted. Most of the Winnebagos were passive. There was, however, considerable hostility on the part of the whites toward the Winnebagos, partly because of the false belief that they had conspired with the Dakotas and partly due to the usual white greed for the good land on which the Winnebago reservation sat. This hostility and Santee threats to exterminate them if they did not join in the uprising motivated a small number of Winnebagos to participate in the outbreak. The Winnebago agent swore to the loyalty of the tribe and enforced that loyalty with two companies of troops stationed on the reservation. But he did admit that some Winnebagos were present at the Lower Agency (probably Chief Little Priest and a handful of warriors) when the August massacre occurred.[13]

In 1862 there were four U.S. Army garrisons in the affected area: Fort Abercrombie, just across the Dakota border on the Red River, fifty miles above Lake Traverse; Fort Ripley, Minnesota, on the Mississippi, forty miles above St. Cloud; Fort Ridgely, Minnesota, twelve miles northwest of New Ulm, on the north bank of the Minnesota River; and Fort Randall, Dakota, on the southwest side of the Missouri, forty-five miles west of Yankton. At the start of the Civil War the regulars at each post had been replaced by volunteer formations.

On the day the uprising began, August 18, 1862, Fort Ridgely was garrisoned by Company B of the Fifth Minnesota Regiment, reporting a ration strength of seventy-seven; Fort Ripley held thirty men of Company C, Fifth Minnesota; Fort Abercrombie held eighty men of Company D, also from the Fifth Minnesota; Fort Randall boasted the largest garrison, 295 soldiers from companies A, B, and C of the Fourteenth Iowa Regiment. In addition, ninety-two men of Company A of the Dakota Cavalry Regiment were stationed at Yankton in the Dakota Territory. Altogether, only 600 volunteers, most of them green and untested, were stationed in the area that would bear the brunt of the Indian rebellion and half of the troops were based at the relatively remote Fort Randall, 200 miles from Fort Ridgely. In 1860–61 there had been 900 regulars stationed in the region protecting the white Minnesota population of 175,000.[14]

Fort Snelling, ninety miles away from the scene of the outbreak, served as a mustering center through which formed and passed the Sixth, Seventh, Eighth, Ninth, Tenth, and Eleventh Minnesota regiments, all destined for Civil War service. On the day disaster dawned for Minnesota, there were some 550 recruits for the Sixth Minnesota gathered at Fort Snelling.

Matched against these sparse garrisons were up to 1,500 men and boys who could be considered warriors, from 779 Santee lodges around or near the agencies. Rarely were there more than half that number active at any one time, however.[15]

On August 18, 1862, all the old and new resentments, all the banked-up fires of animosity, all the dormant dreams and old urges combined to make a combustible mixture and fed the flames that nearly consumed white Minnesota. On that day, beginning at dawn, some 400 Dakotas, transformed by the alchemy of anger from submissive reservation Indians to screeching savages, struck out against every white man in reach and sight. Among the first to die was the tradesman Myrick, killed as he ran from his store, with the grass he would have had the Santees eat stuffed in his mouth. Along with Myrick, twenty-two other whites were killed around the Lower Agency on the Redwood River. (The Redwood River had received its name when the Dakota had marked trees with red paint as a warning to the Chippewas that if they persisted in hunting in Sioux territory the trees of the area would run red with their blood. Now the admonition was carried out with a vengeance, though the blood that splashed the foliage was not Chippewa.)

The Lower Agency massacre was only a prelude. A twenty-three-county area of southwestern Minnesota became a killing ground. Whites were slaughtered without compunction or discrimination as to age or gender. On that first day as many as 400 white citizens of the northwestern state were killed and often killed horribly. Settlers escaping the general slaughter fled in panic. Whole counties were practically depopulated in a matter of days.

The Indians' total war was directed against the white man's army as well. On the first day of the uprising Captain John Marsh, the garrison commander at Fort Ridgely and a veteran of Bull Run, led forty-six soldiers and the post's interpreter out from the fort to investigate the rash of reports of massacres in the countryside. His patrol was ambushed as it prepared to cross on the Redwood River Ferry. Marsh was drowned, the interpreter and half of his men slain, and five more wounded by the Sioux, who, in this first battle of the August uprising, lost only one warrior killed.[16]

Two days later Little Crow sent 400 mostly Mdewakanton warriors against the Fort Ridgely garrison, which had been reinforced to 155 soldiers and 25 armed civilian volunteers, under Lieutenant Timothy Sheehan. Also quartered at Fort Ridgely were some 300 noncombatants who had fled to the fort for protection from the Santee tempest. The Indian attack penetrated to within a few yards of the log buildings of the nine-year-old fort (unprotected by a stockade wall), but four howitzers (two twelve-pounders, one six-pounder, and one twenty-four-pounder) deployed around the parade ground shattered the Sioux assault with canister rounds and saved the day.

After a day of heavy downpour, the Santees returned on August 22, this time 800 strong, including 400 Sissetons and Wahpetons from the Upper Agency. The attackers tried to torch the fort's buildings with flaming arrows, but the roof shingles were still wet from the pounding rain of the day before and the flames sputtered out. The post's artillery again broke up the Dakota attacks. In this double assault, the fiercest attack ever launched directly against a U.S. Army fort in the Indian Wars of the West, as many as 100 Dakotas were killed or wounded. The defenders of Fort Ridgely escaped with relatively light casualties: two killed and nine wounded in the first attack (one of the wounded later died); three killed and thirteen wounded in the six-hour-long second assault.[17]

The Santees next turned their attention to the settlement of New Ulm on the southeastern edge of the Lower Reservation. Some 100 Lower Sioux warriors had probed the town of 900 mostly German immigrants on August 19, but hastily organized defenses and the onset of thundershowers had discouraged the attackers. Five of the defenders and a thirteen-year-old girl had been killed and five wounded. A relief party of sixteen, searching for survivors hiding from the Sioux rampage, had also been ambushed by the Mdewakantons outside New Ulm and eleven had been slain.

On August 23 the Sioux returned to New Ulm, this time 350 to 400 strong. Judge Charles Flandrau had organized 250 armed civilians to defend the town on a bluff west of the settlement, but the Santees managed to penetrate the white line and race into New Ulm. As the attackers set fire to the mostly log structures of the town, Flandrau's men withdrew in a near panic to barricades erected within New Ulm. The resolute judge was able to reform his ranks and fight off the Sioux attack. Though as many as 100 Mdewakanton, Wahpeton, and Sisseton warriors were killed or wounded in the day-long battle for New Ulm, the town was, in effect, destroyed. One hundred and ninety buildings—one-third of the town—were reduced to ashes; only twenty-five structures were left standing without substantial damage at the end of the town's longest day. The defenders of New Ulm had lost thirty-six killed in the two battles and sixty wounded.

On the following day there were only long-range skirmishes with the Indians. Even though 150 reinforcing civilian volunteers arrived, Flandrau decided to withdraw from the devastated town. On August 25, some 1,500 citizens of New Ulm and refugees from the surrounding counties evacuated the settlement in a train of 153 wagons. The column from New Ulm expected a Sioux assault at any moment, but the refugees made it to Mankato, thirty miles away, without incident.[18]

The Sioux, in truth, were very discouraged by the twin failures at Fort Ridgely and New Ulm. The Santee hostiles operated largely in two semi-independent contingents. The lower war party made up the forces that fought at Fort Ridgely, New Ulm, Redwood Ferry, and later at Birch Coulee. The upper war party raided the northern counties and attacked Fort Abercrombie. There was no true plan of campaign, just a general desire to overwhelm Fort Ridgely and New Ulm and sweep away white settlements all the way to the Mississippi, with the expected active aid of the Winnebagos.[19]

While southwestern Minnesota was at the epicenter of the upheaval, its shock waves swept for hundreds of miles across the prairie. Panic gripped the frontier. In Iowa, with memories of the Spirit Lake Massacre only five years old, Lt. Colonel James A. Sawyer organized five volunteer companies into the Northern Border Brigade to man a line of blockhouses stretching from the Chain Lakes to Sioux City. Although rumors of war abounded, the Iowans' only combative contact with the Santees occurred when two volunteers were ambushed and killed three miles from Sioux City. They were the only white casualties in Iowa during the uprising.[20]

In the Dakota Territory five companies, mustering 266 men in all, were raised to support the 92 men of the Dakota Cavalry's Company A. Although the volunteers patrolled vigorously during the uprising, they could not prevent a small number of deadly depredations by the hostiles. Two farmers were slain one mile from Sioux Falls on August 25. This induced panic and flight from that town, which the Sioux subsequently pillaged and burned. Other deadly episodes in the Dakota Territory included the killing of a mail carrier between Yankton and Sioux Falls, a stage driver murdered on the Fort Randall road, and two more civilians slain on a ferry three miles from Yankton.[21]

Fort Abercrombie, on the Red River separating Minnesota from Dakota and far to the north of the Santee reservation, endured no major assault but was often harassed and probed by some 400 Upper Santees, Yanktons, and Yanktonais. Defended by Company D of the Fifth Minnesota Regiment, the post was, like Fort Ridgely, unprotected by a log palisade, and several of its outer buildings were captured by the Dakota. The defenders threw up hasty fortifications in the form of log and earthen breastworks and, with the aid of three howitzers, repelled a series of Sioux probes. The first attack came on September 3, when the Santees fired on the post for six hours without inflicting much damage on either the garrison or the structure. Three days later the Sioux struck again, killing one and wounding two of the men of Company D. On September 21 a dispatch rider and his armed escort of twenty troopers were attacked and two of their number slain. Fort Abercrombie was reinforced and the loose blockade around it was broken on September 23. However, three days later the Santees tried another brief morning probe against the post, after which the reinforced troops there pursued the attackers and burned their camp. Finally, on September 29, an attack in the early evening was repulsed, largely with the aid of several howitzer shells fired into the surrounding woods.[22]

There were several other skirmishes and the war continued to lap over into Dakota Territory even after the storm had subsided in Minnesota. In early September a patrol of the Dakota Cavalry led by Sergeant Abner M. English fought an hour-long skirmish against a small party of Sioux from White Lodge's band, which had murdered two settlers as it moved west from the site of a major massacre around Lake Shetek in Minnesota. Not long after the evacuation of Sioux Falls, Captain Nelson Minor, at the head of a detachment of cavalry based at Vermillion, clashed with and scattered another Dakota war party. The Santees put to flight left behind considerable booty from their Minnesota raids. Late in November, Minor met and parried a Santee party of forty near Sioux Falls. In all these firefights in Dakota the Sioux may have lost forty warriors killed or wounded, more than half of them at Fort Abercrombie.[23]

Fear swept into upper Minnesota as well as west into Dakota Territory. Apprehension that the Chippewas would join in the general unrest ran high in that August of 1862. On August 19 the white agent at the Gull Lake Agency sent out an appeal for help to the tiny thirty-man garrison at Fort Ripley. The post commander, Captain Francis Hall, sent Lieutenant Frank B. Forbes with twenty men to the agency the following day. They encountered groups of fleeing whites who claimed that the Chippewas had taken to the warpath. The troopers proceeded on and tried to arrest Chief Hole-in-the-Day, but he escaped after a brief exchange of gunfire. Although the chief could command 275 warriors as opposed to the 30 at Fort Ripley, he did not attack; he was not sure if he wanted to take that irrevocable step. Governor Alexander Ramsey ordered one company of the Sixth Minnesota and two companies of the Seventh Minnesota to march from Fort Snelling to reinforce Fort Ripley. By the time these reinforcements arrived Chief Hole-in-the-Day had assembled 500 warriors, but the chief's heart was not in an all-out confrontation. The Chippewas held off and let the arrival of the annuity wagon train, led by Commissioner William P. Dole, convince them that a fight with white America was a no-win proposition.[24]

By the end of August panic reigned across a four-state area. Though by far not all of the Lower Santees had taken up the tomahawk and though they had been joined by only a minority of the Upper Santees and a few score Yanktons and Yanktonais, whites in Wisconsin, Iowa and the Dakota Territory as well as in Minnesota, frightened each other with tales of a vast tribal conspiracy, embracing as many as 75,000 Indians, including the entire Sioux nation, the Winnebagos, and the Chippewas. Rumors were rampant of Confederate agents instigating the uprising to divert Minnesota troops from the battlefields in Dixie. Though there was absolutely no evidence of rebel conspirators inciting the tribes to massacre, the effect of the uprising on the secessionist war effort was the same. Bombarded by reports of disasters both current and impending, President Lincoln temporarily suspended the Minnesota draft quota for the Civil War fronts.

Governor Ramsey early on had sought federal assistance. He requested of General-in-chief Henry Halleck, "Could not Minnesota and Dakota be organized into a military department and General W. S. Harney be sent to chastise the Sioux?"[25]

Halleck, weighed down with more important matters (Second Bull Run and Antietam, with their 46,600 casualties, were occurring at the same time as the Minnesota Massacre), refused on August 29. But Secretary of War Edwin Stanton was more receptive to the governor's petitions, and in early September he moved to convince Lincoln that Minnesota was in nearly as much danger of being lost to the republic as were the Southern states.[26]

General John Pope and the Department of the Northwest

Lincoln's response to the pleas coming from Minnesota, Wisconsin, and Dakota was to create, on September 6, 1862, a new Military Department of the Northwest made up of those states and territories as well as Iowa and Nebraska.[27] Departmental headquarters were established at St. Paul, and the commander was to be Major General John Pope, the recipient of Lee's most recent pummeling of the Union army in northern Virginia. Only the week before, Pope had retreated from a second federal disaster at Bull Run and had been relieved from his command, his reputation seemingly shattered. Pope's reassignment to the northwest seemed a form of exile, but in truth Lincoln still had considerable faith in the general who had scored much needed earlier victories in the Civil War's western theater at New Madrid and Island Number Ten. Lincoln thought that Pope's argument that his defeat at Second Bull Run was largely the result of General George McClellan's deliberate failure to support him was not without merit. For the morale of the army and the nation, the president had been compelled to deliver the Army of the Potomac back into McClellan's hands, but Lincoln saw no reason why a general he considered vigorous and aggressive, the very qualities McClellan so woefully lacked, should not be given another active command.

Pope bitterly resented the reassignment at first. A man whose mouth consistently preceded and exceeded his abilities, the two-star general felt the assignment to the frontier was beneath his talents. But by open blandishments to his vanity, Lincoln and Secretary of War Stanton convinced Pope of the importance of the mission. He accepted the command, persuaded

General John Pope. (National Archives photo.)

that a quick "exterminating and ruining [of] all the Indians engaged" would swiftly bring him back to the locus of action against the Confederacy.[28]

Once he arrived on the scene at St. Paul, Pope quickly forgot his resentment and was swept away by the fever of emergency that had seized the region. His adjutant observed that this general, who considered himself to be the "most talented general in the world and the one most wronged," took charge as if Lee himself stood poised outside the gates of St. Paul with the Army of Northern Virginia. The new department commander was soon firing off telegrams to Halleck demanding more troops, more provisions, more everything, to deal with what he had previously considered a minor Indian fracas while he was still in command in Virginia, but now saw as a crisis nearly on a par with the war against Southern secession. Of course, Halleck, dealing with matters that meant the life or death of a united nation, had no more soldiers or bullets to spare and therefore denied all of Pope's requests. Though the forces available were hardly befitting a two-star general, Pope would have to make do.[29]

The man put in charge of detouring disaster and rerouting the Minnesota frontier to security was, in truth, not without ability, though much of contemporary opinion, as well as the judgment of posterity, dismissed him as a windbag. His mouth endeared him to few and obscured his record of accomplishment both before and after Second Bull Run. In fact, the second Battle of Bull Run was the only serious setback of his military career; however, it was on a scale of disaster that transcended all of his many minor triumphs.

Upon first assuming his Civil War command in the east, Pope had openly boasted that he had come from the western theater where, unlike in the east, he saw only the backs of his enemies.[30] The eastern Union ranks did not take kindly to this slur and openly jeered him. Few of them felt pity for Pope when, after Second Bull Run, his enemies saw *his* back. Washington was thrown into a panic following the battle, but Second Bull Run was a defeat, not a rout, and Pope retired his army from the field in relatively good order.

Pope never got over his dismissal following Second Bull Run. Although officially notified of his removal by Halleck on September 5, Pope had already endured the humiliation of his firing as an open secret among the ranks by way of the rumor mill. Pope was probably aware that Lincoln shared his low opinion of McClellan but chose to go with "Little Mac" because he inspired confidence in the ranks where Pope only evoked resentment. To Lincoln, Pope "had many of McClellan's faults in reverse. He was aggressive where McClellan was timid, rash where McClellan was cautions.... McClellan magnified dangers; Pope minimized or did not see them."[31]

The two generals' opinions of one another were as much at odds as were their temperaments, making it impossible for them to serve in the same army. Thus, Pope had to go. Pope's resentment at his dismissal increased when he was not allowed to publish his official report of Second Bull Run because of Lincoln's apprehension that the bitter charges against McClellan and other Union leaders might sink Washington further into demoralization.

Pope's career prior to Second Bull Run had been marked by slow but steady advancement that might have taken him farther faster if he had been able to hold his tongue. His appointment to West Point had come about because of his family's political connections and, although his intemperate personality had not won him many friends, Pope managed to graduate on July 1, 1842, ranking seventeenth out of a class of fifty-six. He spent two years in Florida on topographical engineering duty and another two years surveying the northeast boundary of the United States. His first combat came in Mexico where he was breveted twice for merit and gallantry in the battles of Monterey and Buena Vista. Following the Mexican War, Pope continued his military engineering career path, first surveying in Minnesota, then as chief of topographical engineers in the Department of New Mexico. In 1853 Pope supervised the survey of the Southwest Pacific Railroad route and explored the Staked Plains of New Mexico for artesian wells. A year of lighthouse duty on the Great Lakes brought first tedium, then the acquaintance of Clara Pomeroy Horton of Pomeroy, Ohio, whom he married in 1859.[32]

The next year Pope, by now captain, came close to blindsiding his career with a speech in Cincinnati in which he blasted President Buchanan's vacillating policies for letting the nation slide into dissolution and disaster. Court-martial proceedings were initiated, but Pope had at least one ally in government, Postmaster General Joseph Holt, who pulled Pope's chestnuts out of the fire. Instead of a court-martial, Pope's politics secured him a spot with Lincoln's inaugural escort to Washington, D.C., in 1861. But then, as the Civil War sundered the nation, there came only dull duty for Pope as a mustering officer in Chicago. Pope pestered Washington relentlessly for a general command, and his efforts were rewarded in May with a command of a volunteer regiment.[33]

From then on, west of the Appalachians, against Confederates and Indians, Pope enjoyed general success. He won victories over the rebels at New Madrid and Island Number Ten and in the Dakotas supervised and coordinated a campaign in which Generals Sibley and Sully won substantial victories over the Sioux. He made an honest effort to settle the Indian problem and demonstrated a level-headed handling of civil affairs. But few of these accomplishments would be remembered. History puts Pope in that sad pantheon of Union generals humiliated by Bobby Lee, and there he will undoubtedly always remain.

The Department of the Northwest that Pope took over encompassed the states of Minnesota, Iowa, and Wisconsin and the territories of Dakota and Nebraska. The population of Minnesota, Wisconsin, and Dakota alone in 1860 was 1,500,000—a dynamic and patriotic populace that sent enough men to serve in the Union ranks during the Civil War to equal an army twice the size of McClellan's Army of the Potomac. The Dakota Territory (which in 1860 included Montana and most of Wyoming) was still almost empty of white habitation, able to claim only 5,000 white citizens. But ten years later the population had tripled in what is now North and South Dakota, while Montana and Wyoming, now separate territories, due to the discovery of gold, counted 29,000 white inhabitants.[34]

Prior to March 1815, the United States had been divided into military districts for martial purposes; after that the administrative and geographical units were called military departments. On October 31, 1853, the country was divided into seven military departments. With the advent of the Civil War the number of departments doubled, then fluctuated, and sometimes they were combined into larger entities tagged "military divisions." By 1864 there were eighteen departments, ten of which were further grouped into four divisions. The geographical divisions were dropped from the military map following the war, and the number of departments was reduced to thirteen in 1866. This structure remained until the army was reorganized in 1903/04. Pope's Department of the Northwest was one of the many created in the Civil War for reasons of both necessity and convenience.[35]

Henry Hastings Sibley

Governor Ramsey had already moved to organize a force with the mission of burying the dead and rescuing the survivors in the horror-swept counties of southwestern Minnesota. The governor appointed Henry Hastings Sibley, a prominent citizen of the state, to command the expedition as a colonel in the state militia. A long-time friend and one-time political opponent of the governor, this Henry H. Sibley was not related to Brigadier General Henry Hopkins Sibley, the man who led the Confederate invasion of the New Mexico Territory in 1862.

Though Henry Hastings Sibley had no military expertise, the governor considered him the man most capable of meeting the challenge of the Sioux outbreak and of inspiring confidence among the terror-stricken citizens of Minnesota. For Sibley was a man of integrity and great familiarity with the Santee tribes. His command initially consisted of 400 men in four companies of the newly organized Sixth Minnesota Regiment, mobilizing at Fort Snelling. Within a week Sibley's regiment grew to 1,500 men, including six more companies of the Sixth Minnesota as well as units of mounted rangers and civilian volunteers. The hastily assembled expedition was short of everything—training, rations, weapons, equipment, and most of all, experience—but, beset by strident calls for action, Sibley marshaled his men and proceeded up the Minnesota River toward Fort Ridgely, which he reached on August 28. From Fort Ridgely, Sibley detached on August 31 a burial and reconnaissance force under the command of Major J. R. Brown and Captain Hiram P. Grant to proceed toward the Redwood Agency.[36]

Sibley, at age fifty-one, now faced the most daunting task of his life, but physically and psychologically he appeared to be up to the task. He possessed a commanding presence, and, six feet tall and broad in beam, he carried a girth that was associated in that era with manly power. Sibley had been known to mix it up with any challenger in his younger days, regardless of the opponent's size and reputation. His name had become so synonymous with strength and forcefulness that it was claimed that only a single individual in Minnesota—a trader carrying even a heftier load on his massive frame—dared to take him on.[37]

In addition to his admirable and often intimidating bearing, Sibley knew and respected the Minnesota Indians and was respected by them. Completely at home and at ease in the wilderness, he understood and appreciated the Indian culture and spoke the Indian languages and the French patois that many mixed-bloods spoke. He had known many of the Santee chiefs for up to twenty years, including Little Crow. His dealings with Little Crow had gone beyond the formal and the business-like to an active friendship, which included many hunting expeditions. Probably no other white man in the territory had a more intimate knowledge of the Santees' leader. His Sioux friends called him Wapetonhonska—"the Long Trader"—in reference to his size and his fur trading profession.[38]

Though Henry Sibley had no experience as a military commander he had experience of war almost from his infancy. At the age of one, Henry had been taken by his mother for shelter inside Fort Detroit at the beginning of the War of 1812, while his father, a prominent attorney in Detroit, was absent serving in the army. When General Isaac Brock's British soldiers besieged the fort, Henry's mother did her part by making cartridges for the defenders' rifles. After a brief bombardment, the post surrendered, and Henry and his mother joined all the occupants of the fort as prisoners of war for a brief time before their release could be arranged.[39]

Sibley's natural inclination toward an active, exciting life led him often toward mischief and away from his father's insistence on a classical education and study of the law. After two years, he declared his law study to be but an "irksome task" and at eighteen set his face in the direction of challenge and adventure by fleeing the routine of the city for the excitement of the northwest frontier.[40]

Henry Sibley found both his hoped-for adventure and unexpected wealth on the frontier. After a brief period of hunting and exploration, the young adventurer took a job for a year as a clerk in a sutler's store. But this mundane work was not for him. Sibley secured a position with John Jacob

Henry Hastings Sibley. (Courtesy of the State Historical Society of North Dakota.)

Astor's American Fur Company and began a career of commerce with the Indians in pursuit of furs and pelts. The job required a love of the outdoors, a hardy constitution, and an imperviousness to hardship—all qualities in abundant supply in the makeup of Henry H. Sibley. Within five years he was made a partner in the company and was put in charge of all operations in the northwest.[41]

Sibley was soon living the good life. He married a lady from Baltimore in 1843, and their family eventually expanded to nine children. They lived in a fine stone house complete with fine furnishings, servants, and one of the best private libraries in the territory. Looking for other outlets for his energy, Sibley took up writing and was soon a successful essayist for eastern magazines in which he published stories of adventure on the northwest frontier under the pen name "Hal a Dakotah."[42]

As a leading citizen in his region, Sibley almost naturally turned to politics. Winning a seat, as a Democrat, in the U.S. Congress at age thirty-eight, Sibley represented Wisconsin and then the new territory of Minnesota, into which his district was incorporated. After five years in Washington, from 1848 to 1853, he returned to Minnesota to serve in the territorial legislature. In May 1858 he was elected Minnesota's first governor.[43]

Ironically, for a man who would win his primary and lasting historical fame fighting Indians, Sibley was one of their foremost champions in Congress. He was totally in sympathy with their plight in dealing with the white race and placed much of the blame for Indian misbehavior on the conduct of the federal government and its agents. He considered Indians to be fully as intelligent and moral as whites and advocated giving them complete civil and political rights. Convinced that the Indian must be fully incorporated into white civilization or exterminated, Sibley opposed the reservation system and worked for private ownership of land for the Indians as well as for training and schools to teach the red men the processes and benefits of modern society. Few of the bills he introduced in Congress were even given a good hearing, but Sibley remained a tireless advocate of Indian rights throughout his political career. In August 1862, however, this defender and friend of Native Americans was called upon to be their conqueror.

For the next four years Sibley's life would be centered on the Dakota Indians, either fighting them or negotiating with them. Promoted to brevet major general for his service against the Sioux on November 29, 1865, Sibley was mustered out in April 1866, but he continued to serve as a peace commissioner in talks with the tribes. He settled in St. Paul, where he developed extensive business interests and increased his already considerable wealth. He served a term in the state legislature in 1871, but, like his military career, his best days as a politician were largely behind him. Failing in a run for the U.S. Congress in 1880, Sibley largely faded from public attention and died in St. Paul on February 18, 1891, two days before his eightieth birthday.[44]

The Defeat of the Santees

The defeats and losses at Fort Ridgely and New Ulm convinced many of the wavering Upper Sioux chiefs, such as Standing Buffalo, that the white men could not be defeated. Though many Sisseton and Wahpeton braves continued to fight alongside their Lower Sioux kinsmen, their leaders turned their backs on Little Crow. He would never again be able to muster the 800 warriors he had led in the second assault on Fort Ridgely, let alone the 1,500 he had hoped to one day deploy against the whites of Minnesota.

Certain that white retaliation for their week of rage loomed, Little Crow and his cohorts decided during a council on August 25 to move the Lower Sioux northwest toward the Dakota border. The next day some 3,000 Santees gathered up their possessions, along with some 350 white and mixed-breed captives, mostly women and children, and headed for the villages of the farming and mission-influenced Sissetons and Wahpetons near the Yellow Medicine Agency.[45]

As Sibley marched along the Minnesota, dissension in the Sisseton and Wahpeton camps to which the Mdewakantons had fled split the Santees along generally pacific Upper Sioux and belligerent Lower Sioux lines. The Sissetons wanted to free the captives immediately and negotiate a peace with the approaching white army. Most of the Mdewakantons wanted to continue the war, or at least use the captives as bargaining chips in order to strike the best deal possible. With the dispute escalating almost to the point of violence, Little Crow moved most of his followers away from the farmer Indians, who seemed nearly ready to kill other Sioux in order to prevent the further killing of whites.[46]

Determined to strike Sibley first before he could muster an all-conquering army, Little Crow and his half-brother, White Spider, rode northeast at the head of 110 warriors with the aim of attacking white settlements north of the Minnesota River and then circling around to strike at Fort Ridgely from the rear. At the same time 350 braves and their chiefs—Gray Bird, Red Legs, Big Eagle and Mankato—headed back southeast through the reservation with the intention of looting abandoned New Ulm and then assaulting Fort Ridgely from the front simultaneously with Little Crow's assault.

Little Crow's band encountered and routed a fifty-five-man company of the newly forming Tenth Minnesota Regiment near Acton, where broken eggs a fortnight earlier had broken the peace. Captain Richard Strout's green recruits were pursued eight miles to the town of Hutchinson, which they reached with casualties of six killed and twenty-three wounded. Little Crow tried to capitalize on this victory by storming both Hutchinson and nearby Forest City, but at both places civilian volunteers had erected substantial log breastworks and the Indian assaults on September 4 were easily repulsed.[47]

The other arm of the last Santee offensive of the uprising won greater success. The vanguard force of Brown and Grant—75 men of Company A,

Sixth Minnesota, 51 mounted rangers, 17 wagonmasters, and a 20-man burial detail, for a total of 163 men—had reached the Redwood Agency, where
they buried the scalped and stripped remains of eighty whites, including
the dead from Captain Marsh's command. They then camped the night of
September 1 in the deep, brush-choked ravine of Birch Coulee, which emptied into the Redwood River opposite the agency, sixteen miles from Fort
Ridgely. The position was extremely vulnerable, with poor fields of fire and
thickly overgrown, concealed avenues of approach for hostile forces. The
tactically near-sighted American commanders at least had sufficient savvy
to circle their seventeen wagons in a laager, possible the only thing that saved
them in the dark hours of September 2.

Early that morning, Gray Bird and the other Santee war chiefs directed
some 200 warriors down the green tunnel of the gulch to stage an all-out
assault on the sleeping soldiers. Sentries spotted movement in the coulee
and alerted the camp just as a swarm of Santees descended on the laager.
An hour-and-a-half of close-quarters combat ensued before the Sioux drew
off to concealed positions in the surrounding brush, from which they kept
Major Brown's detachment under almost constant fire. The Minnesota soldiers counted twenty-two dead and sixty wounded in that dreadful predawn
assault. Pinned down, the desperate soldiers scraped out rifle pits with sabers
and bayonets and prepared to endure a long siege.

Rescue was on the way. Sibley sent Colonel Samuel McPhail with 240
men drawn from Companies B, D, and E of the Sixth Minnesota and a 50-
man company of mounted rangers, escorted by a two-howitzer artillery
detachment, to break through the Indian siege. McPhail got to within three
miles of Brown's force before he too was pinned down and surrounded by
Santee soldiers. McPhail unlimbered his howitzers, and the cannonshot
kept the Indians at a distance, but there was little hope for a breakthrough
to Birch Coulee.

With two detachments in trouble now, Sibley formed up the rest of
his command, 1,000 strong, and set out from Fort Ridgely to break the double siege. The colonel reached McPhail's position at midnight but did not
finally secure the demoralized troopers at Birch Coulee until late the next
morning. Brown's men had endured a siege of thirty-one hours and were
down to less than five rounds of ammunition per man. Total white losses
at Birch Coulee were twenty-four killed and sixty-seven wounded (two of
whom died from their wounds), as well as eighty-five of their eighty-seven
horses killed. The Santees had no more than a half dozen casualties, two
of whom died.[48]

Stung by Birch Coulee and still woefully short of every item and ingre-
dient necessary to turn an armed mob into an army, Sibley wanted more
time to train and temper his force. But the hysteria directed at him from

every direction had no patience for preparation. The colonel's inaction for more than two weeks after Birch Coulee was intolerable and inexcusable to the many voices calling for rescue and retaliation. The *St. Paul Press* labeled Sibley "a snail" who "falls back on his authority and dignity and refuses to march." The indignant editor of the newspaper considered Sibley and his army nothing but "the state undertaker with his company of grave diggers."[49] With such admonitions ringing in his ears, Sibley finally moved out of Fort Ridgely on September 19.

Sibley's green regiments had been considerably strengthened qualitatively by the arrival on September 13, of 270 veterans of the Third Minnesota Regiment. Former POWs, they had been captured by General Nathan Bedford Forrest near Murfreesboro, Tennessee, then paroled (though their officers were still prisoners) with the proviso that their rebel-fighting days were over. In addition to these Civil War veterans, Sibley commanded nine companies of the Sixth Minnesota, five companies of the Seventh Minnesota, one company of the Ninth Minnesota, a thirty-eight-man mounted company called the Renville Rangers after the county where they were enlisted, twenty-eight additional mounted civilian volunteers, and sixteen artillerymen, for a total of 1,619.[50]

Sibley advanced to a bivouac near Wood Lake, about twelve miles from where the Dakota camps were located close to the mouth of the Chippewa River above the Yellow Medicine Agency. Once again the Santees debated the fate of their captives and their own fates. The still officially neutral Sisseton and Wahpeton chiefs counseled immediate surrender, and some of the peace protagonists even suggested the execution of Little Crow to placate the white avengers. Others advised a flight to the west to seek succor from their Yankton and Teton cousins in Dakota Territory. The militants urged an all-out assault on Sibley's bivouac and the mass slaying of the captives. Sibley, aware of the almost violent acrimony swirling through the Santee camps between rival factions, tried to keep the pot boiling by dispatching messages to the Indian gathering in which he called for release of the captives and prompt surrender if the white army's wrath was to be avoided.[51]

Finally, though a great many armed and able-bodied men remained in the camp, Little Crow was able to gather 740 braves for a final battle. Though some war chiefs lobbied for a total attack on Sibley's camp, Little Crow knew now—after the hard-won lessons of Fort Ridgely and New Ulm, if he had not known before—that his warriors, though natural-born fighters, lacked the discipline and organization that would be required for a direct assault on Sibley's camp. The martial qualities that distinguished his warriors were their mobility and their expertise at ambush. Consequently, the chief chose to employ those very qualities by organizing on the night of September 22 a loose and flexible ambush in the tall grass and in a ravine lining the road north of Sibley's camp, a road the colonel was sure to take in his march to free the Indians' captives.

Little Crow's carefully prepared trap was tripped prematurely in the early morning of September 23. A group from Company G of the veteran Third Minnesota decided to supplement their dreary army rations by foraging in the nearby Santee pumpkin, potato, and melon patches of the Upper Agency, about one mile from Sibley's camp. Setting out in four wagons without their commander's permission, the troopers proceeded not up the road but directly across the fields toward the hidden Indian positions in the tall grass. Some 200 Santees popped up and opened fire. The soldiers jumped from their wagons to deploy and return a volley of musketry. Three of the Third Minnesota men were hit, one suffering a gushing leg wound from which he later died.

The echo of gunfire soon brought Major Abraham E. Welch and the rest of the Third Minnesota to the aid of the foragers. With the regiment advancing, the Indians wisely withdrew from the soldiers' direct front, but then redeployed along the Third Minnesota's flanks. Sibley sent two messengers to Welch advising his withdrawal to the main camp, but the major was reluctant to pull back with the Sioux seeming to flee before him. When a musket ball shattered his leg and the Sioux seemed to suddenly reemerge like quicksilver from new directions, the regimental commander decided that Sibley's advice was well-founded after all.

As the Third Minnesota began to fall back, the Sioux pressed closer from three sides, and a wrong bugle call confused and rattled the retreating soldiers. A withdrawal under fire is always among the most hazardous of military tactical operations and carries a high potential for disaster. The veteran soldiers of the Third lost their battlefield composure for a few minutes, and their formation came close to dissolving. The Santees' best chance for victory at Wood Lake came at that moment but quickly passed when the Renville Rangers arrived on the scene to buttress the Third Minnesota line and enable the infantrymen to redress their ranks and make a stand on a plateau near the road.[52]

The rest of Sibley's column was now deploying from camp. Colonel William R. Marshall with five companies of the Seventh Minnesota and one company of the Sixth Minnesota moved up on Welch's right just in time to repel an Indian charge from the ravine with the help of canister rounds from a six-pounder howitzer. Another Sioux thrust on the extreme left was met and thwarted by Major R. N. McLaren with two companies of the Sixth Minnesota. A coordinated sweep by the Third Minnesota in the center and the Sixth and Seventh Minnesota on the flanks forced the hostiles out of the tall grass and the ravine and into flight. It was all over two hours after the first forager had fallen to Santee fire.

Because so many of the Santee braves were posted in ambush positions much farther up the road, probably no more than 300 of the 740 warriors deployed actually got into combat. Chief Mankato was killed by a nearly spent cannonball that struck him in the back. The bodies of fifteen other Sioux were left on the battlefield. Later estimates of the Indian dead carried away increased the Sioux toll to about twenty-five killed and thirty to fifty wounded. Several of the Santee dead left behind were scalped by vengeful soldiers, but Sibley made clear his objections to such practices with his general order the next day, "The bodies of the dead, even of a savage enemy, shall not be subjected to indignities by civilized Christian men."[53]

Sibley's casualties were light—seven dead and thirty-four wounded—most incurred by the Third Minnesota. But a lack of cavalry and concern for the captives convinced the colonel that a pursuit of the defeated foe was ill-advised. Making his excuses to Governor Ramsey, he complained that "if only I had 500 cavalry I could have brought the campaign to a successful close."[54] It turned out that he had no need for any horsemen after all as the campaign was, in effect, already over.

After retiring from the Wood Lake battlefield to their camp, the Santees argued about their next move. Some of the firebrands advocated the mass slaying of the captives as a final gesture of defiance and as a way of preventing their testimony in any future atrocity trials. But the vast majority hoped for leniency by a quick capitulation and release of the prisoners. Little Crow remained defiant and, certain by now that the whites had compiled a catalogue of crimes to be used against him, he felt he had little to lose by his defiance. Thus he turned over most of the captives to the peace chiefs Waccuta and Wabasha and fled with 200 followers (including the four young bucks who had broken eggs at Acton to create a bloody omelet) toward Devil's Lake in northern Dakota in search of new allies to continue the war.

The news of Little Crow's departure was the signal for Sibley's final march on the peace camp. On September 25 his companies approached the camp in a long blue line with bayonets fixed. They were greeted by a sudden blossoming of white flags hanging from tepees, wagons, and trees. The 269 captives, including 167 of mixed blood, most of whom were ecstatic about their release, were handed over to the liberators. Sibley established a bivouac at the site, which he christened Camp Release, and proceeded to round up in the next two weeks some 2,000 surrendering Sioux.[55]

The real work at Camp Release was vengeance. With Pope's blessing, Sibley set up a five-man kangaroo court to judge the Santees. The accused were provided no legal representation and hardly given a chance to defend themselves. Simply placing an accused miscreant at the scene of the crime was sufficient to condemn him. Because so many Indian names in their vernacular were similar and because the white man had trouble pronouncing those names, the wrong man was often accused because of mistaken identity. But justice, or some rough frontier variant of it, was swift, if far from certain. Within a month 392 Indians and half-breeds were charged and judged and 307 of them were found guilty of crimes heinous enough to require hanging; another sixteen were sentenced to prison terms.

Though a majority of Minnesota citizens, as well as those of surrounding states, undoubtedly approved of this massacre by tribunal decree—one hardly less calculated and certainly more cold-blooded than that perpetrated by the Santees in August—calmer voices, more modulated by a sense of justice, called for a reconsideration of the verdicts. Among the most influential of those voices was that of Minnesota Bishop Henry Benjamin Whipple, who had long shown concern about the ill-treatment of the Native Americans in his state. He pressed his concerns on President Lincoln, urging him to review the sentences and separate those who had simply fought as combatants in their war against the United States from those who could convincingly be condemned of rape and murder. According to the President, Whipple "came here the other day and talked with me about the rascality of this Indian business, until I felt it down to my boots."[56] After a careful perusal of the convictions, Lincoln reduced the number of the condemned to thirty-nine (one more received a last-minute reprieve) and reduced the sentences of the other POWs to jail time.

Even with this reappraisal, injustices remained. At least three of those still fated for the gallows were men whose names had been confused with those of others. One of the mistakenly condemned, Chaska, had saved and protected a white woman from death or harm during her captivity. She pleaded for his life, but several days after the mass hanging the woman found Chaska's name on the list of those executed, his name confused with that of Chaskadon, who had killed a pregnant woman and cut the fetus out from her womb.[57]

The Indians walked to the gallows at Mankato on the day after Christmas 1862. They were allowed to smoke their pipes one final time; then, shaking hands with one another and with the escorting soldiers, the Dakotas began to chant the tribal death song, and one of the condemned gestured almost ecstatically "Me going up." Stoically, the Santees marched to the gallows, clasping hands as white hoods were pulled down over their faces and waiting for the three taps by a solitary drummer that signaled the moment of execution.

The executioner was a man named William Duley, who had escaped from the wholesale slaughter around Lake Shetek. Three of his children had been killed there and his wife and two remaining children were still captives of the Sioux. At the third drum tap, Duley sprang the traps simultaneously with one lever. The rope of one Indian broke and the body fell to the ground. The Santee, though already dead, was strung up under a fresh noose to join his suspended compatriots. The bodies were buried in a mass grave in a sandy flat alongside the river, but they rested only briefly. Doctors, anxious to use the skeletons of the hanged in research and education, were allowed to dig up the dead. Among the grave robbers was Dr. William Mayo, a physician at nearby LeSueur and the founder of the Mayo Clinic. The Mankato hangings were the largest mass execution in American history.[58]

The hanging of those thirty-eight men was only the beginning of the punishment to be meted out to the Sioux. All the Santees and many other Native Americans as well would do penance for the August uprising. No annuities were paid to the Santee tribes for four years, from 1863 to 1866. The funds saved were used to pay damages to whites who had suffered losses during the uprising. Many damage claims were found later to be fraudulent or at least excessive, and in a good many cases the property loss had been caused not by Indian marauders but by opportunistic white looters. The loss of the annuities, however, was minor compared to all the Santees ultimately were to lose.[59]

Besides the more than 300 Sioux whose destinies were directed toward either the hangman's rope or prison bars, another 1,658 charged with no other crime than being on the war's losing side, remained under Sibley's jurisdiction at Camp Release. The colonel decided to move them to a more secure site at Fort Snelling, not so much because he feared a renewed outbreak from this thoroughly cowed group, but as a protective measure to guard the Indians against white vengeance. His apprehensions about white malevolence were borne out during the march to Fort Snelling. Passing through New Ulm, the beaten, bedraggled group of Santee detainees, who hardly resembled the fearsome war-painted braves of just a few months before, was assailed by mobs of venomous white civilians armed with pots of boiling water, scissors, and pitchforks. The escorting soldiers had to fix bayonets and beat a path through the enraged crowds. Several soldiers and fifteen Indians were seriously injured before the column struggled through the ruins of New Ulm.

At Henderson, which the red raiders had not even come close to during the uprising, an even more vicious throng stoned and clubbed the passing file of Santees. A drunken white woman dashed up to the Indian column to snatch a baby from the arms of its mother and hurl the infant to the ground. The baby later died.[60]

Once at Fort Snelling, where the Sioux were penned inside a stockaded area on the river bottomland beneath the fort, the detainees were relatively safe from the white man's revenge, but not from his diseases. During the winter of 1862/63, some three hundred Santees died of sickness, with measles claiming the most victims. Many of the survivors were converted to Christianity by the zealous missionaries who flocked to Fort Snelling. But the white man's religion offered little protection to the new converts, whose losses continued to mount.

In February and March 1863 Congress passed legislation voiding all the treaties with the Santee tribes, erasing their reservations, and ending their annuities. The Sioux, as well as the Winnebagos, who had remained peaceful if restive during the 1862 uprising, were ordered removed from Minnesota. Over one million acres of Indian land were offered up for sale and settlement to white emigrants. Only twenty-five Santees, who had remained steadfastly loyal to their white patrons and had performed often invaluable assistance to them as scouts, spies, and even rescuers during the uprising, were allowed to remain in Minnesota at the two agencies. Those agencies still exist today as tiny patches of the once extensive Sioux Reservation.

The bitter, deadly winter at Fort Snelling was followed by a sad spring. In May 1863 the 1,318 Santee survivors at the fort were loaded aboard two river transports to be carried along the Missouri to the bleak, impoverished plains at Crow Creek, eighty miles above Fort Randall in Dakota Territory. Along the way the Indians were given one last stoning send-off by a white mob that greeted them with vitriolic passion at the St. Paul dock. Some 2,000 Winnebagos, only a handful of whom had participated in the Minnesota Massacre, were dumped at an equally desolate location nearby. Most of the Winnebagos soon fled the nearly intolerable conditions at their camp to seek shelter with the Omaha Indians in Nebraska, where the refugees were finally settled permanently on a section of the Omaha Reservation in 1865.[61]

Meanwhile, the Santees sickened and died at Crow Creek. A November 1863 expedition to provision the starving Indians at Crow Creek was dubbed the "Expedition to Moscow" after the soldiers in the three escorting companies of the Sixth Iowa almost froze to death in minus thirty-five degrees temperatures. By 1866 more than 300 had been buried in the scraped-bare prairie. A compassionate peace commissioner finally allowed the Dakota Sioux to settle on better, more fruitful land at the mouth of the Niobrara River. At this new Santee Reservation the Indians were eventually joined by those Santees whom Lincoln had rescued from the hangman's noose. Ironically, those imprisoned Indians had passed through easier years in prison, first at Mankato, then at Davenport, Iowa, than had their fellow tribesmen uncharged with any crime. The prisoners were relatively well fed and comfortably housed, while their cousins froze and starved. Many of the prisoners were even granted paroles and allowed to work for pay for local whites.[62]

While the imprisoned and the detained served out their sentences and endured their destinies, other Santees were still on the loose. Few people were certain that the Minnesota War was over. Sibley had tried to resign his command as early as September 29, 1862, but Lincoln had appointed him brigadier general of the U.S. Volunteers and on November 25 made him head of the new military District of Minnesota based at St. Paul, with Pope's headquarters moved on to Milwaukee. In October both Pope and Governor Ramsey put out reassuring statements declaring the end of the war, but Minnesotans protested that such proclamations of peace were premature.

The state was still traumatized. At least 30,000 settlers had fled their homes, leaving behind a smoking swath of devastation fifty miles long by twenty miles wide in twenty-three counties. A year later, no one had returned to nineteen of those counties. Little Crow lurked over the horizon in the Dakota Territory, instigating renewed hostilities and appealing for help from the British who, according to Sioux legend, reserved a cannon captured from the Americans during the War of 1812 for Sioux use in return for their assistance in the course of that conflict. Raiding parties returned to Minnesota in the spring of 1863, and one contingent was so bold as to camp overnight on a hill overlooking St. Paul. Even if no real threat of major revived warfare existed, the people and the press of Minnesota were still unsatisfied by the punishment meted out to the Santee tribes. The *St. Paul Press* insisted, "The war is not over! What the people of Minnesota demand is ... that the war shall now be offensive. In God's name let the columns of vengeance move on ... until the whole accursed race is crushed."[63] Only a new war—the sabers-drawn sibling of the old war—could appease the ghosts of August 1862.

5. The Death
of Little Crow

Though thirty-eight Santees had gone to the gallows, the main culprit of the Minnesota Massacre, with a $500 bounty on his head, remained at large and remained a threat. The winter of 1862/63 was harsh and bleak, but Little Crow's hopes were still high. Having inflicted so much damage on the white race with only a minority of the warriors of the Santee tribes, the man who had led the August atrocities envisioned a grand alliance of the Yanktons, Yanktonais, and Tetons with the Santees, armed and abetted by the British in Canada, to sweep the Americans from his homeland. The seven tribes of the Teton confederacy seemed particularly receptive to calls for resistance. Their warriors still resented their defeat by General Harney at Ash Hollow in 1855 and saw the encroachment of 500 gold miners on their territory in the summer of 1862 as a harbinger of a white wave swamping their people.

But all of Little Crow's grand schemes came to naught. Rebuffed by Standing Buffalo's Sissetons north of Big Stone Lake and then by Yanktons far to the southwest, along the Missouri River, Little Crow then tried to recruit non–Sioux tribes such as the Mandans, Arikaras, and Gros Ventres, also along the Missouri. These tribes, long suffering at the hands of the far more numerous and aggressive Sioux, were, however, more receptive to an alliance with the whites against their old enemies. They demonstrated the direction of their loyalties by firing on one group of Little Crow's emissaries who were attempting to parley with them, killing eight of them.[1]

Seeing his hopes for a grand coalition of the northern tribes aborted, Little Crow turned north to seek aid in Canada. Arriving at Fort Garry on the site of present-day Winnipeg on May 27, 1863, the Mdewakanton leader pleaded with the governor of the Hudson's Bay Company, Alexander Dallas, to repay the services of the Sioux on behalf of the British in the War of 1812 by supporting the Santee resistance fifty years later. But Dallas promised him no weapons and gave him no hope, and soon sent him packing with the understanding that he was no longer welcome in Canada.[2]

Little Crow recrossed the border as Pope's columns began their summer sweeps into the Dakota Territory. As the Santees were chased ever further from their homeland by the converging columns, more and more of Little Crow's party, originally numbering about 300 at the start of the winter of 1862/63, fell away. The remaining Sissetons and Wahpetons, in particular, blamed the Mdewakanton chief for the loss of their annuities and their homeland and eventually deserted his lost cause. Little Crow never came within sight of Pope's armies, but the threat they presented served to scatter his band.

By late June 1863, Little Crow, who had once commanded an army of hundreds of warriors and had led the greatest massacre of white civilians in American history, was now the leader of sixteen men, including his sixteen-year-old son, Wowinape, and one woman. He resolved to go back to the Big Woods of eastern Minnesota where he had spent his boyhood, his grand plans of all-out warfare reduced to horse-stealing schemes. He was to be no Pontiac or Tecumseh of the northern Plains.[3]

The ragged, reduced band traveled 350 miles from Devil's Lake in Dakota Territory to near Hutchinson, Minnesota, north of Yellow Medicine. Now even this tiny remnant of Little Crow's followers split. A few braves still possessed the fighting, or at least killing, spirit and rode off to murder a white man traveling alone. They brought the victim's gray coat back to give to Little Crow, the last loot of his war against the white race. On that same raid the warriors waylaid an ox cart carrying the Amos Dustin family of six. Dustin, his mother, wife and a child were killed; only two children escaped and were rescued a week later.[4]

The killings ended what remained of the little group's cohesion. Now they would not be allowed to remain in peace and isolation in the Big Woods. They would be hunted down and punished, just as their Sioux brethren in Dakota were being stalked and savaged on a much larger scale. Some of the men and the lone woman trekked back to Canada; most of the rest fled south. Only Little Crow and his son Wowinape remained. Little Crow had returned to the Big Woods for good. By passing on his medicine bundles, the symbol of authority and longevity, to his son, Little Crow had already acknowledged the succession of leadership. He was resigned to and prepared for death.

Only six weeks before, Little Crow had paraded before the governor of the Hudson's Bay Company in Winnipeg in all the finery of his Minnesota depredations—black coat with velvet collar, fine shawls, and a showy seven-shooter sidearm. In the arrogance of still considerable power he had made insolent demands of the British, acting more the superior than the supplicant in his negotiations with the redcoats. Now, as evening approached on Scattered Lake, six miles north of Hutchinson, on July 3, 1863, Little

Crow, in the rags of the finery taken from the whites, was picking raspberries for survival in a small clearing in his Big Woods with his son, the last of his legion.

Nearby, another father-and-son-team, farmer Nathan Lamson and his son Chauncy, were hunting. Spotting the two Sioux through the trees, they took cover behind a vine-wrapped poplar tree and opened fire. Little Crow went down, struck in the side by a bullet from Nathan Lamson's rifle, but not willing to release his spirit without a fight. Scooping up first Wowinape's weapon and then his own, Little Crow fired back at the farmers, striking the elder Lamson a glancing blow on his left shoulder blade. The farmer rolled away to reload just as Chauncy and Little Crow fired at the same time. The boy's bullet struck the old chief's gunstock, then penetrated Little Crow's side. He realized immediately that the wound was fatal. Wowinape later testified, "He told me that he was killed and asked me for water, which I gave him. He died immediately after."[5]

Wowinape fled, leaving his father's body in the Big Woods. Less than a month later Sibley's soldiers captured him near Devil's Lake. Though sentenced to death, his execution was stayed, and he was released from prison in 1866. He later turned away from the spirit gods of his father and his people and accepted the white man's religion and a white man's name, Thomas Wakeman. Wowinape/Wakeman founded the first YMCA for the Sioux.

Little Crow's corpse was hardly accorded the honors usually due a fallen leader. The morning after his slaying, July 4, a cavalry detachment found his body, scalped it, and carried it into Hutchinson to use as the centerpiece for the town's Independence Day celebration. Deposited in the center of town, the body drew an inquisitive and revengeful crowd. Firecrackers were lodged in the corpse's ears and nose and set off. When interest and maliciousness waned, the remains of Little Crow were transported to the edge of town and tossed into an offal pit.

The indignities visited on the body of the Santee chief continued. A cavalry officer decapitated the corpse with his saber and presented the head to the town doctor who preserved it in a tub of lime. Later, over the outraged objections of Henry Sibley, the skull, scalplock, and two forearm bones, deformed by earlier gunshot wounds, were gathered for an exhibit at the State Historical Society in St. Paul. Nathan Lamson collected the $500 bounty for Little Crow in 1864.[6]

Only in 1971 were the remains of Little Crow finally granted a measure of respect. With his grandson—Wowinape's son—standing in attendance, Little Crow was consigned to a family plot in South Dakota.[7]

The Last Hangings

The gallows claimed their last two Santee victims nearly three years after the mass hangings in Mankato. Shakopee, one of the first war chiefs to declare war in August 1862, and Medicine Bottle had fled to Canada after Wood Lake. In December 1863 a lieutenant from Hatch's Battalion dangled promises of a substantial reward before two Canadians, John McKenzie and Onisime Giguere, for the apprehension of the chiefs. The Canadians ingratiated themselves with the two exiled chiefs, plied them with wine and whiskey spiked with laudanum, and then subdued them with chloroform-soaked rags.[8]

Delivered to the American officer waiting across the border, the Santee pair were imprisoned and condemned at Fort Snelling and given a date with the hangman on November 11, 1865. An apocryphal story has Shakopee gesturing from beneath the noose as he heard the whistle of the first locomotive in the region echo from the Mississippi River's limestone bluffs and declaiming the end of one era and the beginning of another, "As the Indian goes out, the white man comes in." Though the cinematic speech never occurred, this final hanging did mark a melodramatic end to Santee Minnesota.[9]

The Minnesota Toll

The term "massacre" has been used far too lightly in the literature and rhetoric of the old West, particularly in reference to the victories of red over white. The Battle of the Little Bighorn has often ludicrously been called the Custer Massacre, as if the troopers of the Seventh Cavalry had been helpless, unarmed innocents and not armed and aggressive combatants bent on killing Sioux and Cheyenne. The only noncombatants on the field of the Little Bighorn were the women and children in the Indian camp. The killing of a single frontier family (such as the "German family massacre" in 1874) or of a band of buffalo hunters by Indian raiders was also often grandiloquently overdramatized as a massacre, when the event, though indeed an atrocity, should have been more properly labeled a murder or, at most, a mass killing.

But the calamity that crashed down upon Minnesota during those deadly August days of 1862 is fully deserving of the title of massacre. The killing was wholesale and savage and on a scale comparable to very few such episodes in the history of Indian-white relations in North America. Certainly the massacre was without parallel in the Indian wars fought west of the Mississippi. Contrary to popular conceptions and myths—fostered in large part by Hollywood's need for spectacular cinematic bloodbaths to spice its Western epics—there were few major massacres of white civilians during the Indian wars of the West. Thousands of white civilians were killed by marauding war parties in the half-century of conflict west of the great river, but these killings took place over a vast time and space. Most white victims died in isolated farms, ranches, prospecting sites, or single wagons crossing the prairie. War parties generally stalked single families or small parties of prospectors. Towns, villages, and large wagon trains were rarely attacked.

To find similar large-scale slaughters of white noncombatants, the historian must look back to earlier times east of the Mississippi. A massacre of the size and suddenness of the Minnesota Uprising took place at Fort Mims, Alabama, in 1813, when as many as 500 whites (including about 100 armed militiamen) were butchered by the Creek Indians. In 1711 in North Carolina the Tuscarora killed nearly 300 white colonists in a sudden rebellion and the two Powhatan uprisings in 1622 and 1644 in Virginia each claimed over 300 white lives. But no other sudden mass slaying of white settlers even approaching the toll in Minnesota in 1862 ever took place in the long history of Indian-American conflict in all the vast territory west of the Mississippi. There was at least one major massacre of Hispanic white civilians in the American Southwest. In August 1680 the Pueblo Indians killed about 400 Spanish colonists in a few violent days. Hundreds of civilians were slain in the Sioux, Cheyenne, Comanche and Apache wars of the 1860s and 1870s, but those numbers accumulated over a period of months or even years, while the vast majority of Minnesota citizens slain in 1862 died their horrible deaths within a single week.

There were a great many mass slayings of hundreds of noncombatants in a single event or series of events over a brief period of time in the Western wars, but, with the exception of the Minnesota Massacre, they were all inflicted by the agents of civilization upon the aboriginal "savages."

No one knows for certain the true toll exacted by Little Crow's warriors in revenge for decades of the white man's deceit and encroachment. Estimates of white civilian fatalities range from 400 to a very unlikely figure of 2,000. The Minnesota Historical Society compiled a list of 644 civilian dead, including 221 in Renville County, 204 in Brown County, and 32 in the Dakota Territory. Another count comes up with 413 dead white noncombatants. The strict accuracy of such counts is dubious. No census had been taken of the settlers on the Minnesota frontier; no one knows how many died in isolated rural cabins. The population was growing and spreading and records could not keep up with it.[10]

The number of soldiers slain in the 1862 uprising is less open to argument. The Minnesota Historical Society puts the figure at 113, including

77 U.S. Army soldiers and 36 armed civilian volunteers and scouts. Though the society's calculations for specific battles is often at variance with other records, the overall figure does seem to be close to the mark. Adding up the most reliable counts of the various battles and skirmishes of the uprising almost always arrives at a figure in excess of 100 white combatant deaths.[11]

The Santee toll is the most ambiguous of all the casualty counts. The one precise compilation of Sioux casualties reports a probably low figure of 71 Santee dead.[12] Very few Sioux died in the general massacre of white civilians. Just a handful of warriors fell in the ambushes of Redwood Ferry and Birch Coulee. Even in the battle that broke the back of the Santee resistance, Wood Lake, no more than twenty-five Dakotas were slain. Therefore, the great bulk of Santee slain fell in their unsuccessful attacks on Fort Ridgely and New Ulm. With about one hundred casualties in each battle, surely no more than fifty percent of the fallen were killed. With the maximum of one hundred killed at Fort Ridgely and New Ulm and the twenty-five dead at Wood Lake, surely no more than an additional twenty-five died in all other encounters. To this approximate toll of 150 dead can be added the 38 who died on the gallows and the 600 who died of disease while imprisoned or in subsequent Nebraska exile for the final toll on the Santees for their 1862 paroxysm of rage against white Minnesota.

Part Two

The Dakota War, 1863–1865

6. The Raiding Season, 1863

There may not have been another scarlet season of slaughter on the Minnesota frontier in 1863 to match the madness of August 1862 as so many had feared, but there was considerable hostile Indian activity, a rash of raids, and more than a dozen white deaths to remind the citizens of the northwestern state of the terrors of the summer before.

From the beginning of the Sibley expedition of 1863, there existed considerable doubt among Minnesota officials and citizens that an offensive was the best defense. Governor Ramsey had stressed to Sibley as the latter organized his offensive the high level of anxiety prevailing on the Minnesota frontier. A sudden Sioux attack of even moderate proportions would, he feared, spark a panic that would drive the white population of the western counties back to the Mississippi. But neither Sibley nor his commander shared the governor's worries. Pope, in fact, had advised Sibley that he need not maintain the small posts erected during the winter but could absorb their tiny garrisons into his expeditionary force as his column passed by. Sibley assured the Minnesota governor that he intended to protect the settlers and that the best way to do that was to strike at the Indians in their prairie sanctuaries. The Sioux would be too busy defending their nomadic base to strike across the border.[1]

Sibley was overly optimistic. In mid–April, long before the expeditionary brigade was prepared to strike, a raiding party of Santees struck in the Watonwan Valley, plundering homes, rustling horses, cattle, and sheep, and killing a soldier and two civilians. The raiders were chased to Lake Shetek by Lt. Colonel Marshall with a detachment of the Seventh Regiment and the Mounted Rangers, but they escaped. In the following month another Minnesota citizen was slain two miles from New Ulm, where a company of the Mounted Rangers was based, and the miscreants again evaded pursuit.[2]

Ramsey again pushed the panic button. On May 23 he urged Sibley in the strongest terms to take some forceful and highly visible action against the Indians to soothe his constituents' fears. Sibley was still not convinced. He pointed out that it was impossible to station a sentry at every farmhouse on the frontier and advocated citizen self-defense against the small raiding parties, which, he was still convinced, would cease their mischief as soon as the expedition got underway. Although Ramsey could not fathom why despite 5,000 soldiers in the state it was necessary to mobilize the state militia, he had already sent militia Brigadier General Emil Munch on a tour of the eight counties most exposed to Indian attack to organize the settlers for armed self-defense.[3]

Sibley, under fire from both the governor and the states' newspapers, finally acquiesced. In a June 4 general order he apportioned 2,000 of his troops to an extensive defense belt girding the line of settlement and advanced a line of early warning posts to the very edge of the frontier. Included in this defensive force was the whole of the Eighth Regiment (three companies of which were stationed at Fort Abercrombie to protect the Red River trains of the Hudson's Bay Company), three companies of the Mounted Rangers (two of which were stationed at Fort Ridgely), nine companies of the Ninth Regiment, and a single company of the Tenth Regiment.[4]

Even as the expeditionary force was gathering at Camp Pope and the defensive units were garrisoning their guard posts, the Indians demonstrated, as they had done so often before and would continue to do for another twenty-seven years, that not even thousands of armed men could guarantee a frontier against the hit-and-run guerrilla tactics of a handful of resolute raiders. The raiding season kicked into high gear in June. First a Brown County man was butchered less than a mile from Fort Ridgely. Then on the night of June 7 a raiding party rode into Wright County, only fifty miles from St. Paul, to steal horses. Captain John S. Cady of the Eighth Minnesota saddled up a squad of soldiers the next day to chase the raiders through Wright and Meeker counties to the Kandiyohi lakes where the horse thieves were overtaken. After an exchange of fire the Indians got away, apparently without punishment. The whites were not so lucky. Captain Cady was hit by a Sioux bullet that killed him almost instantly.[5]

On June 29, Wright County settler Amos Dustin was ambushed by members of Little Crow's party as he traveled with his family in an open wagon near Howard Lake, only forty-five miles from St. Paul. Three members of the family were killed immediately in a shower of arrows; a fourth was mortally wounded. Just two days later another traveler, James McGannon, was killed near Fairhaven in Wright County.[6]

Insignificant though it might have been in the larger scheme of things—with the July 3 killing of Little Crow by the Lamsons the only really important event in this season of raids—this spate of killings convinced a great many whites that the Big Woods were teeming with hostile Indians. Although no evidence of Chippewa or Winnebago involvement or even restiveness existed in Minnesota, an imminent outbreak by those tribes was also forecast. In several counties, most particularly in Wright, a panic equivalent to that of 1862 seized the frontier. Much of the population was soon on the roads to St. Paul, with wagons heaped high with their possessions and their livestock driven alongside. When the rash of murders abated, the fugitives began returning to their homesteads, although a good number, tired of living on the knife-edge of fear for so long, abandoned their claims for good.[7]

Convinced now that static garrisons and even patrolling soldiers were not sufficient to protect the frontier, civilian authorities took a series of measures to boost the defense of the line of settlement. On July 4, 1863, Adjutant-General Oscar Malmros issued a general order for the establishment of a mounted corps of "volunteer scouts," consisting of experienced hunters and trappers, to patrol the Big Woods from Sauk Center to the northern edge of Sibley County. The scouts were to serve a two-month tour of duty and provide their own arms, equipment, and provisions. In return, the volunteers were to be paid two dollars a day each, with a greater incentive of twenty-five dollars offered for the scalp of each hostile Sioux Indian collected. The general order did not bother to explain the process by which any particular scalp could demonstrate the degree of "hostility" or even the tribal identity of the Indian from whom it was taken.

To bolster the enlisted scouts and the number of dead Indians a reward of seventy-five dollars was offered to any person not in military service who could produce "satisfactory proof" of the killing of a hostile Sioux warrior. This inducement to "independent scouts" was increased to two hundred dollars a head on September 22. This open season on "hostile Indians" enjoyed little success. In more than three months, bounty was paid for only five scalps. The volunteer scouts were mustered out of service on September 20.[8]

To supplement the forces protecting Minnesota, a gaggle of high-powered state leaders, including Senator Henry Rice and Senator Morton Wilkinson, convinced the secretary of war to authorize, on June 12, the formation of a battalion of two infantry and two cavalry companies (the two infantry companies were quickly converted to cavalry). Recruited in Minnesota and supported by Chippewa auxiliaries, the battalion was to be independent of both Pope's and Sibley's command. Placed in charge of the maverick outfit was Major Edwin A. C. Hatch, a resident of Minnesota since 1843 and a former agent to the Blackfeet Sioux; however, he lacked military experience.[9]

Pope and Sibley were both outraged at this seeming usurpation of their military authority and control. Pope protested to both Halleck and Stanton, particularly about the part of the plan calling for Chippewa auxiliaries. In a letter to Stanton he claimed that "Hatch is but an instrument of Rice." Sibley felt that the raising of the independent battalion was a direct slap at his competence and capability. In his diary entry for July 8 he wrote, "Learned of the order granting authority to Major Hatch to raise two companies of infantry and two of cavalry to serve against the Indians during the existence of this war. The whole thing I regard as a miserable scheme got up by Rice and others, who hate General Pope and do not love me and who wish to annoy and humiliate us both. I have a contempt for the whole humbug inventor and all."[10]

Sibley's and Pope's protestations did lead to a narrowing of the autonomy of "Hatch's Battalion," and it was placed under Sibley's command. At Sibley's suggestion the battalion was posted to the north at what later became the town of Pembina, primarily to guard against a possible incursion by those Santee who had fled across the Canadian border after the 1862 uprising and also as a form of exile to this stepchild military formation. A northward march of four hundred miles from October 5 to November 13, during which many of the battalion's oxen and mules perished, brought it to its posting as winter began its usual early siege of the northern woods. High winds, deep snow, and freezing temperatures plagued Hatch's men on the march and as they constructed their cantonment. The mercury fell to forty degrees below zero as 1863 ended, and on the first day of the new year it fell to sixty degrees below.[11]

The abominable weather and the requirements of construction did not prevent Hatch from aggressive patrolling. For all its efforts, however, the battalion fought only one engagement with hostile Indians. News of a party of Sioux encamped near the old British trading post of St. Joseph, forty miles west of Pembina, sent a dismounted detachment of twenty out on the trail to the trading post on December 15. After a forced march, the white platoon located and closed in, undetected, around the sleeping Indian camp at 3:00 A.M. As the Indians awakened and began to emerge from their tepees, Hatch's men commenced firing. The fight was completely one-sided. Six Sioux were killed even before they were able to return fire, and the rest fled. Two or three soldiers were slightly wounded.[12]

Aside from that incident, Hatch's Battalion passed a largely uneventful, if arduous winter at Pembina. From that post on the Red River in the northeast corner of Dakota seventy miles below Fort Garry, Hatch devoted much of his military activities to luring hungry and haggard Sioux refugees away from Canada. Ninety-one Sioux did recross the Canadian border during the winter to surrender themselves to the garrison. Among the Indians hoodwinked into captivity by agents of the coattail-riding crony of Senator Rice were Shakopee and Medicine Bottle, both of whom were subsequently hanged.

At the end of the long, hard winter, during which three-quarters of the post's stock died of starvation and cold, the battalion was transferred to Fort Abercrombie to garrison that post and patrol the Red River Valley. Commanded after September 5, 1864, by Lt. Colonel C. Powell Adams, the independent battalion served until June 1866, when it was mustered out of service. The battalion claimed a total of 28 Indians killed and 400 taken prisoner. Although hardly the elite strike force that could deal a mortal blow to whatever hostile Indians remained on the Minnesota frontier, Hatch's Battalion did perform a useful defensive and patrolling mission for the northern half of the state and saved the government the trouble and expense of detaching troops for that purpose from the battlefronts of the Civil War.[13]

The Raiding Season in Dakota Territory

In 1863 white civilians suffered from Indian attacks in Dakota and Nebraska as well as in Minnesota. The news of the Minnesota Massacre of 1862 had caused the flight of one-fourth of the white population of the Dakota Territory. Acting Governor and Superintendent of Indian Affairs John Hutchinson prodded federal military and political authorities with frequent requests for more protection for his thin line of civilization scattered across the Dakota prairie. In a letter, dated April 18, 1863, to the district commander, Brig. General John Cook, the acting governor requested three cavalry companies to protect the settlements of Yankton, Vermillion, and Sioux Falls against the Santees. Otherwise, he claimed, the area would probably fall to the Indians.[14] When Sully took over the district command from Cook in May to organize his expedition, he left two companies of the Dakota Cavalry Regiment, led by captains Minor and Tripp, to protect the citizens of eastern Dakota. Those two companies of the Dakota Cavalry vigilantly scouted the Plains and provided some degree of protection. "Without it, the territory would have been depopulated," wrote Hutchinson.[15]

But the cavalry's protective line was stretched too thin to prevent every outrage. On May 6 a man named Jacobson was killed by Indians at Greenway's Ferry. In July, in northeast Nebraska, twelve miles from Yankton in the Dakota Territory, the five children of the Wiseman family were murdered by hostiles while their mother was temporarily absent and their father was marching with Sully. On September 3 the mail coach en route to Sioux City was attacked forty miles west of Yankton, and Sergeant Eugene F. Trask of the Seventh Iowa Cavalry, riding aboard the stage, was killed.

Shakopee (left) and Medicine Bottle. (Courtesy of the Minnesota Historical Society.)

William Tripp's B Company pursued the war party that had attacked the stage two hundred miles into the Dakota Territory but failed to overtake the hostiles.[16]

The most significant Indian attacks on civilians in Dakota were the two conducted against boats on the Missouri River. On August 3, twenty-two miners descending the Missouri River in a Mackinaw boat were killed after a desperate fight with Santees and Yanktonais in the area vacated by Sibley's column two days before. Earlier, in July, much farther northwest and outside the settled region of the territory, the steamboats *Robert Campbell Jr.* and *Shreveport* nearly had fallen prey to the Indians. The *Robert Campbell* had steam-paddled out of St. Louis on May 21, carrying thirty passengers, including two women and two children, and $75,000 in annuity goods due by treaty to various Indian tribes (including $35,000 owed to Indians in areas infested with hostile tribesmen). In its own right the riverboat was nearly as important as the Sully column: the boat steamed to maintain peace with several Indian bands through annuity distribution, while the Sully expedition marched to carry war to other Indian groups.

The two-winter-long drought that was to cause Sully so much trouble and delay also slowed the progress of the annuity boat due to low water, and the *Robert Campbell* did not reach Fort Pierre until June 20. There at Fort Pierre, Indian agent Henry Reed and his associate, S. N. Latta, met representatives from seven Sioux tribes. The Indians at Fort Pierre had been waiting two months for their annuities, and some felt that they were doubly owed because they had taken considerable risks in securing the release of several white Minnesotans from their Santee captors. Also at the fort were members of the Two Kettles and Yankton tribes, angered at the unjustified killing of seven members of their bands by soldiers from Fort Randall. The agents were able to appease the relatives of the slain with special gifts drawn from the annuity stores.[17]

Sailing on, the riverboat reached Fort Berthold on Independence Day to deliver goods to the Mandans, Gros Ventres, and Arikaras. The village of these peaceful Indians had been attacked just a few days before by a Sioux war party, which had also driven off the horse herd of seventy-five mounts from Fort Berthold. The steamboat thus was in dangerous country without military protection (its only military escort had been thirty soldiers aboard to protect against Confederate guerrillas and they had disembarked at St. Joseph). While trying to load wood aboard for its boilers on July 5 and July 6 the *Robert Campbell* twice had to fight off boarding attempts by parties of Hunkpapas, Miniconjous, and Blackfeet. After the second fight, the boat was joined by the steamer *Shreveport*, which was returning from a trip to Fort Benton. Together the two boats proceeded on upriver, with the *Shreveport* usually 150 yards in the lead.

The next day, July 7, at a point above Fort Berthold about fifty miles below the Missouri's junction with the Yellowstone River, the two ships encountered several hundred Sioux lining the riverbank who expressed friendliness and asked the Indian agents to come ashore. Ignoring the combative evidence of animosity of the two previous days, Latta foolishly asked steamboat Captain LeBarge to dispatch his yawl (a small boat) to shore to bring aboard a collection of chiefs for a distribution of gifts of sugar, coffee, tobacco, and other goodies. Six brave and rather foolhardy men landed the yawl, which was immediately grappled by the Indians. Some of the Sioux ran up to the white men to shake hands. Just as the nervous white men let out a sigh of relief at this display of amiability, the Indians suddenly sprang back and opened fire. Three men were killed and two wounded, one of them critically. The sixth threw himself over the side and started swimming back toward the riverboats.

The hundred men aboard the ships, anchored a hundred yards away against a sand bar, replied to this treachery with fire from rifles, double-barreled shotguns, and three small cannon. The Indians abandoned the yawl and fled into the brush lining the shore. After a three-hour ship-to-shore firefight, the Sioux withdrew. Friendly Indians later reported that thirty-eight hostiles had been killed, forty wounded, and five horses killed. The figures may have been inflated to please their white friends who brought them all those welcome annuity gifts, but other reports also speak of twenty or more hostiles killed.[18]

The next day the boats reached the mouth of the Yellowstone. The *Robert Campbell* could proceed no farther because the drought had reduced the river channel to a depth of only two feet. Five days were spent transferring the *Campbell*'s cargo to the *Shreveport*, which had a shallower draft. The *Shreveport* then steamed six miles up to Fort Union to deliver goods to the Assiniboines and store the rest, intended for the Crows, at the fort to await the next spring when mountain run-off would allow navigation up the Milk River to Crow country.[19]

The annuity goods shipped by paddle-wheel steamer helped to maintain peaceful, if often troubled, relations with as many Indians in the Dakota Territory as took to war. Age-old intertribal feuds and animosities also helped to prevent a full-scale northern prairie tribal alliance that could have presented a real threat to white settlement of the Dakota Territory. All the other tribes in Dakota—like the Chippewa and Winnebago in Minnesota, Wisconsin, and Iowa and some of the Sioux—remained on the sidelines or even helped the American army against the Sioux hostiles.

The Poncas, Gros Ventres, Arikaras, and Mandans, though destitute from the drought and poorly provisioned by the whites who were treaty-bound to succor them, remained peaceful, though harassed by both Sioux and Americans. The Yanktons in southeastern Dakota, with the exception of a handful of headstrong young braves, also generally kept the peace. This least combative of all the Sioux tribes certainly had to endure provocation that year of 1863. A cavalry patrol from Fort Randall, searching for horse thieves, had rounded up seven Yankton and Two Kettle men, wrongly blamed them for the thievery, then shot them to death when they attempted to flee. But Yankton agent W. A. Burleigh's ministrations and gifts to the bereaved from the *Robert Campbell* soothed the potentially volatile situation, and Burleigh was able to report a pacific Yankton tribe in a letter dispatched on October 12, 1863.[20]

In the opinion of Hutchinson and other civilian officials the expeditions of Sibley and Sully that summer of 1863 eased the Indian threat but did not eliminate it. Hutchinson felt that although the Santees and the Yanktonais had been discouraged from continuing hostilities by the success of the expeditions, the Miniconjous, Hunkpapas, and other Teton tribes had been incited into taking the warpath by the Sibley and Sully columns. Consequently, if the threat to the Dakota Territory from one group of Sioux was diminished, that result was more than offset by an increased threat from another, stronger group. The acting governor was generous in his praise for Sully's conduct of the campaign, but he felt that further expeditions would be required against the hostiles and that Sully's forces should be quartered in the Dakota district over the winter to protect white civilians and to prepare for a renewed spring campaign in 1864. He also called for the establishment of a chain of military posts to be forged from one anchor at Fort Ridgely, Minnesota, southwest to a second anchor at Fort Randall, Dakota Territory, by way of Sioux Falls and Yankton.[21]

Winnebago Troubles

The Chippewas of the Lake Superior region remained quiet in 1863, but the 400 Winnebagos remaining in Wisconsin evinced restiveness during the season of Santee raids in Minnesota and Dakota. In various incidents one white woman and two Winnebagos were killed. The Menominee tribe living in the same area wanted the wandering bands of Winnebagos corralled so that they would not be unjustly implicated in their forays. In mid–July Pope responded to the pleas of Menominees and whites by dispatching a company of the Thirtieth Wisconsin Regiment to preserve order in the region. This move soon proved sufficient to subdue what few hostile urges remained among the Winnebagos.[22]

7. Into Dakota

The Sibley and Sully expeditions into the Dakota Territory may have had their genesis in the Minnesota Outbreak of 1862, but they were motivated almost as much by a desire to further settlement in Dakota and to protect the Missouri River lifeline to the Montana gold fields as by any desire to punish the Sioux for the Minnesota mass murder and to protect the survivors from a renewal of that terror. One-fourth of the white population of the Dakota Territory had fled following the Minnesota Massacre; more left during the spring raids of 1863. Something had to be done to preserve the remaining white settlements and, if possible, expand them.

Eastern Dakota had acquired a value to white America in its own right quite aside from its worthiness as a buffer between Minnesota and the Tetons. Lieutenant G. K. Warren, in a survey report issued in 1855, judged the soils west of the ninety-seventh meridian unsuitable for agricultural purposes. But a bevy of land speculators and merchants ignored the appraisal and was quick off the mark to exploit the wealth, or potential wealth, of the upper Missouri plains region. Aiding greatly in that exploitation was the cession by the Yankton Sioux in 1858 of fourteen million acres between the Big Sioux and the Missouri rivers. This opened the way for development, and a dozen land companies were offering sites for both towns and farms by the time Dakota was organized as a territory on March 2, 1861. The two largest of those real estate enterprises were the Dakota Land Company and the Yankton Town and Land Company. The two became bitter rivals for the political and economic control of the territory, competing for most of the profits to be gained from land sales, the provisioning of troops, and railroad grants as well as for the patronage ladled out from political and administrative offices.[1]

The value of the Dakota Territory was further increased by the discovery of gold near Bannock, Montana, in 1862, followed by another gold strike at Alder Gulch in the spring of 1863. The Missouri River had once been a major artery for the transportation of the fur trade, but trapping had fallen off after the 1830s as fashions changed and the numbers of fur-bearing animals declined. Although steamboats first plied the river in 1832, there was only light traffic—just one or two boats a year—on the Missouri until the Montana gold strikes. There was access to the diggings from east, west, and south, but the most popular route to the gold fields was by steamboat up the Missouri to Fort Benton, then overland by horse or mule the remaining one or two hundred miles to the prospecting camps. All mining machinery, other heavy freight, most of the supplies for the camps, and a good many prospectors journeyed upriver through Dakota by steamboat. The boats returned downriver with gold dust, increasing the wealth of the general population of the north and thus the economic strength of the Union cause in the Civil War. The movement of the boats up and down the Missouri was often impeded by Sioux harassment and outright attack. Consequently, crushing the Indian menace in the Dakota Territory was important not only for the settlement and business welfare of white Dakota but also for the strength and general welfare of the federal government.

To deal with the Indian problem in Minnesota and Dakota, the War Department had created the Department of the Northwest, embracing Minnesota, Wisconsin, Iowa, Nebraska, and Dakota (with a District of Iowa and Dakota command also organized, but subordinate to the Department of the Northwest). The department commander was Major General John Pope. The creation of the department served a dual purpose: it centralized control of the increasingly more complex and more important military operations on the northern plains, and it provided a convenient banishment of Pope, who had so disappointed his radical friends in Congress because of the fiasco of Second Bull Run.

Pope accepted the frontier assignment only because it offered him a step to rehabilitation. A significant victory over the Indians could rescue his reputation and win him reassignment to the real show in the South. Sibley's quick triumph at Wood Lake not long after Pope had taken over the department encouraged the general into telegraphing a victory message to Halleck. But his hopes for a quick reinstatement were premature, for the inciting of the Yanktonai and the Teton by the fleeing Santee soon made it clear that a further military effort was necessary to secure Minnesota and eastern Dakota.[2]

Consequently, Pope rather reluctantly drew up the plans for a spring campaign. He originally planned a three-column simultaneous advance: one column to advance from the head of navigation on the Minnesota River, the second from the Iowa border via the Big Sioux River, and the third from Fort Randall up the east bank of the Missouri. General Sibley was to head both columns striking from the east; General John Cook was to command the Missouri River force. The two arms of Sibley's offensive were to shove the Indians against the Missouri, where Cook, coming up north from the hostiles' rear, could catch the Sioux as they toppled backward into his arms. If the plan was carried out properly, the offensive columns striking from east and south would crush the Sioux between them.[3]

The plan was amended as spring advanced. Sibley was unable to enlist and equip enough troops to both satisfy the increasing calls for a strong defensive stay-behind force and to staff two full offensive columns. Pope thus reduced the Minnesota and Iowa offensive forces to a single column moving from Fort Ridgely into Dakota by way of Devil's Lake.[4]

Another snag in the smooth fabric of the operational plan arose over the command of the Missouri River column. The original commander, General Cook, was very unpopular with the settlers because of his perceived failure to respond promptly to their demands for troop protection against the savages. Bowing to intensifying political pressure, Halleck removed Cook from his command, practically at the last moment, in the spring of 1863.[5]

Pope wanted to replace Cook with a former member of his Army of the Potomac staff, General C. W. Roberts, who was still serving in Virginia. Halleck tried to placate Pope, but the chief of staff had his own ideas about who was best suited to command the Missouri River column. In a telegram to Pope, he assured Pope that Roberts was to be sent west to join him as soon as he could be relieved of his current assignment at Harpers Ferry. On May 17 Halleck further notified the Northwest Department commander that Roberts was on his way. Also headed his direction, however, was Brig. General Alfred E. Sully, and he rather than Roberts was to take over the command of the Missouri River column. In that same telegram Halleck appended another change to the plan of campaign by suggesting that the column should proceed up the west bank, instead of the east bank, of the Missouri River in order to protect the Nebraska and Overland Stage and Telegraph Route.[6]

Pope was incensed by the chief of staff's interference. He objected to Halleck that Sully's health was not strong enough for active campaigning. Pope insisted that "some officer of experience and activity" should head the expedition. He planned to disregard Halleck's wishes by giving the column command to Roberts if he arrived soon enough. Halleck fired back telegraphically "Orders to Roberts were issued two days ago ... [but] I think you will do wrong to send Roberts in charge of the Missouri Expedition. Sully is the man for that place.... Secretary Stanton directed me to say to you that Roberts should not be assigned as you propose."[7]

Pope's opposition, which bordered on hatred against Sully, had in truth little to do with health or a dearth of experience. Though Sully did suffer from periodic bouts of rheumatism, the attacks were never incapacitating, and few U.S. Army officers had more experience with Indians. He had spent most of two decades, from his graduation from West Point in 1841 to the outbreak of the Civil War in 1861, fighting Indians—the Seminoles in the Florida swamps in 1841 and 1842, the Rogue River Indians in northern California and Oregon in the late 1840s and early 1850s, the Sioux on the northern Plains in the mid–1850s, and the Southern Cheyenne on the southern prairies in 1860. In combat and in treaty negotiations, either as a warmaker or a peacemaker, Sully had accumulated extensive dealings with most of the Plains tribes, including the Sioux, Cheyenne, Crows, Poncas, Pawnees, Arikaras, Mandans, Gros Ventres, Omahas, Chippewas, and Winnebagos.

Sully probably knew the specific region in which he would be campaigning as well as any Union officer (and that knowledge was communicated to Pope by General Sibley, who strongly approved of Sully's appointment). In 1856, while stationed at Fort Ridgely, Sully had led an infantry company on a 350-mile march to Fort Pierre on the Missouri River to join General Harney's expedition against the Sioux. After concluding a treaty with nine Sioux tribes following Harney's campaign, Sully had remained at Fort Pierre to command the garrison there through the winter of 1856/57. In the spring of 1857 he had led the largely unsuccessful punitive expedition against Inkpaduta's bunch following the Spirit Lake Massacre.[8]

Along with the frontier record and Sibley's endorsement of Sully, Pope also knew from personal experience that Sully was a capable field commander. That knowledge had been gained during Pope's darkest hour. On the night of September 1, 1862, following the Union debacle at Second Bull Run, Sully had commanded a regiment that helped hold off Stonewall Jackson's vanguard at Chantilly, keeping clear the Union Army's route of retreat to Washington and preventing Pope's defeat from turning into a rout.

Sully's Civil War record was without the shame of Pope's. He had risen from captain to brevet colonel in just five months (March to July, 1862) and had been twice cited for gallantry and meritorious service during the Peninsula Campaign. Promoted to brevet brigadier general, he had led a brigade of volunteers at Antietam and had gone on to lead a brigade into the hells of Fredericksburg and Chancellorsville.[9]

Quite aside from the painful reminder of his great defeat that Sully as a subordinate would always be, Pope more than likely nursed his grudge against Sully because he suspected that the War Department doubted his own ability to conduct a successful Indian campaign and had assigned Sully to his department to firm up the command structure. If this was true, Pope undoubtedly interpreted Sully's assignment as another personal insult—on a par with his banishment to this frontier assignment—instigated by the swarm of his political enemies in the nation's capital to dig deeper the grave in which they were trying to bury his military reputation.

Sully was in truth hardly more enthusiastic about the prospects of his new assignment than was the department commander. If he was not fully cognizant of the dispute between Pope and Halleck concerning him, he was wearily experienced with what had always been a career-deadening posting on the western frontier. Pulled from the fast track of career advancement in Virginia, he expected things to be little different on the frontier this time. The twenty years it had required to advance from second lieutenant to captain on the Indian frontier had been only typical. His fast climb up the promotional ladder with the Army of the Potomac was now seemingly to be replaced with the usual slow grind up the most gradual of slopes here on the western prairies, while more fortunate colleagues could continue their hurtle toward a major-general's two stars.

If Sully arrived at Sioux City sullen about his reassignment, much of his bitterness must have been ameliorated by the warmth of the welcome given him by the region's citizens. Aware of his reputation as an Indian fighter, the locals looked on Sully as a deliverer from the Sioux menace. Most of the officers and men he was to command also quickly developed a liking for him.

Representative of these views, Colonel Minor T. Thomas of the Eighth Minnesota later described Sully in 1864 as

> an unpretentious man of medium size, and rather past the vigorous days of the prime of manhood [Sully was forty-three at the time although he looked closer to sixty], yet his perceptions were remarkably clear, and he appears to know intuitively just where the Indians were and what they would do. These intuitive qualities, that had been more fully developed by long service in the regular army, rendered him fully competent for the duty to which he was assigned, and added to these a genial temperament made him an agreeable commander.[10]

However, there were dissenting views among the military. Sergeant J. H. Dripps of the Sixth Iowa Cavalry had a low opinion of Sully's geniality. "General Sully had no superior as an Indian fighter, but he had one enemy he never conquered and that was his ungovernable temper. If he was crossed or criticized he would fairly foam with rage."[11]

Indeed, Sully was rumored to possess a vocabulary to match his disposition. On the other hand, given the job confronting him, a few choice expletives were not only understandable but necessary. The general faced the monumental task of whipping a collection of raw recruits with little or no training, hastily organized and indifferently equipped, into an efficient Indian-fighting army.

On paper Sully was provided with a powerful force: detachments of the Forty-first Iowa Infantry and the Thirtieth Wisconsin Infantry, the Sixth

Iowa Cavalry Regiment, eight companies of the Second Nebraska Cavalry, two companies of the Dakota Cavalry, and one company of the Seventh Iowa Cavalry, for a total authorized strength on paper of 2,000 cavalry and 300 infantry. Because of detachments, illness, and understrength units, the actual number of soldiers available for offensive operations was considerably smaller. In a telegram to Halleck on July 27, 1863, Pope reported that Sully's troops "were not even 1,200 strong."[12]

Nonetheless, when combined with Sibley's command of 2,200 infantry and 800 cavalry, the units involved in Pope's 1863 Dakota campaign constituted a force nearly half the size of the entire U.S. Army prior to the outbreak of the Civil War. It was to be one of the largest offensive commands ever to take the field against American Indians.

Pope's grand plan envisioned Sibley moving 600 miles from Fort Ridgely to Devil's Lake in Dakota, where most of the hostiles were reported to be concentrated. Should the Indians choose to stand their ground (always unlikely), they were to be engaged and destroyed there. If, as was much more likely, they chose to flee, the hostiles were to be herded toward the Missouri River. At the same time, Sully was to proceed upriver by steamboat to a point southwest of Devil's Lake to place his force between the retreating Sioux and the Missouri. According to the strategy's second phase, Sully, after snaring the Indians pushed west by Sibley, was to return to the Missouri and traverse the country on both sides of the river to the Black Hills.

The strategy seemed solid on paper, but time, distance, and the unpredictability of the Indians rendered it difficult to execute. As usual, intelligence about Indian movements and locations was late or wrong. By the beginning of the campaign, the Sioux were not at Devil's Lake anymore in any significant numbers and had not been there for several months. Pope's estimates of Indian intentions and willingness to fight were also badly off. The Santees who had fled to Dakota Territory in the fall of 1862 had gathered Yanktonais and Tetons to their cause and may have numbered 6,000 warriors or more by spring—which would have made it the most powerful concentration of Indians in the history of the western frontier up to that time, a force so powerful that many of its leaders boasted that no white soldier would dare set foot on the Dakota prairie.

Pope, on the other hand, believed that

> most of the Indians assembled near Devil's Lake and on the James River are planting Indians, who had been accustomed to depend upon their crops of corn for a large part of their food supply. The moment they find they will be prevented from raising any crops at all by the advance of our forces, and that they must fight so large a force unsuccessfully, I do not doubt that a very large part of them will come and deliver themselves up."[13]

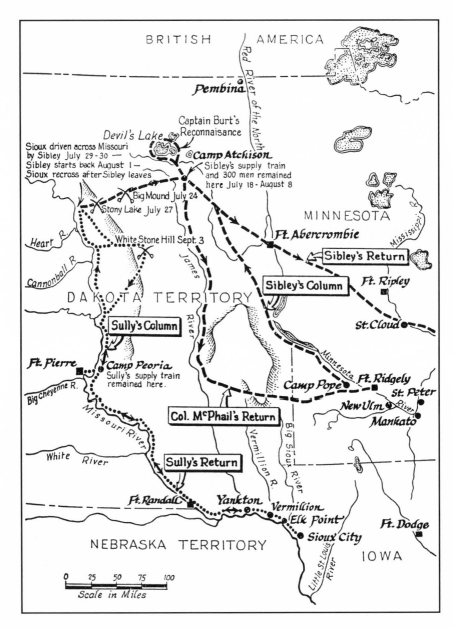

The Sirocco Campaign, 1863. (From *The Civil War in the Northwest* by Robert H. Jones. Courtesy of Robert H. Jones.)

The department commander obviously expected the campaign to be an anticlimax to the Minnesota uprising, more a matter of sweeping up the stragglers—no matter how numerous they were—than a new war against a formidable fighting force. He confidently predicted that by fall he would be able to send nearly all of the troops involved in the Dakota campaign south to the Civil War theater of operations.

In addition to underestimating the Indians' willpower and belligerency and miscalculating their location, Pope failed to factor in the unusual logistical difficulties his strike force would encounter. The unusually severe winter of 1862/63 had delayed the arrival of both troops and supplies at the assembly points for the Missouri River expedition. The lack of the normal run-off from a far below average mountain snowfall, combined with a continuance of the extreme drought of the spring and summer, caused the Missouri River to be lower than at any time in the previous thirty years. In consequence, supplies sent upriver from St. Louis were greatly delayed.

8. The Sibley Brigade

The war had been declared over by General Sibley in October 1862, but he was quick to assume a second war had spawned from the hatred and bloodshed of the first. A second season of horror on the Minnesota frontier seemed likely to him and a great many other military and political observers.

Sibley had collected more than 2,000 prisoners at the stockades at Mankato and Fort Snelling in the fall of 1862, but he had hoped for a more massive surrender. Of the 2,312 Lower Sioux (including 627 adult males) on the annuity rolls in 1861, about 700 remained at large on the prairies between the Red and Missouri rivers during the winter of 1862/63, the largest concentration burrowing in for the frigid months on the Missouri River near Fort Rice. The Upper Sioux, with a head count of 4,026 (including 909 adult males) in 1861, had fled completely from their villages on Lake Traverse shortly after Wood Lake.[1]

Sibley had tried to corral the Upper Sioux. On the day after Wood Lake he had promised in a letter to Sisseton Chief Standing Buffalo safety for his people if they showed a willingness to submit to the Great Father. The victor of Wood Lake had followed this with a second message urging a council to bring about some accommodation. But although the chief and his braves had endured enough of war, they were not ready to deliver themselves into the hands of an army hot for vengeance. The Upper Sioux had, consequently, fled north to huddle in winter camp around Devil's Lake.

The winter was rife with rumor. Various combinations of hostile Indians were reported here or there, as Yanktons and Yanktonais supposedly rushed to bolster the ranks of the renegade Santees. The Yanktonais were, according to rumor, being armed with weapons supplied by half-breed Canadian traders, trappers, and buffalo hunters and were receiving further sustenance and supplies from Fort Garry (present-day Winnipeg). The numbers of this phantom force, all set to descend once again on white Minnesota, escalated from Sibley's October 1862 estimate of 2,200 warriors to General Pope's February 1863 guess that Little Crow had assembled more than 7,000 braves for round two in the spring, although the department commander admitted that the "number ... [was] perhaps overestimated."[2]

Beyond the Yanktonai-Dakota threat coiled a second snake of hostility in the Hunkpapa and other Teton tribes west of the Missouri. They were led by such rising young war chiefs as Sitting Bull, Gall, and Two Moons, all embittered by the increasing wagon traffic through their lands. The wagons were filled with miners headed for the Idaho and Montana gold fields. The Tetons claimed that the passing prospectors frightened off the buffalo and left the microbes of white men's diseases in their wake.

Those hostile thousands waiting over the horizon certainly suited Pope's personal needs and ambitions. A man habitually underappreciated, according to his own estimation, Pope was bitterly disappointed by the distinct lack of praise from Washington for his successful resolution of the Minnesota War. He had hoped that a victory in the north woods would purchase him a ticket back to the Civil War center of the storm. But when no such recall came, the department commander resigned himself to a peripheral role in the northwest. If there was to be no new command against the secessionists, Pope was determined to at least make his distant department and himself as important as possible by continuing major combat operations. The Indian threat looming in Dakota was as much an opportunity as a danger, and Pope hoped to make the most of it.

In order to deter any second Indian assault on white civilization and also to punish the Sioux for the first attack, Pope had weaved a converging campaign of advancing columns into Dakota Territory. The columns would hopefully both push the hostile Santees and Yanktonais a safe distance from the Minnesota frontier of settlement and intimidate the Tetons who threatened the gold routes along the upper Missouri River. Endorsed by the War Department, the plan called for a column of mostly infantry to march northwest from Fort Ridgely towards Devil's Lake, while a second expedition, composed mainly of cavalry, headed up the Missouri River from Fort Randall and then northeast toward the same lake to act as the anvil against which the Indians retreating from the Fort Ridgely hammer would be smashed. Original campaign plans had called for a third column striking north from the Big Sioux, but a shortage of troops and Pope's fears that this extra arm of the assault would make timing and coordination too complex led to its elimination.

Pope was so anxious for a grand outcome to his grand campaign that he intimated that hot pursuit of the hostiles across the Canadian border might be justified. The general was particularly focused on groups of fugitive Sioux who had crossed the border, ragged and hungry, to beg for rations at Fort Garry and then recrossed to worry northern Minnesota. Pope wanted to end this use of Canada as a sanctuary and protect his northern flank, and he was ready to violate Canadian sovereignty to do so. Pope's request for the right of hot pursuit across the border had been passed on to the British minister to the United States, Richard Bickerton Pemell, Earl Lyons, but permission had been denied. Halleck, worried that Pope was not completely disabused of the notion of a Canadian caper, had to dispatch a restraining advisory to the department commander, reminding him that the president "directs that under no circumstances will our troops cross the boundary line into British territory without his authority."[3]

Sibley was given command of the Minnesota column, which was to include all troops in his district except for those already posted to defend the frontier line. Though the choice of Sibley as commander was a generally popular one, there was some opposition to it. Most prominent among Sibley's opponents was Minnesota Senator Henry Rice, a rival of Sibley since his fur trading days. When Rice's machinations to remove Sibley from his command came to naught, the contentious solon (who, as a Democrat, had little hope for reelection in an increasingly Republican state and Republican era) plotted to supplant Pope as department commander. Though backed by Minnesota's other senator, Morton Wilkinson, Rice's attempted coup made little headway with Halleck. The chief of staff agreed with Pope's evaluation of the Minnesota senators and their clique as "unscrupulous speculators and traders" who wanted the department command solely for their personal profit.[4]

Sibley had gathered a formidable force by early June 1863 at a bivouac he christened Camp Pope, sited at the junction of the Redwood and Minnesota rivers (near present-day Redwood Falls). Units collected for the great enterprise to come included nine companies of the Seventh Minnesota Infantry, commanded by Lt. Colonel William R. Marshall; eight companies of the Tenth Minnesota Infantry, led by Colonel James H. Baker; the Sixth Minnesota Infantry, under Colonel William Crooks; nine companies of the First Minnesota Mounted Rangers, armed with long-range rifles and commanded by Colonel Samuel McPhail; the Third Battery of Light Artillery, led by Captain John Jones (who had handled the howitzers in the defense of Fort Ridgely); 100 pioneers (engineers) from the Ninth Minnesota Infantry, under Captain John Chase; and 70 Indian and mixed-blood scouts, led by majors Joseph R. Brown, George A. McLeod, and William J. Dooley. Ration strength was reported at 2,200 infantry, 800 cavalry, 150 artillerymen, 100 pioneers, and 70 scouts, for a total of 3,320. To supply and sustain the expedition a train of 225 six-mule-team wagons was gathered, carrying provisions for ninety days. Supplementing the wagon-borne supplies was a herd of hundreds of cattle, to be driven along to furnish fresh meat to the column. In addition, another 100 wagons were collected to carry the column's camping gear, ammunition, bridging material, and quartermaster and medical supplies. It was the largest single force ever to take the field in the history of the Western Indian wars.[5]

Included among the officers accompanying Sibley's column were quite a few who later were to have distinguished legal or political careers in Minnesota, Dakota, or Washington. Colonel William Marshall served as governor of Minnesota. Colonel John T. Averill and Captain Eugene M. Wilson were later elected members of Congress from Minnesota. Colonel Samuel P. Jennison at one time served as the Minnesota secretary of state. Colonel James Baker was to be appointed commissioner of pensions. Captain Alonzo J. Edgerton became in later life chief justice of the Dakota Territory.[6]

There were a number of critics, among them Minnesota senators Rice and Wilkinson and other prominent Minnesotan political enemies of Sibley, who had complained to Halleck that the expedition was far too large and cumbersome to have any real hope of bringing the evasive, fleet-footed foe to decisive battle. They feared that while a majority of the trained armed soldiers in the state were traipsing around the Dakota prairies seeking an enemy who would snipe and steal from the lumbering column with abandon, too few troops would remain to patrol the frontier and defend the civilian population against savage raiders. Pope came under considerable pressure to whittle Sibley's force down and had earlier advised Sibley that a column of much more than 2,000 men would become both tactically and logistically unmanageable and unprofitable in operations against the Indians, as past Indian fighting expeditions had shown. As late as July 18 Pope advised against an expeditionary force of any more than 2,800 and was surprised when informed that Sibley had embarked into Dakota's grassy sea with a column considerably larger.[7]

Sibley's brigade had departed from Camp Pope on June 16 in a creaking and creeping column five miles long. The expedition had been delayed from the onset by the need to wait for the prairie grasses to grow abundantly enough to support the quartermaster stock and cavalry horses. The drought of the summer of 1863 was a continuation of the one from the year before and the worst in Dakota history. Consequently, the plains were painfully parched and bare. Dust enveloped the column, coated and choked men and horses. The lakes and streams were dry or so alkaline that the expedition's dogs all died of thirst or were shot when thirst drove them to snarling madness. Horses and mules also weakened and many died. Prairie fires added to the intolerable heat.

The march was almost entirely a morning affair due to the heat and dryness. Trumpets sounded reveille at two o'clock in the morning, and the march was commenced at the first flush of dawn. By around noon the march ground to a halt as soon as a campsite could be located near some low-lying area close to a lake or a marsh. It usually required the rest of the daylight hours to find enough grass to feed the stock. Horses, mules, and cattle could not be allowed to graze at night for fear of an Indian stampede and thus had to be tied to picket ropes and the sparse grass around the camp had to be scythed and brought to them. Finding enough water to sustain men and beasts was also a problem. Often the soldiers had to dig wells ten to twelve feet deep at the end of marshes in order to obtain water that was drinkable. Even the typical prairie fuel—the buffalo chip—was in short supply because the drought had dispersed the herds.

The march routine was particularly exhausting for the cavalry. Though they got to ride during the march while the infantrymen walked, once camp was reached the advantage switched sides. While the infantryman had considerable time to rest, the cavalryman had to take care of his mount's needs during the afternoon and then often had to ride picket guard outside the camp perimeter at night. Adding to these tiring duties was the anxiety produced by a potential Indian attack from outside, and the dangerous annoyance of dodging bullets from inside, fired by the green infantry standing guard on the camp's perimeter who often mistook the cavalry sentries for approaching Indians. This almost nightly affliction was finally cured by the cavalry pickets when, with the tacit approval of their officers, they returned fire to give the infantry guards an incentive to identify their targets more accurately.[8]

With regiments regularly alternating at the head of the column, the brigade proceeded slowly across southern Minnesota. It took ten days for the invasion force to reach the Dakota border, 119 miles from Camp Pope, at a point between Lakes Big Stone and Traverse, the site of the future village of Brown's Valley. The column rested for three days while cracking wagons and leaking barrels constructed from green lumber were repaired. Some of the doomsayers' predictions about an overlarge expedition accomplishing nothing but the burial of victims of the 1862 rising found along its route and the rapid consumption and depletion of its own supplies, seemed borne out as the hard bread supply shrank by 17,500 rations before the column had even waved good-by to Minnesota. A wagon convoy was sent north to Fort Abercrombie to replenish supplies for the expedition. It was escorted by three infantry companies, a cavalry battalion, and an artillery section— 600 men in total.[9]

Another five days' tramp over desert-dry prairies stripped bare by a Great Plains plague of locusts carried the column to the Big Bend of the Sheyenne River, seventy-four miles from Lake Traverse, by Independence Day. The expedition, rapidly exhausting itself without having yet encountered a single hostile Indian, had to interrupt its halting progress for another six days at what was dubbed Camp Hayes to await the return of the detachment sent to Fort Abercrombie for provisions. The ration train pulled into

Camp Hayes on July 9, and two mornings later the expeditionary force resumed its march on a northwest axis generally paralleling the Sheyenne River.

Sibley later described the terrible terrain his column had to traverse during this phase of the march in a letter to the Acting Assistant Adjutant-General in Milwaukee.

> The region traveled by my column between the first crossing of the Sheyenne River and the Coteau of the Missouri is for the most part uninhabitable. If the devil were permanently to select a residence upon the earth, he would probably choose this particular district for an abode, with the redskins' murdering and plundering bands as his ready ministers, to verify by their ruthless deeds his diabolical hatred to all who belong to a Christian race. Through the vast desert lakes fair to the eye abound, but generally their waters are strongly alkaline or intensely bitter and brackish. The valleys between them frequently reek with sulphur and other disagreeable vapors. The heat was so intolerable that the earth was like a heat furnace and the breezes that swept along its surface were as scorching and suffocating as the famed sirocco. Yet through all these difficulties, men and animals toiled on until the objectives of the expedition were accomplished.[10]

The Coteau des Missouri country, to which Sibley referred in his letter and toward which his column was now headed, is an area of elevated rolling plains located along a geological fault line that runs from close to the Canadian border generally east of the Missouri River to the James River and south to the present-day northern border of South Dakota. It was in the Coteau country that the major battles of the 1863 campaign were to be fought.

The Sheyenne River was forded again by the expedition, from east bank to west, on July 17 after a march of eighty-three miles through what are now Cass, Barnes, and Ransom counties. On that day three Red River buffalo hunters rode into Sibley's bivouac to inform the general of their sighting of a swarm of Sioux—up to 600 lodges—who had in recent days migrated from the Devil's Lake area to an encampment some seventy-five miles in the direction of the Missouri River.

These Indians were the Sissetons and Wahpetons of Chief Standing Buffalo's band, a group that from first to last in the 1862–65 conflict was, with a handful of headstrong exceptions, a reluctant participant in the Indian war and that had almost always been more interested in flight than in fight. It was these Indians' poor luck to constantly meet up with and become entangled with more belligerent bands. That fate held true again in this July of 1863, when they fell in with Wahpekutes and other Sioux led by the infamous Inkpaduta, who, like the Sissetons, were hunting buffalo. Several frontier chroniclers claimed that the old renegade had not participated in the

1862 uprising, but others were certain, though lacking proof, that the perpetrator of the Spirit Lake Massacre had to have a part in the horror of the Minnesota Massacre (if only on the periphery, in the Sioux Falls area raids). In any case, Inkpaduta was certainly present for the looming conflict in the summer of 1863 and was rarely out of the picture again.[11]

The Indian sighting by the buffalo hunters was the news Sibley had been waiting for. Enlisting the Red River hunters as guides, he moved twelve miles on the morning of July 18 to a defensible position he called Camp Atchison on Lake Emily, in order to secure all soldiers and animals invalided, as well as all supplies not needed for a forced march. The general left Colonel William Crooks of the Sixth Minnesota Infantry in charge, with orders to entrench the position and guard the site with two companies drawn from each of the three infantry regiments, a company of cavalry, and an artillery section. The rest of his stripped-down force Sibley organized into light march order—1,436 infantrymen, 520 cavalrymen, 100 artillerymen and pioneers, for a total of 2,056—accompanied by wagons reduced to 1,500-pound loads to carry enough rations for 2,300 men for twenty-five days. After a day of rest and reorganization, Sibley led his strike force out of camp early on the morning of July 20.[12]

Marching southwest toward the Indian concentration, Sibley encountered not hostile Indians that first day, but a herd of mostly Chippewa half-breed buffalo hunters, some 200 in number, who rode into the army's camp behind an American flag "like Arabs of the desert" from their own base of 500 butchering carts three miles to the west. They were led by former Minnesota legislators Charles Grant and John B. Wilkie, the latter serving as captain of these Red River rovers. The hunters' priest, Father André, speaking with Sibley in fluent French, confirmed the intelligence reports of the earlier hunters. After relating the hunters' own litany of hardships inflicted upon them by the Sioux, Father André wished Sibley happy hunting. Some of the Chippewas even volunteered to help fight the Sioux if rations were provided. Sibley tactfully declined their offer and boasted that he would soon overtake the Sioux and "give them a whipping they would long remember."[13]

The Battle of Big Mound

The first battle of the Dakota War erupted four days later. The column had made its dusty way for fifteen miles since breaking camp early that morning. Shortly after noon scouts alerted Sibley to Indian sightings two to three miles ahead and reported a large Sioux camp to the south. Rather than rush headlong into an attack, the rarely impetuous Sibley decided to encamp and entrench and give the Indians an opportunity to show their intent. The general believed that Standing Buffalo and other peacefully inclined chiefs were among the Indian concentration, and he hoped that a show of force might induce a parley. He sent scout Joe LaFramboise with a message to Standing Buffalo to meet him in council.

While hoping for talk, Sibley prepared for combat. He circled his wagons in a corral on the east side of a small alkali lake, deployed the Sixth Minnesota on the northern face of the perimeter, the Seventh and Tenth Minnesota on the east side, and the cavalry along the southern rim, while directing ten men from each company of the Seventh Minnesota to begin putting up sod earthworks. While this deployment was taking place, more and more Indians were seen to gather on a range of rocky hills about a mile east of the army's entrenchments.

The largest group assembled on the summit and near (western) slope of the highest hill, called Big Mound (northeast of present-day Bismark, North Dakota). Several of the Sioux—a dangerous mixture of conciliatory Sissetons and combative Wahpekutes and Yanktonais—rode down from this height toward the camp and signaled a willingness to talk. They were met by a group of Sibley's scouts on a hillock three to four hundred yards from the soldiers' perimeter. The scouts received assurances of the Indians' peaceful intentions. They were told, however, that some of the young warriors looking on were raring to fight. Nevertheless, the scouts urged the Indians to talk Standing Buffalo into negotiating with Sibley. Squawman scout Gabriel Renville was informed by his father-in-law, Scarlet Plume, a Sisseton chief, that a plot was afoot to lure Sibley and his regimental commanders into a council in which they would be murdered. Informed of this plot, Sibley sent word to the negotiators on the hillock that he would only talk to Standing Buffalo in the soldiers' camp.[14]

As a result the talk turned less than friendly and hostile words rent the air. The group on the low hill was joined by Dr. Josiah S. Weiser, the surgeon of the cavalry regiment. Sighting several Sisseton friends, he had remarked to a comrade, "Let us go and shake hands with our friends; I know them."[15] His friend remained behind when the doctor rode out to exchange pleasantries with red friends he had known under vastly different circumstances in Minnesota. Weiser's friend doubted the benevolence of these Indians, and his doubts were confirmed tragically. As Weiser spoke in Sioux to the Indians and offered them bread and tobacco, one of them, a Santee named Tall Crown, approached the surgeon from behind. A follower of Inkpaduta and a participant in the Minnesota Massacre, he apparently feared that the soldiers had come to arrest him. He also may have mistaken Weiser for Sibley. At close range Tall Crown put a bullet into the doctor's heart.[16]

Scouts and Sioux panicked, exchanged volleys, and dispersed following

Standing Buffalo. (Photo published by J. G. Whitney Gallery of St. Paul, Minnesota. Courtesy of the State Historical Society of North Dakota.)

the discharge of Tall Crown's weapon, and the Battle of Big Mound had begun. The murderer of Weiser was the target of the first shots directed at the Indians, but he dismounted quickly and used the cover of the broken terrain to escape. However, several old chiefs, arrayed in tall headdresses, who had been approaching for the council with Sibley, were hit by the scouts' fusillade. Sibley's camp was made aware of Weiser's assassination by the doctor's black servant, who rode back to the bivouac, leading the surgeon's horse and shouting, "Da shot Dr. Weiser! Da shot Dr. Weiser!"[17]

Sibley directed Colonel McPhail to send out three companies of the Mounted Rangers to recover Dr. Weiser's body. Under an ominously gray sky, rent with rolling thunder and rapid-fire lightning but little rain, Sibley's soldiers deployed for battle. With a company of the Seventh Minnesota on the left and two companies of the Seventh on the right, the three-company squadron of the Rangers, led by Major Parker, dismounted and moved across the rocky ground toward Big Mound. Sibley himself led Lieutenant Whipple's artillery section forward to an elevation halfway to Big Mound. From this rise, the six-pounder howitzer tossed spherical case shot against the Indians on the mound and in the ravine in front of it. Several Sioux were killed or wounded by the howitzer fire and others were seen fleeing.

Major Parker's men then surged forward to occupy Big Mound, while Lt. Colonel Marshall deployed five companies of the Seventh Minnesota in a long skirmish line to push beyond Big Mound in order to clear the hills immediately south of the mound. Wheeling to the right, Marshall drove the Indians from the eastern slopes while the cavalry swept up the western slopes.[18]

At this point McPhail ordered Captain Horace Austin's Company B of the Mounted Rangers to remount and charge the hills. As the Rangers galloped spiritedly toward the hills south of Big Mound, they suffered their only fatal casualty of the battle. A Minnesota cavalryman, Private John Miller, fell victim not to a Sioux bullet or arrow but to one of the weapons in God's arsenal. A lightning bolt struck Miller and his mount, killing them both and knocking down two more troopers, one of whom was seriously burned. A second bolt nearly unhorsed Colonel Marshall. Austin's men were momentarily thrown into confusion, thinking that one of Whipple's six-pounder rounds had landed short. But the cavalry line was restored and, reinforced by three companies, the push was resumed. The hostiles were quickly driven two miles south to their camp.[19]

The charge by the Rangers and Marshall's regiment decided the battle. Sibley rode up a rise to witness the hostiles, estimated by him to number 1,000 to 1,500, breaking contact and retreating westward. Though about equal in numbers to the American soldiers, the Sioux were definitely outgunned. Marshall reported that "probably not one half had firearms," and

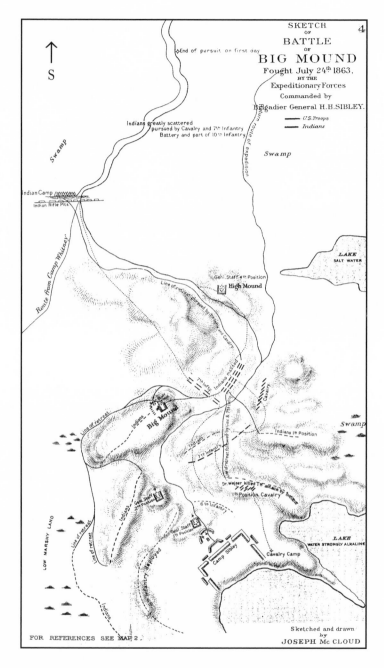

Battle of Big Mound. (U.S. War Department map.)

their ammunition supply was similarly limited. In clearing Big Mound and the intertwining ridges and ravines to its east and west, the Rangers had suffered only a few men wounded, besides those casualties inflicted by nature. The Seventh Minnesota had only close calls to report: one soldier had his hat shot off his head, another had the stock of his rifle shattered by a musket ball.[20]

As soon as battle had been joined, the Sioux women in the Indian camp south of Big Mound had rushed to strike their tepees and load their possessions on travois and horseback. As the women and children fled toward the Missouri, the warriors fought a delaying action. Sibley ordered all the Ranger companies to remount and reform and sent them in pursuit of the Indians, with the Seventh Regiment, a company of the Tenth, and Lieutenant Whipple's single six-pounder in support. Colonel Robert McLaren was detached with several companies to destroy the large amount of materiel left behind by the fleeing Sioux in their abandoned camp.

Five times McPhail's men regained combative contact with the Dakotas and Yanktonais, and each time the cavalry carbines struck down several warriors. Finally, near dark, the Rangers drove the Sioux into the bulrushes and wild rice skirting Dead Buffalo Lake, thirty miles east of the Missouri River. There the final Indian line of resistance was shattered by a well-aimed volley of carbine fire, and the Sioux warriors dispersed.

Sibley's men had won a considerable victory. The Indian body count by the Rangers alone was listed as thirty-one. The Rangers estimated that several other Sioux had been killed, but their bodies remained unrecovered in the thickets of the marshes around Dead Buffalo Lake. A great deal of Sioux gear had been destroyed at the camp or was left strewn all along the fifteen-mile retreat to the lake. The Rangers had fought with enthusiasm, and McPhail was intensely proud of his command for the bravery displayed. His only criticism of their conduct was the very excess of their enthusiasm in the many mounted charges, which made it difficult for him at times to rein in his troops and control their zeal. All in all, though, the Mounted Rangers had demonstrated a fighting prowess that veteran troops would have been proud to emulate.[21]

Unbeknownst to McPhail and the other officers, several Indian scalps were taken, either by men seeking vengeance for their loved ones butchered in Minnesota or by soldiers who had been hunters and trappers and were acquainted with the Indians' repugnance at entering the spirit world without all of their body parts.[22]

Total Sioux casualties were estimated at eighty killed or wounded. White losses in this opening battle of the Dakota War were only three killed and four wounded.[23] Besides Dr. Weiser and the ranger killed by the lightning bolt, the third death was that of Lieutenant Ambrose Freeman of Company

D of the Mounted Rangers. The lieutenant's death, however, was not even a result of the main battle. Shortly after Weiser was gunned down and combat had commenced, firing was also heard to the rear of the American forces. It was not until the following day that the source of this gunfire was discovered. Freeman had been a member of an antelope hunting party that included G. A. Brackett, the expedition's beef contractor and a prominent citizen of Minnesota, as well as two Indian scouts. Suddenly surrounded by Dakotas, the hunters tried to flee when the volley that killed Weiser echoed over the prairie. The Indians opened fire on the hunters, mortally wounding Freeman as the riders made for the concealment of the tall rushes bordering a small lake. The party hid in the rushes until nightfall. After Freeman died, the scouts crept from the rushes and made it back to camp. Brackett, left alone, wandered around lost the next morning before finally finding the expedition's track back to Camp Atchinson, which he reached four days after the battle. He had survived on brackish water and raw frogs.[24]

As combat petered out, McPhail's Rangers prepared to camp for the night and resume the pursuit of the hostiles in the morning. Five miles to the cavalry's rear, Marshall's Seventh Minnesota, on their feet since before dawn, weary from battle and a five-mile pursuit in double-time, also prepared at nightfall to bivouac. For their supper, the soldiers gathered dried meat left by the fleeing Indians and fashioned beds from discarded buffalo skins. A knock-out blow at dawn seemed likely, for the exhausted Indians had little likelihood of gathering their families and escaping at daylight before the rangers and the infantry would come upon them. The Sissetons and Wahpetons of Standing Buffalo and the other peace chiefs seemed particularly likely to have surrendered in mass. Thousands of POWs might have been rounded up, and Sibley might have won a victory to overshadow the triumph Sully was to gain two months later on Whitestone Hill. But a grievous communications failure, possibly the worst mistake of the 1863 campaign, cost Sibley his chance at battlefield renown.

McPhail had just tended to his few wounded when Lieutenant Frederick J. H. Beaver from Sibley's staff reached the rangers with an order to march the cavalry back to Sibley's camp at Big Mound. The supremely weary rangers, in the saddle since before dawn, with only one two-hour break, with nothing to eat since the beginning of the battle but a few tough scraps of dried buffalo meat, had to saddle up once again and head back the fifteen dusty miles they had already traveled.

Reaching the Seventh Minnesota bivouac, McPhail imparted the unfortunate order to Marshall, who also broke camp and led his men back toward Sibley. Driven by thirst, the American companies reached the abandoned Indian camp at midnight to scoop up dirty water from the marshy lake there, then continued on to Sibley's bivouac, which they reached at dawn.

All told, the rangers had covered more than forty-five miles, much of it over horrid terrain in combat and in pursuit, with little food or water in just over twenty-four hours.[25]

Beaver's message saved the Sioux. Sibley had to rest his worn-out warriors a day, and the Indians, with twelve to fifteen miles between them and the soldiers—another day's march—were given, in effect, two days to get their families away toward the relative safety of the Missouri River.

The responsibility for the order to McPhail and Marshall to return to camp is unclear. Sibley later insisted that he had intended both regiments to bivouac where they stood for the night and to resume the pursuit in the morning. He claimed that Beaver had simply misunderstood or misdelivered that message. Beaver, a thirty-three-year-old Englishman who had volunteered for the expedition as a staff aide to Sibley, was unable to defend his actions. He was killed four days later at Stony Lake.

It is also possible that McPhail misinterpreted the order Beaver carried from Sibley and subsequently convinced Marshall—who seemed to have understood Sibley's intentions as remaining in place for the night—of the advisability of following the rangers back to camp.

Sibley's aims were more than likely misdirected by someone along the chain of communication, for he had indeed made plans to march the rest of his command to Dead Buffalo Lake. His advance elements met McPhail's and Marshall's returning men just as this vanguard was starting out in the morning. The exhaustion of these returning units required Sibley to cancel his plans for any further advance on July 25 and to rest his command. Whatever the origin of the misunderstanding, the chance for a quick and decisive end to the campaign had passed.[26]

The Battle of Dead Buffalo Lake

Sibley moved his men out again on the next day, July 26. There were still a great many Sioux to fight, but among them would not be the never very belligerent Sissetons and Wahpetons of Standing Buffalo, Sweet Corn, and Red Plume. Those had gathered their families, left Inkpaduta's band, the Yanktonais, and the Tetons, and had fled northwest toward the Mouse River. They managed to avoid the converging American military columns for months and attracted other Dakotas, Lakotas, and Yanktonais anxious to avoid combat with the bluecoats. The group, some 3,000 in number by early 1864, finally crossed the Canadian border to seek refuge with the redcoats at Fort Garry. Though later urged by agents and military men to return to America and settle on reservations, the battle-shy Sissetons and their companions rejected these blandishments and remained in Canada. Eventually,

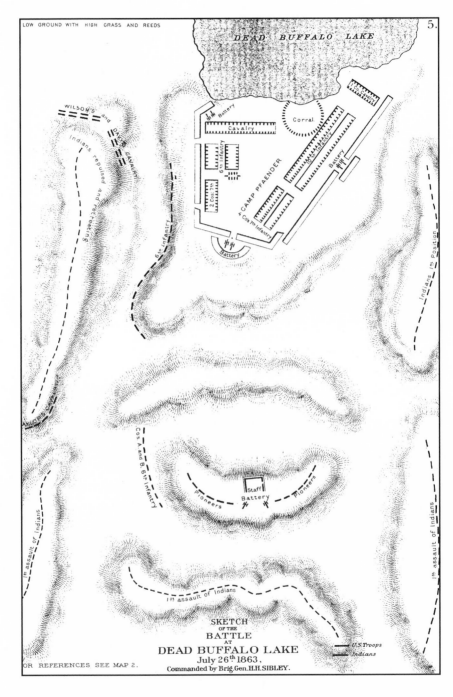

Battle of Dead Buffalo Lake. (U.S. War Department map.)

they moved west to hunt buffalo on the Canadian prairies and ultimately settled on reservations in the provinces of Manitoba and Saskatchewan.[27]

While Standing Buffalo's Sissetons were fleeing the Dakota War, many other Sioux were galloping toward it. Joining Inkpaduta was a large camp of 650 Hunkpapa and Blackfeet Teton warriors hunting buffalo east of the Missouri. The Teton arrivals more than replaced the scurrying Sissetons, both in numbers and in zealousness. Unlike the Dakotas retreating with Standing Buffalo, these Tetons, who included Sitting Bull, were more than ready to take on the white man, and they were certain that, with a total of 1,600 warriors under arms, they could drive the invaders from Dakota.

The men the Tetons were ready to challenge rose to reveille on July 26 and began their march before dawn. Sibley's column struck southwest and for miles the route was strewn with discarded buffalo robes, dried buffalo meat, buffalo tallow, and other items of the Indians' buffalo-based culture as well as with plunder taken from the white victims of the Minnesota Massacre. The troops reached the abandoned Indian camp of the 24th and torched what remained, then proceeded on for fourteen miles to the shore of the small lake that received its name for the hundreds of buffalo carcasses scattered about, including at least one still rotting so fragrantly in the hot sun "that we did not need sight to be aware of its presence."[28]

Soon after noon, swarms of Lakotas and Dakotas started appearing to the front and around the flanks of Sibley's vanguard, which consisted of Colonel Crooks' Sixth Minnesota Infantry. Crooks deployed two companies into a skirmish line, supported by Captain Chase and his pioneers and Whipple's battery section of six-pounders. Fire was exchanged at long range, and the Indians fell back one and a half miles.

Inkpaduta's braves and his Teton allies then attempted a sortie on the Sixth's left flank, but Captain Taylor and his Mounted Rangers slapped them back. A second surge of painted warriors hit two companies of the Sixth led by Lt. Colonel Averill, but this attack too was repulsed, again with the aid of Taylor's Rangers.

Fighting faded by midafternoon as the soldiers prepared to bivouac at Dead Buffalo Lake. However, one large Sioux force made a final dash at the soldiers, striking at the hay cutters and teamsters grazing their mules on the lake shore some distance from the camp. Having assumed that the battle was over and that the Indians had fled, most of the foragers and muleteers had foolishly left their arms behind when they left on these work details (they would never do so again). Fortunately for the foragers, Captain Eugene M. Wilson's ranger company was mounted and nearby. They galloped to the rescue, joined promptly by Captain Peter B. Davy's company, which had quickly saddled up and dashed to the fight. Major McLaren also brought up six companies of the Sixth Minnesota, which maneuvered in a "color line" (a line of deployment for battle with the regiment's colors flying) to protect the rangers' left flank.

The fighting was hot and furious for half an hour. Gunsmoke mingled with the dust kicked up by cavalry horses and Indian ponies to create a choking haze in which the combatants mingled. Unit cohesion broke down in the physical and mental fog of battle, and the contestants had trouble telling friend from foe. The Indians fought hard, but their aim in the smoke and swirl of the battle was faulty, and only one cavalryman received a mortal wound. That trooper, Private John Platt, in the exchange of gunfire that cost him his life, wounded the opposing warrior, who was subsequently killed by Private Joe Campbell.

Two Sioux in particular distinguished themselves. One unidentified warrior, claimed later by many to have been Sitting Bull, galloped out from the others at the beginning of the attack on the mule skinners and charged single-handedly downhill toward the mule herd. Avoiding the fire of the few muleteers who were armed, the warrior rode down on a mule skinner armed only with a blacksnake whip. He counted coup on the teamster and rode off with a saddled mule as his battle trophy. A second warrior, Grey Eagle, a prominent war chief, bravely led the Indian attack, his body and head covered only by war paint and feathers. His death broke the spirit of the Sioux, who then fled the close-quarters combat, leaving fifteen of their dead behind.

Sibley had earthworks thrown up to protect his camp from a night attack, but there was no starlit sequel to the Battle of Dead Buffalo Lake.[29]

The Battle of Stony Lake

Sibley was determined to delay the Indians' flight across the Missouri until Sully could come up from the south to snare the Sioux in the very pincers movement on which the whole campaign had been predicated. The general had heard nothing recently from Sully, but he assumed that the southern column was just a march of one or two days away along the Missouri from effecting a junction with his brigade. Inkpaduta's recalcitrants and their Teton allies seemed to be following the script perfectly, fleeing from Sibley's hammer directly into the anvil of Sully's force, against which they would be destroyed. The only change from the original conception of the campaign was the switch of the site of that destruction from Devil's Lake to the banks of the Missouri River.

Though many of the hostiles' families were able to escape because of the misinterpreted order delivered by Lieutenant Beaver on July 24, most of the warriors remained behind to take on Sibley. Because of the boost to their numbers and confidence gained by the continuing arrival of more Teton combatants, the Sioux had forfeited the headstart they had gained from the foul-up following Big Mound. Only a few hundred warriors were actually required to fight the delaying action against the Americans that would give their families time to cross the Missouri River, but, according to the report of a captured squaw, ten times that number sought the thrill and glory of battle against Sibley and thus presented the white army with its chance to close a giant trap.

Sibley continued hot on the Indian trail on July 27, covering twenty-three miles further southwest to Stony Lake. The brigade pitched camp on the stony shore of the sweet-water lake, designating the site Camp Ambler. After a predawn reveille, the column had just resumed its march when about two hours later, on July 28, the Battle of Stony Lake commenced.

Sibley was in the forefront of the column with the scouts and a few headquarters staff wagons, followed by Colonel Baker's Tenth Minnesota Infantry, one-half mile ahead of the rest of the brigade. As this vanguard was ascending a long sloping hill rising from Stony Lake, scouts sent ahead to reconnoiter galloped from over the hill to shout, "The are coming! They are coming!" Baker quickly deployed his troops left and right of the trail. A Sioux brave then popped up on the brow of the hill and shouted, "We are too late; they are ready for us." A second warrior joined him and replied, "But remember our children and families; we must not let them get them."[30]

Moments later more Indians appeared, first on the crest of the hill, then in gathering numbers on the flanks to quickly form a vast crescent five to six miles in length around the march column. This enveloping line of Indians, forming two-thirds of a circle, numbered, according to Sibley's estimate, 2,200 to 2,500 (and the total number of Indians in their camp he estimated at almost 10,000).[31]

Though the Sioux had arrived too late to catch the white expedition while it was still breaking camp, as they had hoped, the bluecoat column was still vulnerable. The wagon train had just rolled out of its overnight corral and was forming in its designated place in the line of march to the rear of the Tenth Minnesota when the Sioux mounted their attack. The regiments assigned to protect the train's exposed flanks had not yet had time to assemble and deploy. The Sioux, painted for battle and naked except for their shot pouches and knife belts, seemed to have a determination to match their numbers this time and were as disciplined as they were bold. Individual warriors waved signal flags to control the movements of the Sioux force and knots of warriors responded with alacrity to those directions.

Scattering two companies as skirmishers, Baker advanced with the rest of his regiment in line, the soldiers spaced an arm's length apart and most of them having fixed bayonets without being ordered to do so. The encircling arc of mostly mounted Indians, barking war whoops and shaking lances and long-barreled muskets at the soldiers, seemed an overpowering force, and many of the men of the Tenth Minnesota thought they were about to be overrun.

The Tenth moved forward to hold the hostiles at bay, while the wagon train closed up and the other regiments deployed. Supported by Lieutenant Whipple's two-gun section, the men of the Tenth advanced at double-time and released two volleys at the Sioux. Three Indians were seen to topple from their ponies under the discharge of the infantry fire. Other warriors dismounted to toss their fallen comrades across the backs of their horses and lead them away. The long-range rifle fire and the spherical case artillery shells, which had inflicted so much damage on the Indians in the previous two battles, seemed to disabuse the Sioux of any notion of mounting an all-out assault on the Minnesota infantry. They returned heavy fire on the Tenth Regiment, but except for a few sallies did not attempt to charge the advancing infantrymen. For fear of moving too far forward and thus exposing the wagon train's still open flanks, Baker had to halt his advance. He had trouble restraining his eager men, having to order a cease-fire twice in the face of the long-range Indian volleys, because the soldiers were eager to close in on the enemy and because his line over the broken, rocky ground was very long.

The wagon train finally closed up and Colonel Crooks' Sixth Minnesota and Colonel Marshall's Seventh Minnesota, with McPhail's cavalry attached, deployed to the train's right and left. The Tenth Minnesota was then ordered to advance again in a broad skirmish line, with two companies held in reserve. Firing was hot and heavy, but Sibley, after getting his brigade deployed in line of battle in echelon with the able assistance of his regimental commanders, did not stop his march. The Indians probed for any weakness to penetrate the white line. Sallies against the soldiers' flanks and rear were repelled with musketry volleys and the shells of Captain Jones' howitzer battery. Most of the warriors returned to the front of Sibley's formation, where white skirmishers lying in the prairie grass heard Sioux war chiefs urging the Indian rank-and-file to attempt a final all-out charge. But the Sioux had lost heart for further battle. Yelling in disappointment and rage, they fired a few parting volleys and began to withdraw.

The Tenth passed over the hill from whence the Indians had first massed to attack and found the Sioux gone. They appeared for a moment in great numbers on a distant hill, then disappeared. The Americans' cavalry mounts were too jaded to continue pursuit. The Battle of Stony Lake was over.[32]

The Push to the Missouri

Following a two-hour rest, the march was resumed in combat formation.

The column proceeded on unmolested for eighteen miles. The only Indian the soldiers encountered was asleep beside his pony. He was dressed in a breechcloth and moccasins and was lying on a buffalo robe. Claiming he was a Teton from west of the Missouri who had taken no part in the recent fighting, the Indian was released with a warning. Sibley later claimed eleven Indian bodies recovered (although Sergeant J. W. Burnham, in his memoir of the expedition, reported seeing no bodies at all).[33] Rather remarkably, the army incurred no casualties at all and only one weakened horse was captured. The horse was recaptured that evening, and the Indian who had taken the mount was gunned down and killed. With just a few mounted Indians in sight, the brigade settled into camp on the Apple River, a tributary emptying into the Missouri about ten miles south of present-day Bismark.

Reveille came early on July 29 as Sibley sent Colonel McPhail's rangers and a two-gun section of six-pounders ahead to harass the Indians as they tried to retreat across the Missouri. Sibley followed with the main column. A twelve-mile march brought the brigade to the thick woods lacing the river about four miles above Burnt Boat Island by noon. The Sioux had ferried most of their families over on the night of July 28 on rafts called bullboats made of buffalo hides stretched across frames of flexible willow boughs. Those Indians who could swim had waded into the water to pull the bullboats, loaded with the non-swimmers and their gear, by ropes held in their teeth. Now on July 29, the hills and bluffs opposite the soldiers were aswarm with Indians, some shouting taunts at the cavalrymen to cross over and fight, others pleading, "We do not want to fight the whites."[34]

With the signal mirrors held by the Indians on the bluffs and the barrels of the soldiers' Springfields glittering in the searing sun, skirmishing broke out. The cavalrymen were initially repulsed by Sioux warriors armed with bows and arrows and positioned in a dense grove of prickly ash and thorn on the east side of the river. The brigade's howitzers speedily shelled the hostiles out of this gnarled stronghold. Colonel Crooks was then sent with his Sixth Regiment to clear the woods to the river. Though his men received heavy fire from the Sioux across the river, the infantrymen found few Indians remaining on the near side and they accomplished their mission without loss. The Sioux still on the east side of the river were then exposed to heavy rifle and howitzer fire from the Sibley brigade as they took to the river, the swimmers clinging to the tails of their horses, the non-swimmers trying to paddle across on bullboats. According to later testimony by Standing Buffalo (who was probably not present on the scene), more Indians drowned while trying to cross the Missouri under fire than died in all the preceding battles (a figure he listed as only thirteen killed in action). Sibley later disputed these figures, however. In a letter to the Acting Assistant

Adjutant-General, he commented on "the remarkable dislike to acknowledge how many are killed in action characteristic of the race," claiming, in contrast to Standing Buffalo's figures, to have counted at least forty-six Indian bodies in the three fights prior to the Sioux crossing of the Missouri.[35]

While the Sixth Minnesota was thrashing its way through the tangle girding the Missouri, Sibley dispatched Lieutenant Beaver, an Oxford graduate, with a message to Crooks. Although the young Englishman had been the bearer of the misinterpreted message recalling the rangers from their long pursuit on July 24 after the Battle of Big Mound, he was persistent in his duty and generally well-liked by Sibley's staff. Beaver delivered the message to Crooks and then headed back with the colonel's reply. Unfortunately, he took the wrong trail, and as night fell he was reported missing, along with Private Nicholas Miller of the Sixth Minnesota, who also went down this wrong path.

In their push to the river Crooks' men had found masses of Indian equipment left behind. From across the river, the Sioux continued to proclaim their peaceableness, but this was belied when a canteen detail from the Sixth Regiment approached the water and received hundreds of rounds from the Indians, all of which fortunately fell short. The day was waning and weariness among all was growing. Mules, horses, and men were exhausted from heat, exertion, and combat. Soldiers were dropping from exhaustion, to be picked up by mule-drawn ambulances, and several horses had to be shot. Sibley gathered up his tired troopers and proceeded the short distance down the Missouri to the nearest point on Apple River opposite Burnt Boat Island (so called from the wreckage of the steamer *Assiniboine*, grounded and burned in an accident while carrying Prussian Prince Alexander Phillip Maximilian of Weid on a naturalist expedition in May 1834). There the brigade made camp for the night.

The night was not restful. If Lakota and Dakota warriors were not all around, they seemed to be. Shots often rang out in the darkness, usually fired by spooked sentries, but several of the guards insisted that at least some of the fire was incoming. Twice drums rolled to sound the men to quarters. Several mules were untethered and run off by Indian skulkers. Rockets and guns were also fired in the forlorn hope of signaling the camp's location to the two missing men.

On the morning of July 30, the brigade commander sent Colonel Crooks with eleven companies of infantry and dismounted cavalry and three of Jones's howitzers and a detachment of pioneers—700 men in total—back to the site of the Indian crossing of the day before to destroy the wagons and other materiel left behind by the Sioux. Crooks' force was also to search the woods for the missing men. Crooks' men swept the river thickets and found no Indians, but they did come under fire from warriors concealed in the tall grass on the other side. The foot soldiers and dismounted rangers returned this long-range fire and claimed several hits on Indian targets while sustaining no loss themselves.[36]

The fate of the missing men was determined when Crooks' soldiers discovered their bodies not far apart along that wrong trail taken by both. Lieutenant Beaver's body carried a deadly decoration of iron-tipped arrows. His horse lay dead beside him, killed by a bullet. The lieutenant had been armed with three revolvers and, according to Crooks' report, must have fought hard, based on the expended cartridge cases strewn about, probably killing some of his attackers before he died (although there was no body count evidence of this).[37] Beaver's killers had apparently tried to scalp him, but his hair was cropped too short, so the Indians satisfied themselves with slicing the Englishman's long whiskers from one cheek. Private Miller's corpse was also pinioned by arrows, but the private, with longer locks, was scalped in the usual manner.[38]

While a detail gathered the mortal remains of the two dead men, most of Crooks' command went about the business of setting on fire the 150 discarded wagons and carts, many of them still filled with loot taken during the Minnesota Uprising. Having completed his mission of destruction, Crooks led his men back to Sibley's camp, which he reached after dark.[39]

The news Crooks brought back of Beaver's death greatly grieved Sibley's staff. According to Beaver's messmate, Dr. J. W. Daniels, "He was a genial, well-educated English gentleman, who won the love and respect of all those having the pleasure of his acquaintance. To meet and not have him with us was a bereavement that filled our hearts with sorrow."[40]

Beaver, an ordained clergyman of the Anglican Church, had spent two years in New York City when he first came to America, cultivating an influential crowd. In his search for Western adventure he had jumped at the opportunity Sibley's expedition presented and came to the Minnesota general's headquarters armed with letters of recommendation from J. J. Astor and Hamilton Fish. Beaver's body was buried in a grave shaped in the form of a rifle pit to prevent desecration. Ten years later, Captain J. C. Braden, the Masonic Grand Master of Minnesota, removed the body from its Bismark location and had it transported to St. Paul, where it was reinterred in a grave maintained at the expense of General Sibley. Each Memorial Day, Beaver's grave was decorated by veterans of the Grand Army of the Republic.[41]

There were still enough Indians on the east side of the Missouri to keep most of the men of the Sibley expedition bleary-eyed from lack of sleep for the next two nights after the discovery of Beaver's body. On the night of July 30–31, hostiles took advantage of a strong wind to set the grass on fire. The soldiers had to form a skirmish line of men slapping the ground cover with wet blankets to douse the flames. The next night constant sightings of hostiles signaling to one another kept the brigade on alert through most of the dark hours. After midnight, a considerable number of Sioux crawled across the ground burnt black from the previous night's fire to shoot a heavy volley that shredded many tents at the north end of the camp. The Sioux fire killed a mule and stampeded a herd of cattle. Men of the Seventh and Tenth regiments formed a living wall to turn the panicked steers and drive them back into the corral. Colonel Marshall reported that this was the only time during the campaign that he thought the expedition was ever truly in peril. Though the Indians maintained an oftentimes heavy fire until dawn broke, no U.S. soldiers were hit during the night's combat.[42]

Sibley remained at the campsite opposite Burnt Boat Island (now called Sibley Island) for two days and three nights. His men baked during the day and shivered at night as the ricocheting weather made the thermometer seem "to be affected with delirium tremens."[43] He had expected Sully's column to have long since reached this point on its northward progress up the Missouri. Firing rockets at night and cannon by day, Sibley hoped to signal and unite with the sluggish Sully, and, with a relatively fresh and reinforced column, resume the pursuit of the Sioux. It was too late to spring the trap, to pound the hammer down on the anvil, but it was not too late to combine the freshest elements of the two columns and reinvigorate the chase. But Sibley waited and signaled in vain. There was no Sully. Sibley charitably ascribed Sully's failure to appear to being "detained by insurmountable obstacles."[44]

General Sibley decided against continuing the campaign by fording the Missouri. His command had marched 585 miles from Fort Snelling and had fought three pitched battles and several skirmishes in a season of killing heat and unprecedented drought, an accomplishment that many seasoned veterans of the prairie had thought impossible under such circumstances. But to continue was probably impossible. The expedition's transport animals were miserably worn down. Many mules were so weakened that a good number of army wagons had to be burned. There were only sufficient provisions for the return trip. Any resumption of the pursuit by his debilitated brigade, Sibley decided, would easily be evaded by the Indians, who could cross and recross the rivers of the territory with their lighter loads and consistently put more distance between them and their pursuers. Thus the general issued an order for a return march. In that same written order he warmly praised all of the expedition's regiments and commended the officers and men of his brigade for their bravery, fortitude, and success in destroying either the lives or the livelihood of so many savages. Sibley was particularly laudatory for the work of the Mounted Rangers, who had fought the hardest battles with the enemy and inflicted the heaviest losses.[45]

The number of those losses and the number of the Indian foe from whom those losses were extracted was a matter of some speculation and dispute. In his official report Sibley estimated 2,200–2,500 warriors were congregated against his column, the largest hostile native concentration ever seen in North America. From his analysis of information provided by his half-breed scouts, Sibley calculated that this force had developed from a union between Little Crow's people with Sissetons, Cut-Heads (a band of intermarried Sissetons and Yanktonais), Yanktonais (which he erroneously referred to as the most powerful band of the Dakota people), and Tetons, to compose a total population of 10,000. This force had, as a result of "three desperate engagements," been disabused of their contempt for any invading army and of their sense of invulnerability. By his lights, Sibley had not only utterly broken the Sioux, but had also taught a tough lesson to all the tribes of the northwest.[46]

In a letter to Pope, Sibley furnished more specific figures for his Lakota and Dakota opponents. The Indian order of battle was figured thus: remnants of Minnesota River bands: 250; Sissetons: 450; eastern Yanktonais: 1,200; other bands (including Teton Sioux from west of the Missouri River): 400; for a total of 2,300 warriors.[47] The Sioux estimated their own numbers at 1,600, including 650 Tetons.

The estimates of Indian fallen varied widely. No definitive figures exist, though several body count totals were reported. The Sioux were definitely outgunned, armed as they were with mostly bows and arrows, buffalo guns, and some arms taken from white soldiers and civilians in Minnesota, while the white soldiers countered with modern rifles as well as muskets and howitzers. Because so much of the fighting at Big Mound was at close range, Sioux losses in that first battle were probably fairly heavy and almost certainly the most numerous of the three major engagements. After Big Mound, the Indians were more wary of the howitzer and massed musketry fire of the white brigade and subsequently fought generally at long range. Nathaniel West, Sibley's biographer, places the number of Indians killed and wounded at Big Mound at eighty, "twenty-one being scalped in the last charge." West also records the killing of nine warriors by a single soldier.[48]

In his diary, Sibley somewhat contradicts this last figure by writing "nine were killed by *our* [italics added] men, and I am ashamed to say all were scalped.... God's image should not be thus mutilated or disfigured."[48] Ranger commander Colonel McPhail in his report claimed thirty-one hostiles killed by his rangers, "all found with the peculiar mark of cavalry upon them" (undoubtedly implying that they were scalped).[49] McPhail seems to have been of two minds about the efficacy and morality of scalp taking. According to Colonel Marshall, the ranger leader admonished his men that it was wrong to lift the enemy's hair, but that a full-size scalp was a surefire method of proving the killing of a warrior.

Dr. J. W. Daniels rode with the cavalry in pursuit of the Sioux after the Battle of Big Mound. Though he acknowledged that twenty-one Indians were later found dead on the trail in the wake of the battle,[50] he reported sighting only four during his ride: a lame warrior of his acquaintance, one old woman, and two old men, one of whom was wrapped in a shroud of the U.S. flag. According to at least one account, the old warrior arrayed in the stars and stripes put up a grand fight before he fell. Thrown from his horse during the pursuit following the Battle of Big Mound, the elderly brave stood his ground against the oncoming blue troopers and got off two musket rounds, which struck the saddle and the overcoat of two charging cavalrymen. Aiming his third shot at the heart of a soldier just several paces away, the warrior discharged his musket but nothing other than the flash of the igniting powder emerged from the muzzle. In the heat and fury of the moment, the old Santee had forgotten to ram a musket ball down the bore. As a squad of cavalrymen swarmed around him, the flag-draped warrior reversed his empty musket to club at the enemy. A dozen rifle and carbine shots from the cavalry troopers failed to bring him down. It required the slash of several sabers to end the stalwart Sioux's resistance.

Specific figures for the fights at Dead Buffalo Lake, Stony Lake, Apple River, and the crossing of the Missouri are hard to come by. In a report and dispatch to Pope of August 7, Sibley gauged Indian losses as at least 150 for the whole campaign. In his general order of commendation to his command, the brigade commander placed Sioux casualties between 120 and 150, including 44 bodies counted. In his letter of September 2 to Adjutant-General Meline, he recorded the body count at forty-six. West in his biography of Sibley states that nearly 150 Indians were killed or wounded in the battles of late July 1863.[51]

The figure of 150 thus seems to be a fairly consistent estimate for Sioux losses in the Sibley campaign, at least from the white soldiers' perspective. Although this figure was later interpreted to mean that 150 Indians were *killed* in the Sibley battles, it seems much more likely that the number represents the total *killed and wounded* (though the reports in the Official Records do not make this clear).

The Sioux did not concur with these casualty claims. Standing Buffalo insisted that no more than thirteen Indians were killed by Sibley's army, though he conceded that many more were drowned attempting to cross the Missouri. Other Indian participants claimed a total of twenty-four of their kinsmen killed in the July battles. The Sully column came across a lame Indian in late August who reported that the Sioux lost fifty-eight killed in the battles with Sibley.[52]

Because Indian witnesses very often did not bother to include in their casualty counts those whose names they could not recall, their estimates are questionable. Based upon the body counts taken by the Americans and the agreement by both sides that a considerable number of Indians died while crossing the Missouri, the actual number of Sioux dead from the Sibley campaign of 1863 was probably in the neighborhood of seventy to eighty.

Sibley's losses in the campaign were minimal. Six officers and men had died: Dr. Weiser, murdered in the parley at Big Mound; Private John Miller, struck down by lightning; Lieutenant Freeman, ambushed while hunting; Lieutenant Beaver and Private Nicholas Miller, killed along the trail near the Apple River; and Private John Platt, mortally wounded at Dead Buffalo Lake. Four other soldiers were wounded in battle.

The losses of the Sibley expedition really seem insignificant next to the fact that more soldiers died in defensive operations against the hostiles in Minnesota than did in Sibley's offensive march. Seven soldiers died in Minnesota, including one Eighth Minnesota private shot down in the brush by a comrade who thought he was taking aim at a bear. Six of the seven dead soldiers came from the Eighth Minnesota, including three men killed on May 2 when a squad from Company D was ambushed by Santees near Pomme de Terre. In that same spring and summer of 1863 at least nine Minnesota civilians were also killed by hostiles.[53]

Mackinaw Massacre

The largest massacre of civilians during the Dakota campaigns and the worst such incident since the August 1862 outbreak occurred on August 3, 1863, after Sibley had left the Missouri. Trailing in the wake of the departing soldiers, the Dakotas salvaged what remained of their huge cache of hidden supplies not found by Crooks. While recovering the remnants of their property, the Indians sighted a large river raft, called a Mackinaw boat, coming downriver and prepared to attack it.

The Mackinaw boat carried twenty-two civilians who had traveled from the Boise, Idaho, gold mines with up to $100,000 in gold dust in their possession. Originally, the party had numbered twenty-seven miners, two half-breed Sioux, a woman, and two children, but after Indian attacks on the group near Fort Union and other points, ten of the miners had left the boat at Fort Berthold. Rafting into an ambush set by hundreds of Dakota warriors, ten of the remaining seventeen miners were killed or wounded in the first volleys, according to Dakota witnesses. The survivors, armed with a small cannon, bravely and accurately returned the Indians' fire, but when the group's leader fell with a fatal wound and their ammunition ran out, the defenders of the raft were doomed. The ambushers, some in canoes, some wading into the river on horseback, rushed the raft and killed the rest of the mining party.[54]

Dakota losses were heavy, though undetermined, for there are only the counts of Indian witnesses or Indian second-hand accounts to go on and, as was often the case, their figures were not reliable. One Indian claim put their losses at thirty-six dead and thirty-five to forty-two wounded. Another Dakota captive told Sully, who discovered the wrecked raft upon his late arrival at the Missouri with his expedition, that ninety hostiles had died under the miners' fire. Red Blanket, a Santee woman who claimed her brother had been among the warriors who had slain the one woman aboard and had himself died in the river fight, said that thirty Dakotas had been killed. More than likely these casualty figures were just examples of Indians telling whites what they thought the Americans wanted to hear. Though the miners may well have given a good account of themselves before they died, it seems very unlikely that they could have worked such execution before they were overwhelmed, particularly if the claim that more than half their number fell in the Indians' first volleys is true.[55]

Red Blanket testified that the bodies of the slain whites were stripped and some buckskin belts filled with gold dust, which the Indians took to be spoilage, were ripped open and spilled across the ground. Several of the Indians, however, aware of the white man's reverence for the yellow flakes, took up to $20,000 in gold dust and some greenbacks with them to buy arms from undiscriminating traders at Fort Garry.[56]

In a footnote to this bloody incident, Whistling Bear, an Arikara Indian scout, said in 1876 that two weeks after the ambush a Fort Berthold trader named Fred Gerard, who was married to Whistling Bear's sister, sent him to the site to recover gold dust, showing him a sample so that the Indian would recognize it. Reaching the wrecked boat, Whistling Bear and his companions found a coffee pot filled with gold dust as well as several belts still heavy with gold. The Arikara handed over the dust to Gerard, who rewarded him with a treasure far more useful to the Indian, a horse. Gerard then sent word to nearby Sioux that he would give full value in trade for all the gold dust they could recover. It is not recorded if Gerard was able to further profit from the Mackinaw massacre.[57]

The Conclusion of the Campaign

Sibley had done an about-face and headed homeward on August 1, 1863. Although some braves followed the Sibley column until it crossed the James, the return march was uneventful. Upon reaching Camp Atchison on Lake Jesse on August 10, Sibley was able to interrogate Little Crow's son, Wowinape, about the death of his father. Wowinape had been captured by a detachment of two infantry companies and one cavalry company led by

Captain Burt of the Seventh Minnesota. They had been sent on an eight-day scout on July 24 from Camp Atchison in search of a band of fifteen to twenty lodges, which according to Red River buffalo hunters had stayed behind near Devil's Lake when the rest of the large Sioux assemblage had moved west.[58]

From Camp Atchison on, the brigade commander sent off several large detachments from the main column. Colonel McPhail was dispatched with four ranger companies and a section of artillery to sweep the region between the James River and Fort Ridgely in search of a small band of Yanktonai who had been committing depredations in the area. Before reaching Fort Abercrombie, a three-company battalion of the cavalry was separated from the main column to proceed north to Fort Ripley via the Otter Trail Lake route as a reminder to the Pillagers and other Chippewa bands in the region to maintain their peaceful ways. Sent on a similar mission to deter the Chippewas was the Tenth Minnesota and another cavalry detachment, leapfrogging along the chain of frontier posts to Fort Ridgely. The main column, now reduced to the Sixth and Seventh regiments and two howitzer sections, terminated the march and the campaign when it reached Fort Snelling on September 13. The eighty-nine-day-long march of the Sibley expedition had carried it nearly 1,040 miles from Camp Pope to the Missouri and back to Fort Snelling.[59]

Sibley returned from the expedition generally pleased with the results of the campaign, although any exultant feelings of triumph the general may have had were considerably dampened by the deep sense of loss afflicting him when he received news while on the march that his young son and daughter had died from disease. Though his campaign had not resulted, as he had hoped, in the utter destruction of the hostile Sioux, Sibley could boast that the enemy had been "driven in confusion and dismay, with the sacrifice of vast property, across the Missouri River, many, perhaps most of them, to perish miserably in their utter destitution during the coming fall and winter."[60]

In the general's view, the Indians had been taught that the long arm of the government could reach the most distant haunts and punish them, that they were utterly powerless to resist the attack of any decent-sized U.S. force, and that only the interposition of the Missouri River prevented the utter destruction of a great camp. Sibley wished that all of the murdering Mdewakanton and Wahpeton bands had been "extirpated, root and branch; but as it is, the bodies of many of the most guilty have been left unburied on the prairies to be devoured by wolves and foxes."[61]

Although in actuality the mostly Mdewakanton perpetrators of the Minnesota Massacre were little punished by the Sibley expedition, department commander General Pope was greatly pleased by the campaign. In a letter to Sibley, Pope remarked that the spirit and strength of character with which his troops had overcome the hardships of the campaign "reflected the highest credit upon them and upon you."[62] The reward for their success in the Dakota campaign would be, Pope promised, a transfer to the Southern battlefields, where their Indian fighting experience would help them garner even greater laurels. The infantry regiments were indeed sent south, while the ranger regiment, within a few months, was largely demobilized.

In truth, the results of Sibley's campaign were a decidedly mixed bag. One of the major accomplishments of the expedition was the expulsion of the main horde of the Sioux from Dakota east of the Missouri. That accomplishment lasted, however, only until Sibley began his eastward homebound march. Though the Tetons followed their holy men southwest to their Mecca in the Black Hills, Inkpaduta, within days of the Sibley withdrawal from the Missouri, led his band, accompanied by a large number of Upper and Lower Yanktonais and Cut-Heads, back across the river to resume their interrupted hunt for winter meat.

Nonetheless, though small bands of raiders had terrorized the Minnesota frontier in the rear of Sibley's campaign, thereafter Minnesota was largely secure from significant Indian attack. Huge quantities of Indian (as well as stolen white) provisions and equipment had been destroyed. A large number of Santees had fled across the Canadian border to take up permanent residence and never again presented a threat to white Americans.

On the other hand, a great sum of the taxpayers' money had been expended to kill or capture only a relative small number of hostile Indians. Even if the highest figure offered for Indian combat deaths, 150, is accurate, the toll, plus a handful of POWs, represented only a tiny fraction of the thousands of Sioux involved. Sibley's trio of battles with the Sioux were all one-sided contests. The soldiers had modern rifles and artillery, while the Sioux were primarily armed with bows and shotguns. Though a considerable faction of the Sioux ambitiously aimed for an all-out contest with the blue-shirted invaders, most were chiefly concerned with protecting their families and delaying the soldiers until their women and children could escape across the Missouri. In this they were largely successful. Sully's failure to move up the Missouri River fast enough to link with Sibley allowed the bulk of the Sioux to cross to the west side of the river. Thus Sioux losses, even accepting the highest estimates, were insignificant compared to what they could have been had the pincers of the original battle plan closed.

The Sibley expedition also justified to a certain extent the fears of those citizens of Minnesota alarmed that the offensive into Dakota would leave the state unprotected and vulnerable to renewed Indian attack. Even though some 2,000 soldiers and militiamen remained behind to safeguard the Minnesota frontier, small Sioux war parties managed to penetrate the protective military screen and carry out numerous raids through the late spring and summer of 1863, raids that resulted in at least sixteen whites dead.

Finally, and possibly most important in this list of negative results from the Sibley campaign, there is the impact of the expedition on the future of U.S.-Lakota relations. From the Sioux point of view, the Sibley expedition represented another aggression, a westward extension of white encroachment upon their territory. Rather than engaging and annihilating the Santee subjects of the Minnesota Uprising, the expedition had mainly fought Sioux bands that had not participated in the 1862 war, and had initiated hostilities with the powerful Teton tribes that would endure until Wounded Knee twenty-seven years later.[63]

9. The Battle
of Whitestone Hill

General Alfred Sully

This history of the man in command of the Missouri River column, forty-three-year-old Brigadier General Alfred Sully, is one of public accomplishment and private pain. The son of painter Thomas Sully, Alfred was born in Philadelphia, Pennsylvania, in 1820. He spent his childhood in the Quaker city and at seventeen was sent to West Point. Sully spent the rest of his life in uniform, but he did not scorn his heritage or his father's influence. Throughout his military career he as often held a painter's brush in his hand as an officer's sword. In the course of his duties, which took him across the length and breadth of his country as well as into Mexico and Europe, he broadened his military experience and expanded the subjects and landscapes for his sketches and watercolors. His forty years in uniform resulted in a respectable record of military service and a rich visual collection of the scenes and scenery of nineteenth-century America.[1]

Sully graduated thirty-fourth in a class of fifty-two from West Point in 1841 and immediately got a taste of combat as an infantry officer in the swamps of Florida, where he engaged in low-level warfare with the last hostiles in the last year of the Second Seminole War. Five years of the more common experience of the professional soldier followed—garrison duty in Sacketts Harbor, alternating with recruiting service.[2]

The Mexican War broke the monotony of the peacetime army, sending Sully to the siege of Vera Cruz in 1847. His next assignment took him to California, where at the age of thirty Sully eloped with Manuela Jimeno, the fifteen-year-old daughter of a wealthy Spanish ranchero. To supplement his income, Sully developed a third skill to go along with his military and artistic talents by becoming a surveyor. Sully's father-in-law further boosted the young man's prospects by turning over part of his vast land holdings to Sully for development.

General Alfred Sully and his favorite horse. (Courtesy of the State Historical Society of North Dakota.)

It was now that pain entered a life of rather happy prospects, leaving Sully embittered for a time and prone to greater eruptions of an already volatile temper as well as increasing the eccentricities that had always marked his character. Sully's teenage wife suffered the fate of so many women in the past; she died at the age of seventeen soon after the birth of their son. The son did not long survive the mother. He died in the embrace of love when he was accidentally smothered to death by his grandmother, who was sleeping beside him.[3]

Though Sully's private life was shattered, his public life remained on course. Promoted to captain in 1852, he was given command of Company F of the Second Infantry at forts Ridgely and Pierre and was put in charge of the construction of Fort Randall. After spending most of 1858 in Europe on detached duty observing other armies, Captain Sully returned to the American prairie to briefly take the field against the Cheyenne. Made a major early in 1861, Sully was awarded the colonelcy of the First Minnesota Regiment on March 4, 1862.

With his regiment Sully distinguished himself in many of the great battles of 1862; he served in the Peninsula and Second Manassas campaigns and at the battles of Antietam and Fredericksburg. Promoted to brigadier general of U.S. volunteers on September 26, 1862, he was given command of the First Brigade, Second Division, Second Corps of the Army of the Potomac. Less than three months later, he was awarded command of the Second Corps' Third Division. The only stain on his record occurred after Fredericksburg, when he was relieved of his brigade command by the divisional commander, General John Gibbon. A regiment in Sully's brigade, the 34th New York, had come close to mutiny, and Sully had hesitated to force the New Yorkers' compliance with orders because he was uncertain of his right to use force against volunteers under regular army rules. Sully requested a court of inquiry to clear his name and was fully exonerated on May 16, 1863. Aside from this bump in his career path, he seemed well on his way to a major command position when he was yanked from the very core of large-scale combat with the Army of the Potomac and ordered to the periphery of Indian fighting. Though given command of the Military District of Iowa as well as the punitive brigade, Sully, like his predecessor and commanding officer, General Pope, was disappointed and resentful that he had to chase Indians while his fellow officers were determining the fate of the nation in Virginia.[4]

To make matters worse, Sully and Pope, initially at least, maintained a mutual detestation. Secretary of War Stanton had turned down Pope's own preference for brigade commander, and Pope, still nursing the psychological wounds of Second Manassas, suspected in the full flush of his paranoia that his superiors in Washington considered Sully a better field commander than himself and thought Sully would be capable of carrying out a successful campaign against the hostiles even under Pope's clumsy overall direction. Sully, for his part, had little respect for Pope as a man or a leader of men. His regiment had helped defend at Chantilly the rear elements of Pope's beaten army after Second Manassas, and Pope's grandiloquent boasts matched against his humiliating defeat rendered him in Sully's opinion little more than an arrogant fraud.

The commander of the Missouri River column was thus a man of distinguished service and of an independent and, some would say, eccentric mindset. He was not afraid of innovation and of taking the road less traveled. He was instrumental in recruiting "galvanized Yankees" (Confederate POWs enlisted into Union service for Indian fighting) and had demonstrated aggressiveness and initiative in his battlefield tactics. In the field, Sully shed his uniform to dress comfortably and informally in corduroy pants, white shirt and undershirt, and white slouch hat. He extended his penchant for civilian comforts and pleasures to the arena of rations as well, carrying with him on campaigns hutches of hens for fresh eggs. Nor was he averse to a sense of irony and wit in coping with the problems of field command, both tactical and logistic. Once, when Sully had a surplus of mules and a shortage of horses, he promoted several mules to the honorary rank of "brevet horses" to balance his record books.[5]

Sully's moment in the sun was to take place on the Dakota prairies. The campaigns of 1863–65 were to bring him three distinctive victories, but they neither catapulted him to fame, like Crook, Custer, or Nelson Miles, nor did they boost his future career. After the Civil War, Sully, like his mules, lost his brevet rank and was returned to the regular army with the permanent rank of major. During a long leave of absence he repaired his personal life and patched over some of the pain by meeting and marrying Sophia Webster, with whom he later had a son and a daughter.[6]

Garrison duty interspersed with Indian fighting marked the remainder of Sully's years. His biggest fight after Killdeer Mountain and the Badlands came during the 1868/69 campaign against the Cheyenne, when he commanded units of the Seventh Cavalry and the Third Infantry in a long-running fight through the Sand Hills of Nebraska, September 11–15, 1868. At a cost to his command of three killed and five wounded, Sully stung the Southern Cheyenne, inflicting losses, by his count, of twenty-two killed and another dozen wounded.

The victor of Whitestone Hill and Killdeer Mountain's last Indian campaign was as the commander of one of the many columns that hunted but did not find Chief Joseph's Nez Percés in their epic trek toward Canada in 1877. Through the intervening years, Sully regained his colonelcy and held several administrative posts. His last assignment was as commander of Fort Vancouver, Washington Territory, where, after several years of failing health (and forty-four months of internal bleeding), he died in 1879. The man who arguably won the U.S. Army's two greatest victories over the Plains Indians passed largely unremembered from American history.[7]

Sully died a bitter man, his early victories forgotten and his career dribbled away to a series of lackluster postings that never afforded him the opportunity to shine again. He had made too many enemies among reporters, who he felt distorted the facts, and among superiors, whom he had too often criticized. Sully had carried on a public feud with George Armstrong Custer, whom he considered arrogant, impulsive, and undisciplined, and had consequently incurred the ill will of Custer's powerful sponsor, General Phil Sheridan. He had earned deeper displeasure from Sheridan and from General Sherman as well for advocating a lenient policy toward the Indians, instead of the policy of extermination favored by the generals and the War Department. Sully went to his grave at age fifty-eight, a man of history, but one passed over by the purveyors of myth.

The March of the Sully Column

General Alfred Sully's slow march up the Missouri River in July 1863 short-circuited the grand strategy of the U.S. Army's Dakota campaign and seemed to justify Pope's lack of faith in him. But Sully's victory at Whitestone Hill a little over a month later served to both redeem his reputation and restore the luster of the campaign. Although there was no Cannae on the prairie in July, no annihilating decisive battle on the banks of the Missouri (just as there was never any annihilating decisive battle anywhere in the West during the decades of U.S.-Indian warfare), Sully's triumph at Whitestone Hill was a victory of considerable proportions. Indeed, though there are critics who dispute the size of the victory, never again in nearly three decades of sporadic warfare would the Sioux nation suffer such a costly defeat at the hands of the American army. But the campaign at its commencement hardly looked promising, as the painter's son, sporting the single silver star of a brigadier general, seemed to flounder in his first major independent command.

For all its sluggishness (due in large measure to circumstances beyond the commander's control), the Sully column was built for mobility. Unlike the column of General Sibley's expedition, consisting predominantly of infantry, Sully's brigade was heavy on cavalry. The two primary elements of the column were the Sixth Iowa Cavalry Regiment, commanded by Colonel David S. Wilson, and eight companies of the Second Nebraska Cavalry Regiment, led by Colonel Robert W. Furnas. Two companies of the Dakota Cavalry and a single company of the Seventh Iowa Cavalry, under Captain Willard, supplemented the two cavalry regiments. The expedition's only infantry were three companies of the Forty-fifth Iowa Infantry Regiment. In support was an eight-gun mountain howitzer battery, seventy-five army wagons loaded with gear, ammunition, and provisions, and seventy-five civilian employees, mostly teamsters and scouts. Total personnel strength was about 1,200 (compared to the 3,000 of Sibley's column).[8]

Though the Second Nebraska had already been in service, the Iowa units were, in the main, newly formed. The Sixth Iowa, mustered in Davenport in early 1863, was composed of farm boys and working-class youths from the towns, all itching to fight with Johnny Reb. When they heard that they were destined for duty in the west instead of the south, and against redskins rather than graycoats, the news fell on them with all the morale-muffling impact of a "cold blanket."[9] The Seventh Iowa was mobilized about the same time, jerry-built of eight new companies married to four old, formerly independent companies. The single company of the Seventh Iowa designated as part of the Sully expedition was one of the veteran units, formerly called the Sioux City Volunteer Cavalry. The rest of the regiment was scattered into frontier posts in Nebraska to defend the territory in place of the Second Nebraska as it marched northwest up the Missouri with Sully.[10]

On June 20, 1863, three weeks after assuming command of the Missouri River expedition, Sully marched his green and underequipped column out of Sioux City. He was not encumbered by a long supply wagon train as was Sibley; the rations for the troops and grain for the livestock were stored aboard steamboats. This supply system harnessed the expedition to the river and to the speed by which the boats could make headway up the shallow channel. As the column filed out of its cantonment outside Sioux City, the citizens there openly expressed skepticism. Because of the lateness of the season, low water, and the consequent slow progress of river traffic, most of the doubtful civilians predicted that the expedition would accomplish little.[11]

The march progressed indeed at a snail's pace. It took three weeks for the column to traverse the 250 miles from Sioux City to Fort Randall, in part because Sully was forced to pause midway, near the Crow Creek Reservation, to rest and wait for the supply boats to catch up with him.

In a letter to the secretary of the interior, dated July 16, 1863, Sully blamed the slow pace of the expedition on low water in the Missouri. He also reported visits by Winnebago chiefs who, along with their people, had been forcibly removed from their homeland in Minnesota after the 1862 massacre even though they had not taken part in it. The Winnebagos remembered Sully from when he had been posted to Minnesota before the Civil War, and they implored his help. They claimed that the land they had been given for a reservation was too rocky for farming, that water and rainfall were inadequate, that the hunting was poor, and that neighboring Sioux often harassed them. Sully was sympathetic and felt that the best resolution for their problems was to relocate them with the friendly bands on the Omaha Reservation.[12]

Sully's concern for the race he had alternately fought and negotiated with for twenty years was heartfelt. He had long lobbied for an even-handed and consistent treatment of the Indian nations. Though he had never refused to obey the often contradictory and confusing orders issued by his military and civilian superiors in their dealings with the Indians, Sully was often openly exasperated by the vacillating Indian policy of the Interior Department. A satirical statement he penned at the end of the 1864 campaign expressed his frustrations.

> If a war of extermination is called for, it will be necessary to shoot everyone that wears a blanket, but it would be very expensive and I know such is not the wishes of the government. The cheapest and easiest way to exterminate the wild Indian is to bring him into a civilized country in contact with the whites (the women would soon become prostitutes and the men drunkards).[13]

In that summer of 1863, many things combined to slow down the column. The tributaries of the Missouri were almost dry, and the Missouri itself dribbled down in places to the size of a rivulet. The almost unbearable heat and dust made the daily march of the infantry an ordeal. On July 25, the day designated by Pope for the link-up with Sibley in northern Dakota, Sully's column had reached only Fort Pierre, hundreds of miles to the south. While his troops rested at Fort Pierre, Sully waited for the river to rise sufficiently for the steamboats to reach him with desperately needed supplies.

On August 7 the correspondent from the *Weekly Dakotan*, who accompanied the expedition, reported that the supplies had still not arrived. Most vitally required was grain for the mounts. The prairie grasses had been almost burned away by a scarcity of rainfall and a surplus of sun, making it necessary to haul most of the livestock's feed by boat. The delay caused by the inability of the boats to steam upriver drove Sully to distraction. The reporter from the *Weekly Dakotan* wrote, "All that mortal man can do will be done by General Sully, and it is his intent to make one bold strike at the Indians—grass or no grass."[14]

In Milwaukee, Pope was even more incensed at the column's creeping progress and, naturally, blamed it all on Sully. He expressed his disappointment to Sully in a letter dated August 5:

> I never had the slightest idea you could delay thus along the River, nor do I realize the necessity of such delay…. I never dreamed you would consider yourself tied to the boats if they were obstacles in going up the river. As matters stand, it seems to me impossible to understand how you have stayed about the River, delaying from day to day, when time of all things was important, and when you have wagons enough to carry at least two months' subsistence for your command.[15]

Sully's slowness seemed to vindicate Pope's prior doubts about his competence, which were further confirmed when the column commander expressed his doubt that he would be able to unite with Sibley on time. Pope wrote to Sully, "Such failure as you anticipate must not happen, as it will be impossible for you to explain it satisfactorily."[16]

Pope was hardly hesitant about reminding his superiors that Sully had been imposed on him. Praising Sibley and pummeling Sully, he wrote Halleck on August 20:

> General Sully has not made the progress expected of him, and which it was in his power to have made, but the Indians were so badly worsted by Sibley, and are in so destitute a condition, that he has nothing to do except follow up Sibley's success with ordinary energy and the whole of the Indians on the upper Missouri will be reduced to a state of quiet which had not been obtained for some years.[17]

Pope's condemnation of Sully was as unfair as his praise of Sibley was overly generous. The Indians were hardly on their last legs because of Sibley's campaign, and Pope obviously had little idea of the extent of the logistical difficulties confronting Sully. With his cavalry-heavy force and because of the drought, Sully was far more dependent on transported provision for his livestock than Sibley. Ironically, at the very moment Pope was writing his missive to Halleck, Sully was beset by a new vagary of the tempestuous prairie weather as driving rain and hail pounded his brigade at the mouth of the Little Cheyenne.

Even after Sully, in late August, finally got his column moving across country in a belated effort to join with Sibley's force, Pope continued his harassment by dispatch rider. In a letter changing his orders, Pope wrote, "It is painful for me to find fault, nor do I desire to say what is unpleasant, but I feel bound to tell you frankly that your movements have greatly disappointed me, and I can find no satisfactory explanation of them."[18]

According to Pope's new orders, Sully was to head back immediately for the Missouri, load his wagons for an extended campaign, and then operate west of the river until winter set in. His force was then to be parceled out in garrisons at Fort Pierre, Fort Randall, and Sioux City to block any further Indian raids across the river into eastern Dakota and Minnesota. Pope's orders came too late, however, (or, possibly, Sully chose to ignore them). The Sioux had already recrossed the Missouri, and Sully, after two months of frustration and futility, was about to embark on a successful sortie that would render full restitution for a summer of aggravation.[19]

Whitestone Hill

Sully had set his column in motion from his advance base above Fort Pierre on August 14, although there was still no sign of the supply steamers

Shreveport and *Belle Peoria*. He directed his brigade toward the mouth of the Little Cheyenne River, where he hoped the steamboats would finally catch up with him and deliver the provisions that would allow his column to cut its tie to the Missouri and strike inland. The column reached its destination on August 16, and three days later the *Belle Peoria* finally met up with the troops. Wagons were loaded with the supplies necessary to strike out across country in accordance with the long-delayed strategy of linking up with the Sibley column. Excess baggage, the sick, and the unmounted, were placed aboard the steamboat to be sent downriver to Fort Pierre. This trimmed the force considerably and enabled the brigade to load rations and forage for the transport animals sufficient for twenty-three days, even with the "wretched mules furnished." Because the grass to the north was reported to be in much better condition than anticipated, Sully planned to provide forage for his cavalry and artillery horses by grazing them along the route of march.

For the first time in weeks, optimistic that the campaign could be salvaged, Sully was ready to strike off northeast toward Devil's Lake in accordance with Pope's original strategy, but the Dakota weather delivered another blow. On August 20 heat, dust, and dryness were chased from the scene by a momentous rainstorm. Hail fell like volleys of white musket balls. The storm struck as the brigade was crossing the Little Cheyenne, flooding the steep-banked river and upsetting a wagon. The hail grains, some as large as hen's eggs, pelted the column for twenty minutes. Part of the expedition's herd stampeded; many rations were destroyed in uncovered wagons, and several troopers were tossed from the saddle by their panicked mounts. A bugler caught an icy chunk on the temple and was sent sprawling into the mud. Private Milton Spencer, Company L, Sixth Iowa Cavalry, reported in a letter to his father that although he covered himself with two blankets, a rubber rain jacket, and a woolen coat, his shoulders and arms were sore for a week after the hailstorm.[20]

The rain continued to pour and the flat area around the river was completely inundated. Sully had to lead his men to the top of the bluffs overlooking the river to find a dry campsite for the night. After recovering the stampeded animals, Sully finally got underway on the afternoon of August 21, but the ground was so soggy from the thunderstorm that progress was very slow.[21]

The first day's march covered only eleven miles up the Little Cheyenne River. On August 22 the column continued to follow the Little Cheyenne, but for only seven miles this day before settling into camp on a slough in the prairie, denuded entirely of any wood. The following day the column veered northwest to the outlet of Swan Lake. The brigade managed to cover eighteen miles, bearing northward, on August 24 before bivouacking on

Bois Cache Creek. The expedition was now in buffalo country, and a hunting party was organized to supplement the daily rations. Although the hunters managed to kill a good number of buffalo on the 25th, that success was unusual, and the party was soon disbanded when the wear and tear on the horses exceeded the limited benefits of the extra meat ration. The hunters, in their wide sweeps, did discover many signs of recent Indian presence in the vicinity of the Missouri, convincing Sully he was on the right track.

Still headed north, Sully's column made twenty-two miles on August 25, reaching Bird Ache Creek. His scouts rounded up two squaws and their children the next day. They reported a fight at Long Lake (the headwaters of the Apple River) between the Sioux and Sibley (who was by then on his way back to Minnesota) as well as the presence of an Indian encampment near the Missouri. Acting on this information, Sully detached Companies F and K of the Second Nebraska Cavalry, led by Captain D. La Boo, toward the Missouri to try to pick up the Indians' trail. The main column slogged on for a record thirty-five miles to the Beaver River before Sully could find a campsite with water. The column got a late start on August 27 because of the inherent delay of a river crossing and managed only a five-mile march north. Company F of the Second Nebraska rejoined the main body that day, having become separated from its sister company and having uncovered no further Indian signs. Frustration mounted again as a successful contact with the enemy seemed to always loom just beyond view.[22]

But fortune came again to flirt with Sully's brigade on August 28 in the form of a lame old Indian. After a hard march northwest for twenty miles, Sully's soldiers encountered this elderly "good" Indian, who was well known by whites in the Sioux City area. He reported that hostiles had robbed him of his horse after he had become separated from his band in an isolated area, and that as a result he had nearly starved to death. He also spoke of Sibley in action around Long Lake, fifty miles to the northeast, gave details of Sibley's campaign—including the claim that the Sioux had lost fifty-eight killed against Sibley—and reported that Sibley had recrossed the James River and was on his way back to Minnesota. The old Indian also gave an account of the destruction of the Mackinaw boat and claimed twenty-one white men, three white women, several children, and ninety-one Indians were killed in that episode (all figures higher than most counts, particularly the number of Sioux dead). According to his account, some of the hostile Indians had drifted north, but most, after learning that Sibley was headed homeward, recrossed the Missouri to their old hunting grounds; most of them migrated to the head of Long Lake, but some camped on the east bank of the Missouri, to the west of Sully's present position.[23]

Several of Sully's guides who were acquainted with this region corroborated the old Indian's story. They pointed out that a large body of Indians could not survive the winter on the largely barren west side of the Missouri unless they moved a great distance west. The Sioux customarily camped at this time of the year to the southeast on the Coteau des Missouri, an area near the tributaries of the James River replete with lakes and fresh water springs full of fish, where the grass was tall and the buffalo plentiful. Traditionally, the Sioux would hunt and fish and prepare meat for the winter, then move back to the Missouri, whose timbered banks provided plenty of fuel to warm them during the winter. Armed with this information and now certain that a union with Sibley was impossible, Sully decided to change direction. He determined to move southeast as rapidly as possible and as far as his rations would permit.

As Sully was about to set out on what finally appeared to be a truly hot trail, anxiety about the fate of Company K of the Second Nebraska kept him in camp for two more days. Captain La Boo and his fifty men had been gone on their search for Indian signs for two days without rations. Major Pearman was sent out with five companies to try to locate Company K. Much to Sully's relief the company returned to camp after a mounted march of 187 miles, during which the Nebraska cavalrymen had lived on buffalo and other game while searching the area to the north of the main column. Captain La Boo did locate the Indian camp his force of originally two companies had been sent to find and destroy. The ten-lodge encampment had been abandoned and no Indians were in sight. After torching the tepees, La Boo led his weary horse soldiers back to the expedition's camp. After a march of ninety miles, Major Pearman's detachment, sent to find La Boo, also returned to camp.

With all his units accounted for, Sully was ready to move toward the Coteau. First, though, he sent two companies of the Sixth Iowa to proceed to the mouth of the Apple River to confirm the various reports of Sibley's movements by finding both Sibley's vacated camp and the wrecked Mackinaw boat.[24]

An energetic march of three days duration carried the column into present-day Dickey County, North Dakota, by September 3. According to Indian POWs taken at Whitestone Hill during the battle, stealthy groups of Sioux braves had followed the Sully column undetected all the way to the Coteau, with the larcenous intent of stampeding the soldiers' horse and mule herds. Sully had prevented this, however, with his march tactics, perfected from twenty years of frontier experience. The marching column was protected by both an advance guard and flankers. The wagon train moved in two lines sixty paces apart with troops on either side. All loose stock was herded between the wagon lines, and the howitzer battery was placed in the center of the column, from whence it could be rushed to provide heavy fire support to whichever section of the column might come under attack.

During the entire march, Sully lost only a dozen head of stock that wandered from camp during the night. The trailing Indians never had the opportunity to attempt either a harassment attack or a stampede.

By mid-afternoon on Thursday, September 3, Sully had reached a small lake beside which several buffalo had recently been butchered. This and other Indian signs indicated that the Sioux were indeed headed for their favorite late summer haunt. The brigadier had detailed the 300-man Third Battalion of the Sixth Iowa Cavalry, led by Major A. E. House, to scout five miles ahead, with Frank La Framboise as his guide. House's orders were to engage and destroy any small Sioux force he might encounter, but to hold back and simply observe any substantial Indian congregation until Sully could bring up the main column. If House could keep his presence unknown to any such Sioux camp, Sully planned to leave his train under a heavy guard and move the rest of his force up during the night to surround the Indian village and attack at dawn.[25]

House's scout mission had begun at 5:30 A.M. on September 3, about thirty miles northeast of Whitestone Hill (which is located twelve miles northwest of present-day Ellendale and fifteen miles west of present-day Monango). His battalion consisted of companies C, I, F, and H (which was detached from the Second Battalion to replace Company M, whose horses were too worn out from prior scouting duty to accompany the advance force). The battalion proceeded southward, halting hourly to dismount the men and allow the horses to graze for ten minutes. At 1500 the battalion guide informed House that an Indian camp of 400–600 lodges nestled in the ravines around Whitestone Hill three miles ahead, where (according to the later testimony of Indian POWs) the Sioux, apparently unaware of the white soldiers' approach because the warriors who had hoped to stampede Sully's stock had not informed them, felt secure. They assumed that Sully was still on his way up the Missouri.

The battalion commander ordered his men to load their carbines and pistols and proceed at a slow gallop. Within one mile of the camp he halted his 300 men to form his companies in line—I in the center, H and F on the flanks, and C in reserve. The battalion closed up to a position behind a ridge about 280 yards from the unsuspecting camp. Captain C. J. Marsh from Company H and Lieutenant G. E. Dayton of Company C were sent forward to reconnoiter. They returned to report 400 lodges; it was subsequently estimated that there were 1,500 braves (950 according to the Sioux) and 3,000–4,000 Sioux in total.[26]

The guide, La Framboise, and two men from Company C were sent to summon the brigade, some ten miles in the rear. La Framboise rode right into a party of 200 Sioux. Surrounding the guide, one of the Indians declaimed that "they had fought General Sibley, and they could not see why the whites wanted to come fight them, unless they were tired of living and wanted to die."[27]

La Framboise spurred his mount into a gallop and succeeded in escaping from the Sioux. He quickly covered the ten miles to Sully, reaching the site designated Camp 33 at around 1600 to report the impending confrontation at Whitestone Hill.

The general quickly mobilized his men, many of whom were grazing their horses when the scout rode in. At the blare of the bugle, the troops saddled up, let out a cheer, and formed into line in a few minutes. Sully detailed Major Pearman, the commander of the Second Battalion of the Second Nebraska Cavalry, to take charge of four companies, and all those men whose mounts were worn out, to remain in camp to strike the tents and corral the wagons. The Second Nebraska (eight companies with 350 men) was formed up to the front; the Sixth Iowa (minus House's battalion) in the rear; the single company of the Seventh Iowa and the howitzer battery were placed in the center. Then at full gallop, the brigade covered the ten miles to Whitestone Hill in less than an hour.[28]

Sully arrived just in time (almost in cinematic, cavalry-comes-to-the-rescue fashion). House's position had deteriorated from promising to perilous once he discovered the true size of the forces opposed to his battalion and the Indians became fully aware of his presence. House had wanted to surround the camp, in keeping with Sully's plan of containment until the whole brigade could arrive, but that seemed impossible because the Indian lodges were so spread out. Inhabiting those lodges were Santees, Cut-Heads from the Coteau, Yanktonais, some Blackfeet Sioux from west of the Missouri, and Hunkpapas and others who had fought Sibley and ambushed the Mackinaw boat. Letters and papers of the victims of the Indians found later in the camp confirmed this identity.[29]

Because the ground was so broken and uneven, making it difficult to determine the exact layout of the Sioux camp and the numbers he faced, House decided on a reconnaissance-in-force while he awaited Sully. First he sent Captain L. L. Ainsworth and Company C to the left, supported by Captain Marsh's Company H. When those companies returned, reporting ten-to-one odds, House dispatched Captain S. Shattuck with Company F to the right to scout the ground.

While the scouting was taking place, the Sioux sent out a delegation to talk with the battalion commander under a flag of truce. House, though obviously heavily outnumbered, boldly demanded an unconditional surrender. The negotiating chiefs offered to turn over a few of their leaders as hostages, but rejected total capitulation. They claimed they were only interested in drying meat for the winter and had no desire to fight the white soldiers. House suspected that the negotiating team was using the parley only

Major Albert E. House, Sixth Iowa Cavalry, 1863. (Courtesy of the State Historical Society of North Dakota.)

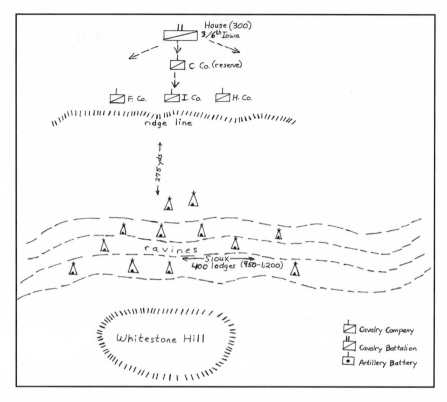

Whitestone Hill, Sept. 3, 1863, 1500 hours. Initial deployment. (Numbers in parentheses show troop strength.)

as a delaying tactic to give the village time to prepare an evacuation of the noncombatants, for he noticed a great deal of activity among the camp's women and children. Both sides were probably using the parley only as a stalling tactic to prepare for battle.[30]

The prospects for that forthcoming battle became ominous for the Iowa cavalrymen. Although they presented a bold front, the men of House's battalion soon found themselves outflanked by the gathering Sioux and nearly surrounded. The Iowa troopers readied themselves to make what many of them felt would be a last stand.

The Indians, led by the old warhorse, Inkpaduta, certainly acted as though a triumph of major proportions was only minutes away. Though many women and children were indeed packing up and preparing to flee, other women were cooking, in obvious anticipation of a victory celebration, while their men daubed themselves with mud and warpaint and decorated their bodies with feathers and battle amulets in eager preparation for battle. If the Sioux seemed motivated by different impulses—some of them parleying with the soldiers to avoid an attack while their noncombatants made ready for flight, while others, predominantly of Inkpaduta's ilk, made joyful and confident preparations for battle—it must be remembered that the Sioux, like all Plains Indians, always maintained their individual options, that chiefs and leaders could only advise and lead by example, never command. Thus, while a considerable number of the Indians in the Whitestone Hill camp were plainly in no mood to fight, the majority by their enthusiastic preparations and jeers and taunts directed at the Iowa troops, were just as plainly thoroughly psyched for battle. Outflanked and outnumbered four- or five-to-one, House's cavalrymen faced a predicament no less perilous than that confronting the men of the Seventh Cavalry thirteen years later on another prairie battlefield several hundred miles to the west.

Depending on what Indian was asked later, the Sioux were either just getting ready to launch an overwhelming assault or were in the process of fleeing wholesale when Sully arrived on the site at around 1700 with the main force. Thus—again according to the interpretation—the brigadier approached Whitestone Hill in time to prevent the total escape of the Indian camp or in time to rescue one of his battalions from utter annihilation. There was no doubt, however, on how the frightened and grateful soldiers of House's battalion felt about Sully's arrival. Up to the moment of the main column's appearance, they had considered themselves, not unsuccessful pursuers but ensnared prey.

To Sully's eye, as he rode up to the site, the Indian reaction seemed more flight than fight. Having come this close to finally snagging the enemy, the general was not about to let them get away. At the same time, he wanted to make sure that House's Third Battalion was secure. Consequently, he ordered Colonel Furnas to push his Second Nebraska at a full run to the aid of House. Aiming for House's left flank, the Second Nebraska moved to the southeast and was soon lost in a cloud of dust.

Sully deployed his other units to coordinate with the Second Nebraska and surround the camp. Colonel Wilson, commander of the Sixth Iowa, was sent to the right flank with his regiment's First Battalion (commanded by Major J. Galligan). Sully himself led the center, which consisted of two companies of the Sixth Iowa's Second Battalion under Major Edward P. Ten Broeck, Captain A. J. Millard's company of the Seventh Iowa, and the howitzer battery, toward the middle of the camp.[31]

On the left, Furnas of the Second Nebraska directed Major J. Taffe's First Battalion toward the head of a ravine where he saw warriors gathering. Taffe's mission was to cut off any possible flight in that direction. The Second Battalion, commanded in Major Pearman's absence by Captain La Boo, was ordered to advance directly on the Sioux.

After securing the head of the ravine without encountering resistance,

François LaFramboise and his children. Left to right: Fannie, 12; George, 10; and John, 8. (Courtesy of the State Historical Society of North Dakota.)

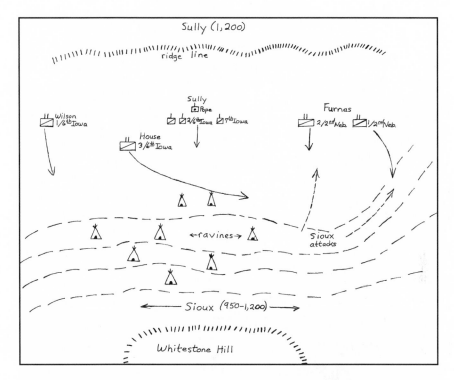

Whitestone Hill, 1700 hours. Sully reaches the battlefield and deploys.

Taffe's battalion was then ordered to move forward with the Second Battalion, the line of the two battalions forming an obtuse angle. Within 400 yards of the camp the Nebraska soldiers were ordered to dismount. At 300 yards the Second Battalion was ordered to open fire. The ripping volley from the cavalrymen's Enfield rifles downed several Sioux and rattled the rest.

At this point in the battle, Furnas spotted House's battalion, one and a half miles away. Just an hour ago, House's men had been surrounded themselves. Now they were threatening to turn the tables on the Indians by advancing on the rear of those engaging the Second Nebraska. Seizing on this development, Furnas pushed his line forward as heavy firing rose from both sides. Within thirty yards, the regimental commander ordered his men to halt in the rear of a slight elevation before which ran a Sioux-held ravine. Battle became general now and the entire battalion line was hotly engaged. As dusk descended, House's battalion could be seen by Furnas' men striking the left flank of the Indians facing the Second Nebraska. Furnas now ordered Taffe to extend his left to cover a ravine that, with approaching darkness, Furnas feared the Sioux could use as either an escape route or as an avenue to get behind the Second Nebraska and strike the regiment from the rear.

Colonel David S. Wilson, Sixth Iowa Cavalry, 1863. (Courtesy of the State Historical Society of North Dakota.)

As the day waned, the Indians did indeed try to strike on that left flank of the regiment, as well as on the right flank, but both attacks were repulsed by the Nebraska troopers, with considerable losses inflicted on the charging warriors.[32]

House's Third Battalion of the Sixth Iowa was also now fully engaged. The first appearance of the Second Nebraska on a hilltop off to their left had transformed the situation for the men of House's battalion from one fraught with peril to one ripe with opportunity. The battalion had advanced on horseback to within 100 yards of the rear of the threatening swarm of Sioux warriors, while the Nebraska troopers had dismounted on their left to fight on foot. House had his men dismount and marched them down the hill to within thirty yards of the Indians. The Sioux were now contained from their front by the Second Nebraska and the Sixth Iowa's First Battalion, while the Sixth Iowa's Third Battalion covered their rear.[33]

At this point, Colonel Wilson, commander of the Sixth Iowa, arrived on the scene to take direct command of the Third Battalion. Instead of continuing the fight on foot, Wilson ordered the men of the Third Battalion to remount. According to the eyewitness account of Private Milton Spencer, Wilson was in such haste to organize a mounted charge in the gathering dusk that he neglected to even give the order to load weapons, and one of the companies—for whatever reason—had not yet done so. Wilson advanced the battalion in column at a trot, then a gallop, and finally a full charge.[34]

Several Sioux fired on House's men, who then discharged several volleys "with terrible effect, covering the ground with dead men and horses." On the opposite side, the Second Nebraska also shot off a volley that, according to Private Spencer, did as much damage to House's battalion as it did to the Indians. The impetuous Colonel Wilson at one point found himself some distance in front of his Third Battalion and came under considerable fire. His horse took a fatal bullet, but lived long enough to carry him thirty yards back to the battalion line.[35]

The heavy firing caused the horses to bolt and become unmanageable and therefore the charge broke down. House pulled his men back 140 yards to dismount and fight on foot. As darkness fell, the major formed his men in a hollow square, with a line of soldiers in front of the horses. Fighting continued for some time on the Third Battalion's front, with several of House's soldiers distinguishing themselves by their valorous conduct. The major later particularly singled out Captain L. R. Wolf, who stood in front of his company and "killed an Indian every shot he made."[36]

Furnas too pulled back as darkness settled in, mainly out of fear that House's men, behind the Indians who were to Furnas' front, might accidentally start firing into the ranks of the Second Nebraska (just as the Nebraska troops had helped to disrupt the Sixth Iowa's charge by inadvertently firing

"The Sioux War—Cavalry charge of Sully's brigade at the Battle of Whitestone Hill, September 3, 1863—sketched by an officer engaged." From *Harper's Weekly*. (Courtesy of the State Historical Society of North Dakota.)

into its ranks). Consequently, he ordered his men to remount and fall back out of range of House's guns. The skittish horses, unnerved by several hours of intense firing, kicked and caused confusion during the withdrawal, but the regiment was able to backup 200 yards to reform on a line of hills to the rear. The Indians facing the Nebraska regiment had had enough; they fled rapidly up a ravine and away from the soldiers.[37]

While the Second Nebraska and the Sixth Iowa's Third Battalion had been hotly engaged, Sully had led the brigade's center toward the middle of the Sioux camp. He first encountered the "good Indian," Chief Little Soldier, with a group of his people. Claiming to be innocent of any belligerence toward the whites and reaffirming his reputation of friendship with the Americans, the chief and his band were placed under guard and conducted to the rear. Proceeding on, the brigadier next found the lodges of the "notorious chief," Big Head, who along with several of his warriors was dressed for battle. Sully surrounded the tepees and quickly forced the chief's surrender, collecting thirty braves and ninety women and children as prisoners.[38]

During this roundup, firing broke out one half mile to the left front of Sully (this was the Sixth Iowa's charge on the rear of the Indians). Soon the

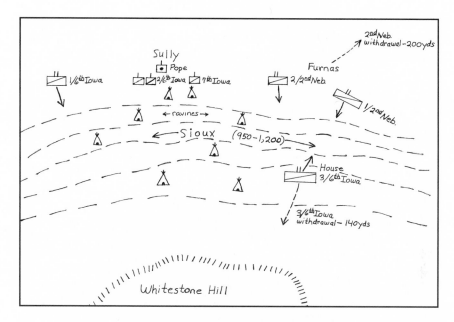

Whitestone Hill, 1800–2130 hours.

general received the false report that his units were being repulsed. To serve as a firebreak or rallying point in case this proved true, Sully formed a line with the howitzers in the center on the highest knoll in a collection of hillocks.

Firing remained spirited all along the brigade front as the warriors, though with little or no coordination or control, rallied from point to point to cover the flight of their families. Sully later reported "a very desperate resistance" on the part of the Sioux soldiers, making Whitestone Hill, in his words, quite a "respectable engagement."[39]

It would have been more than just a respectable engagement, and possibly a huge victory for the U.S. Army, if the battle had commenced earlier in the afternoon, but darkness made it possible for the Indians to break contact and withdraw and too dangerous for the cavalry battalions to pursue in the broken, ravine-rich terrain around Whitestone Hill. Sully thought he could have annihilated the enemy if he had been granted just a few more hours of daylight. But rather than risk a loss of control over his troops, a possible ambush, or another blind friendly-fire encounter between units of his brigade, he reluctantly called off any further advance or pursuit. The general had his buglers blow the rally recall and had fires built to rein in all pursuing units. Although confusion briefly ruled as the Dakota night lengthened, Sully managed by about 2130 to collect all his troops and end the battle.[40]

Private Spencer, in his letters home, expressed a dissenting point of view about the brigade's failure to utterly destroy the Indians. From his perspective, it was not so much the onset of darkness that enabled the Sioux to escape as it was the incompetence of Colonel Wilson. Spencer pointed out that once House had gained the rear of the Indians, "They were now completely in our control and everyone supposed they would surrender, or else be obliged to fight us at a great disadvantage, as they were within easy rifle range while we were completely out of reach of their arrows and shotguns."[41]

But Wilson's appearance on the scene and his headlong, mounted charge resulted in confusion and withdrawal by the Third Battalion and allowed the Indians to slip out of the snare. As Spencer put it, "Mr. Indian, seeing the gate open, was not long in going out."[42] Although Sully, in his official report of the battle, did not blame Wilson for the Sioux escape, the general may have shared these misgivings about the competence of the Sixth Iowa's leadership. In a letter written a few weeks after the battle, Sully complained that many of the regiment's officers were ignorant and inefficient and threatened them with a board of examination to test their military qualifications.

Spencer was pessimistic about the outcome of any such examinations. "That is a trial to which our officers have never been subjected, and as the most of them are more familiar with a deck of cards than they are with Cavalry tactics and army regulations, I am afraid it will go rather hard with some of them."[43]

Whether Wilson's actions at Whitestone Hill provoked Sully's rather intense displeasure with the officers of the Sixth Iowa is unknown. If all of Spencer's claims against Wilson are true, it seems that the official reports of the battle, which mention no error of judgment on the part of the colonel, cover up what amounted to a serious failure of leadership by the commander of the Sixth Iowa at Whitestone Hill. Certain is only that most of the twelve Sixth Iowa soldiers killed on September 3 died in the charge of the Third Battalion, including several who died under the misdirected fire of the Second Nebraska.

The brigade camped for the night on the field of battle. The horses were corralled, reinforced pickets were set up to guard the perimeter, and those men who slept did so with their weapons in easy reach. The night was very dark, almost starless, and quite cold. One of the picket details killed two Indian stragglers near the camp's perimeter, but otherwise the night passed in apprehension but without incident.[44]

Sully must have rested easy, certain that the Sioux had been punished too severely to attempt a nighttime counterattack. He regretted that darkness had curtailed the scope of his victory but was nonetheless well satisfied with what his men had achieved. His mounted men, armed with long-range rifles instead of the normal cavalry armament of carbines, sabers, and pistols, had functioned smoothly—with the glaring exception of Wilson's charge—dismounting to fight until the Sioux broke, then remounting for pursuit. Their coolness under fire, the bold and proficient leadership of their officers (again, with one exception), and their deadly marksmanship, all had combined to produce a significant victory and to cause heavy losses for the Santee, Yanktonai, and Teton enemy.[45]

Those losses became clearer with the dawn on September 4. Sully first ordered the wagon train, left behind under the charge of Major Pearman of the Second Nebraska, to be brought up to join the brigade. Then he sent out scouting parties to overtake the Indian fugitives. The net was cast wide, but pulled in only a disappointing catch. A few small groups were tracked down and dispersed after brief skirmishes, but most of the Sioux from Whitestone Hill were long gone. However, there was bloody evidence in all directions of the execution the men of Sully's brigade had inflicted on September 3. At sun-up Furnas marched his Second Nebraska one mile to the upper end of the Sioux camp. The fleeing Indians had abandoned all but their dead, "whom they carried away as fast as they fell."[46] Even children had been lost and left behind in the deserted camp. Furnas's men collected a mass of plunder—a few minié rifles and ammunition, boxes of army revolvers and rifle cartridges, numerous articles from the Minnesota Massacre, including letters, two gold dollars, and bags of gold dust.

Although Furnas found few bodies in his sweep through the center of the camp, the other units discovered many in all directions, some of them miles from the battlefield. One search party scoured the countryside to the James River and found eleven dead Indians there. Many dead ponies were also found. Many ponies and dogs harnessed to travois were found running unattended over the prairie. Packed on the travois were baggage, dried buffalo meat, and other provisions. Sully's men spent September 4 and September 5 burning plunder and Indian gear, including 300 lodges and a winter's supply of 400,000–500,000 pounds of buffalo meat (representing at least 1,000 butchered buffalos). Captain R. B. Mason, the wagonmaster, stated that "fat ran in streams from the burning mass of meat."[47]

Quite apart from their casualties, the Indians had thus suffered a grievous blow in the loss of their food and possessions, a blow that would ensure a winter of misery for them. According to Sergeant Drips of the Sixth Iowa, "To show the extent of their loss in measure I will just say that it took a party of 100 men two days to gather up the stuff and burn it. It was our policy to burn everything we could."[48]

Several more Indians, mostly women and children, were rounded up on the 4th and 5th, so that the final tally of Sioux prisoners from Whitestone Hill was 156, 32 men of fighting age and 124 women and children.

Sully personally questioned several of the Indian POWs. The men said little, except for claiming to be good Indians and reporting that the other "bad ones" who had resisted the cavalry brigade had joined their camp against the will of the majority. The squaws were more forthcoming. They related that the Sioux, after recrossing the Missouri, had sent a party to follow Sibley back to the James River. After making sure that Sibley was gone for good, the Indians had returned to camp near Long Lake to secure a large cache of provisions and had then moved to the campsite on White-stone Hill.[49]

Although this information helped confirm the general's overall under-standing of the movement of the Sioux during the campaign, he hardly showed his gratitude. The POWs, most of whom had surrendered at the first American charge, had offered no resistance and cooperated fully with their captors. But they were soon sent on a forced march across the burn-ing plains to Crow Creek on the Missouri, where they were herded onto the reservation where the Dakotas from Fort Snelling had been sent into exile. Several of the Sioux captives died on the torturous journey, and a cen-tury later their ancestors were still to refer to the trip as a "death march."[50]

There was a violent sequel to Whitestone Hill on September 5. On the night of the battle, Dr. Bowen, the regimental surgeon of the Second Ne-braska, had been sent with an escort, consisting of Sergeant Newcomb and eight other Nebraska troopers, back to the old camp to bring up the ambulances for the white wounded. When this party had not returned by the morning of September 5, Sully worried about their fate and dispatched a search party of twelve men of the Second Nebraska and fifteen of the Sixth Iowa, under the leadership of Lieutenant Charles W. Hall of the Second Nebraska. The missing men rode into the Whitestone Hill camp in the afternoon, but by then the search party had already left and was already in trouble.

About fifteen miles northeast of the battlefield, Hall's patrol was sud-denly attacked by about 300 Sioux. The lieutenant had his men fall back slowly. The horse soldiers returned an effective fire and held steady, until a sudden surge by the Indians pressed their painted ranks so close to the cav-alrymen that panic set in, succeeded by flight. Hall tried to check the dis-organized flight, but the pursuing Sioux gave him no opportunity to reform his ranks. The chase continued for many miles, with the Sioux trying to cut the patrol off from the brigade camp. The Indians did not break off their pursuit until they were only four miles from Sully's bivouac. The exhausted and demoralized soldiers made it back to camp by midnight, having lost six killed in action—two from the Sixth Iowa and four from the Second Nebraska—and another Nebraska trooper wounded; four of their horses had also been killed.

Sully had sent Colonel Furnas out from camp with five companies of the Second Nebraska after he heard the gunfire of the running fight approaching his position. Furnas, after a great deal of marching about, found that the Indian force had fled, but his men did manage to overtake and kill three warriors trying to conceal themselves in the tall grass. Hall claimed, probably on the basis of wishful thinking, that his battered patrol killed six hostiles and four ponies and wounded "many" in their multi-mile skirmish.[51]

Sully's victory at Whitestone Hill was considerable, but the precise extent of that victory in terms of Indian casualties was difficult to gauge. Sully stated in his official report of the battle that the fight was so scattered in expanse and that dead Indians were found in so many places that it was impossible to give accurate figures. He estimated, however, that the Santee, Yanktonai, and Teton combatants lost 100 killed, including those slain on the primary battlefield on September 3 and those killed on the 4th and 5th by scouting parties. On another occasion, however, he referred to total Indian casualties of 150 killed *and* wounded, one of the smallest casualty counts offered by any of the army officers involved.[52]

As an example of the sanguinery quality of the battle, Sully offered the image of the Second Nebraska, afoot and armed with rifles—"and there [were] among them probably some of the best shots in the world"—engaging the Sioux at sixty paces and pouring a murderous fire into a ravine packed with Indians—"The slaughter, therefore, must have been immense."[53]

Sully pointed out that he had been unable to use his artillery because much of the combat was at such close quarters that his own men would have been greatly endangered: "If I could [have used artillery], I could have slaughtered them."[54]

Other calculations of Sioux losses ran from the 150 killed and wounded guessed at by some of Sully's staff officers and guides to later estimates by some frontier historians and chroniclers of as many as 300 killed. More than likely this figure represents a considerable exaggeration, but given the size and intensity of the battle, it is not entirely unrealistic. Major House calculated 100 Indian dead; Colonel Furnas, who estimated the number of Indian combatants at 1,000, placed Sioux casualties at 150 killed and 300 wounded; other unit leaders talked of figures of 200 killed and 200 wounded. Indian witnesses and participants most often settled for a figure of around 200 killed and wounded.[55]

Whatever the true toll taken by his men, Sully had praise for those soldiers; he thought they had reacted well in what was the first fight for most, and the general felt that "in time, with discipline, they will make worthy soldiers." He regretted his own relatively heavy loss, but judged that the casualties could hardly have been less because the "Indians had formed a line of battle with good judgment, from which they could be dislodged only by a charge."[56]

Those heavy troop losses to which Sully referred were, like the casualties incurred by the Sioux, a matter of some confusion and dispute. Sully originally reported twenty men killed, including one officer, Lieutenant T. J. Leavitt of Company B, Sixth Iowa, and thirty-eight wounded. The combat deaths included six killed in the fighting on September 5. Later, in his official report, Sully revised the toll down to one officer and seventeen enlisted men killed, two officers and thirty-four enlisted men wounded. In the main battle on September 3 the Second Nebraska had reported two killed, thirteen wounded, plus five horses killed, nine wounded, and nine missing; the Sixth Iowa suffered twelve men killed, twenty-one wounded. Sully reported that those losses were taken by 600–700 men directly engaged in the battle out of his total force of 1,200.[57]

On the markers circling the granite monument erected later on Whitestone Hill the names of twenty men of the Iowa and Nebraska cavalry regiments are inscribed. Many subsequent military and journalistic reports and historical accounts reckon the final white toll at twenty-two killed, thirty-eight wounded, with a few of those accounts going as high as twenty-five killed and fifty wounded. The discrepancy between the combat death figures can probably be attributed to a number of soldiers who died from their wounds days or even weeks after the battle. The higher figure of fifty wounded sometimes given can probably be accounted for by factoring in the number of men only slightly wounded who were not normally counted among the more seriously hit combatants.

There were also disputes about the nature of the Indian casualties and the battle itself. Most of the dissenting voices were Indian, but at least one white man added his protestations to the generally accepted version that Whitestone Hill was a hard-fought battle resulting in a major white victory and considerable Sioux combatant casualties. Many Sioux insisted that their village was filled mostly with Indians intent on peace, that they resisted only enough to cover the escape of their families, and that most of the Indian dead were noncombatants. Whitestone Hill, in their view, was simply another Sand Creek, Marias (Blood) River, Camp Grant, or Wounded Knee. Whitestone Hill, from their perspective, was a massacre, not a battle.

This view was supported by Samuel J. Brown, a nineteen-year-old interpreter at the Santee agency at Crow Creek. In a letter dated November 13, 1863, to his father, Joseph R. Brown, he put forth his dissenting opinion.

> I hope you will not believe all that is said of Sully's successful expedition against the Sioux. I don't think he ought to brag of it at all, because it was

what no decent man would have done, he pitched into their camp and just slaughtered them, worse a great deal than what the Indians did in 1862, he killed very few men and took no hostile ones prisoners, he took some but they were friendly Yanktons, and he let them go again…. It is lamentable to hear how those women and children were slaughtered, it was a perfect massacre, and now he returns saying that we need fear no more, for he has wiped out all hostile Indians from Dakota; if he had killed men instead of women and children, then it would have been a success, and the worse of it, they had no hostile intention whatever, the Nebraska 2nd pitched into them without orders, while the Iowa 6th were shaking hands with them.[58]

The number of Sioux noncombatant casualties at Whitestone Hill is indeed a bit of a mystery. Brown, an obvious sympathizer to the plight of the red man in America, provides one of the few white versions of a peaceful village attacked by vengeful whites. His sources were Santee friends, unwilling, as Indians often were, to give credit to white soldiers who had defeated them and anxious to put their own spin on their considerable losses. That there were Indians at Whitestone Hill who had not fought and did not want to fight Americans was undoubtedly true. But it is almost equally certain that a great many of the Indians there, probably a majority, had taken part in either the Minnesota Massacre, the raids on Dakota and Minnesota in 1863, or the fighting with Sibley. Among the many items recovered from the Dakota and Minnesota raids were letters from the passengers of the ambushed Mackinaw boat as well as a considerable amount of gold dust.[59] There can be little doubt that most of the Indians fought hard at Whitestone Hill and fought effectively, given the heavy casualties among the soldiers, and that most of the Indian casualties came from that spirited resistance.

On the other hand, with minor exceptions, there is a conspicuous lack of references to Sioux noncombatant casualties in the official reports or the later accounts or memoirs of the officers and men of Sully's brigade. In that era the distinction between hostile and nonhostile Indians was often obfuscated or ignored. In June at Fort Randall men of the Sixth Iowa had arrested eight Indians for allegedly stealing horses and had shot seven of them to death when they tried to escape—according to the official report. Private Spencer, however, claimed that the Indians, who had been part of a band that rescued eight white prisoners from hostile Sioux the winter before, had been, in effect, gunned down in cold blood.[60] But unless there was some vast conspiracy of silence on the part of the white participants in the battle, it seems extremely unlikely that any kind of deliberate, large-scale massacre of Indian women and children occurred that would be comparable to Sand Creek or the Marias River.

Given Sully's long demonstrated concern for the Indians and his overall spotless record of honor and integrity, it is hardly believable that he would have countenanced or commanded any such massacre. It is true that throughout history there are many examples of honorable and effective commanders losing control of their troops whose bloodlust had boiled over. But Sully's troops seemed fairly well disciplined and were led, generally, by strong-willed and competent commanders who were not inclined to let things get out of hand. Unlike in Sibley's force, there were few men in the ranks who had lost loved ones in the killings of 1862 and were consequently predisposed toward revenge.

However, given the circumstances of the battle—fought in gathering darkness in the midst of an Indian camp filled with thousands of Sioux women and children—it is inconceivable that not a few Indian noncombatants were, if not deliberately killed, caught in the crossfire. In the chaos and confusion of combat, it was inevitable that a good number of unarmed Indians, attempting only to hide or flee, were killed.

In none of the official reports do the battalion or regimental commanders make any effort to distinguish the noncombatant dead from the combatant dead. This may have been partly due to a desire to enhance the quality of the victory or to sincere notions that because it was a hostile camp and most, if not all, of the slain women and children were killed accidentally, there was no need to differentiate between armed and unarmed Indians killed. The fight at Whitestone Hill had been against armed and very belligerent warriors, not against women and children, and if anyone needed proof of that, all that was required was a look at the number of white casualties.

It is true that several of the white casualties might have been due to friendly fire, as was indicated by Spencer's letter and implied by Furnas's decision to withdraw his regiment out of range of the guns of House's battalion. But the possibility that many, or even most, of the U.S. Army losses at Whitestone Hill were the result of crossfire between friendly units (as would happen at Wounded Knee) is unlikely in the extreme. Sioux fire, not friendly fire, did the real damage.

In the final analysis, as many as one quarter of the Sioux casualties at Whitestone Hill may have been noncombatants hit by some of the thousands of nondiscriminating bullets that whizzed across the ravines of the battlefield. Somewhere between Brown's version of innocent villagers slaughtered by vengeful men in U.S. Army uniforms and the American commanders' sanitized official reports, cleansed of anything that might detract from the glory of their victory, lies the truth.

The Conclusion of the Campaign

Whatever the true number and nature of the Sioux losses, Sully was convinced that they could have been far heavier, possibly heavy enough to settle forever the contest with the Sioux, if he had possessed provisions enough for just two or three more weeks of campaigning. His scouts reported that the hostiles were scattered; some were heading for the James River area, others, mostly Blackfeet Tetons, were recrossing the Missouri; still more were headed northward to seek refuge among the Canadian Métis (half-breeds). But after all the rapid marches without fodder, the column's cavalry mounts and team horses and mules were played out, and the rations were too diminished to conduct a probe in any direction. In fact, Sully had only enough rations to return to his rear base at Fort Pierre and that only if he did it in a series of rapid marches. Thus on the morning of September 6 Sully aimed his column homeward and set out for Fort Pierre.

After a march of 130 miles, Sully reached the mouth of the Little Cheyenne River on September 11 to find the steamboat he had ordered to be there by September 8. The general put his wounded aboard the boat, as well as his empty wagons, while loading the supply of grain brought by the steamboat aboard the rest of the wagons to feed his stock. Without that grain he would not have been able to bring his wagons back to his base, because from several miles north of the Little Cheyenne all the way to Fort Pierre most of the grass was burned away. As it was, a great many of the column's horses and mules died on the last leg of the return march, and many more were killed by the expedition's rear guard on the orders of Sully to prevent the exhausted animals who could not keep up from falling into the hands of the Sioux.[61]

The column made it back to Fort Pierre by the middle of September and prepared to go into winter quarters. To expand the army protection of the Dakota frontier, Sully commenced construction of a new post, sited on the east bank of the Missouri, north of Fort Pierre and a short distance above Farm Island. Completed by October 13, it was named Fort Sully "in compliment to our brave commander, Brig. General A. Sully, U.S. Volunteers."[62]

Part of the brigade was detached to garrison this new bastion for the winter; the rest wintered at Fort Randall. Sully intended to move on to reestablish his headquarters at Sioux City, Iowa. Prior to leaving his namesake fort, the brigadier acknowledged that his campaign and the Battle of Whitestone Hill had not entirely ended the Indian threat. In a public letter he warned settlers in isolated areas to be ever vigilant or to relocate to more defensible sites, for the hostiles he had hammered at Whitestone Hill were now "destitute and they must necessarily steal or starve this winter."[63]

This recognition that an Indian menace still existed on the Dakota frontier amounted to a confession that the campaign had not achieved the complete success Pope had hoped for when drawing up his strategic plans the previous fall. Still, after Pope had heard of Sully's victory at Whitestone Hill, he was in a vastly improved mood compared to that which had darkened the departmental headquarters for two months while he lambasted Sully for his slowness. Sully must have glowed with the warm rays of redemption upon receiving the following letter, dated October 5, 1863, from Pope:

> The results are entirely satisfactory, and I doubt not that the effect on the northwestern Indians will be, as you report, of the highest consequence. Whilst I regret that difficulties and obstacles of a serious character prevented your cooperation with General Sibley at the time hoped, I bear willing testimony to the distinguished conduct of yourself and your command, and to the important service you have rendered to the Government.... To yourself and your command, I tender my thanks and congratulations.[64]

Thus did three months of condemnation make way for a moment of commendation.

There was other praise to warm Sully's winter. Indian agent W. A. Burleigh summarized the scale of the mountain that Sully had to and did climb to achieve success in 1863.

> The arrival of General Sully in our Territory, although late in the season, and under the most discouraging circumstances, inspired confidence in the hearts of our citizens. With the Missouri now almost unnavigable from the low stage of the water, with a scarcity of land transportation, the broad prairies where he hoped to find abundant forage to supply his horses and cattle dried to a crisp and in many places burned over, he pushed forward with extraordinary energy almost 400 miles into the country inhabited by the hostile bands, met the savages upon their own chosen ground and defeated them in a well-contested battle.

Burleigh concluded by urging the retention and reinforcement of Sully for a summer campaign in 1864 to finish the job.[65]

John Hutchinson, Acting Governor of the Dakota Territory, seconded these sentiments in a missive to Indian Commissioner Dole: "I believe no officer in the army could have led the expedition ... with better success than General Sully. He had to encounter many obstacles, yet he has overcome them all, and fought a glorious battle.... I hope he may continue in command of this military district for another year."[66]

Other official voices, however, were not so laudatory. The Indian agent at the Upper Missouri Agency, Samuel N. Latta, had opposed the whole strategic concept of the campaign initially, and its results had not changed his mind. Latta had cautioned that the expulsion of the Santees from Minnesota would only expand the war as the fleeing Minnesota Sioux incited previously peaceful bands into belligerency against white America. He believed that drought and distance and the mobility of the Sioux would combine to prevent any decisive success. Latta pointed out that, although

Newton Edmunds, governor of Dakota Territory 1863–1866. (Courtesy of the State Historical Society of North Dakota.)

a few victories had been won, the Indians had not been subjugated by a campaign that cost hundreds of thousands of dollars, and that, in fact, there were now more hostile Indians on the Dakota prairie than there had been before the Sibley-Sully campaigns.

He did not believe that a reprise in 1864 would be any more productive, and suggested that negotiations leading to treaties would come considerably cheaper and bear brighter fruit. The money necessary to outfit another military expedition could, he postulated, be more profitably spent in building homes and farms for the Indians to civilize them as well as in establishing military posts to discipline them.[67]

Newton Edmunds, governor of the Dakota Territory in 1863, also gave the campaign of 1863 poor marks. In a report to Commissioner Dole he presented his case.

> Since the outbreak of the Indian War in Minnesota, two years ago last August, but little progress has, in my opinion, been made towards its extinguishment. I believe this fact to be owing to the extent of country over which these hostile Indians roam, rather than [to] a want of appreciation on the part of officers placed in charge of the various expeditions of the magnitude and extent of disaffection, and the seeming necessity of vigorous measures on their part to thoroughly subdue them, in order to accomplish the desired end. Of the two campaigns made against the Indians last summer, one under General Sibley of Minnesota, and one under General Sully, starting from Sioux City, Iowa, I am fully convinced that little, if anything, was accomplished towards the subjugation of the Indians. These two expeditions were immensely expensive to the government, and ought, in my opinion, to have brought about more decisive results. I am not prepared to say why they were failures; I leave this subject where it properly belongs, to the War Department, to make the inquiry; of the fact, however, I have not the least doubt.[68]

Edmunds did not believe that any conventional military campaign would bring about any positive long-term results, because of the nature of the Indians, the land they roamed, and the character of so many of the whites they came into contact with. The governor blamed the "War of the Outbreak" (as he and many other contemporaries called it) primarily on two factors: the influence of disloyal individuals, many of them outright rebel agents "who are so generously permitted by the government to have intercourse with them," and the widespread practice of allowing such persons to sell whiskey to Indians in exchange for furs.[69]

The Dakota governor, then, was convinced that full-fledged military expeditions like those of Sibley and Sully in 1863 and the succeeding campaign by Sully in 1864 could accomplish little due to two factors: the extent of the country traversed by the Sioux hostiles, and the magnitude of Indian disaffection, which seemed to spread and harden exponentially with each invasion. Edmunds did not blame the military commanders for their failure to subdue the Sioux, but he intimated that the uniformed authorities did not fully comprehend the task at hand, which could not be settled by purely military actions.

The war, he argued, retarded settlement in Dakota more than in any other of the Great Plains territories. Settlement was tenous and confined to the Missouri River at twenty to thirty mile intervals, which Edmunds considered little more than a "picket-guard" to stake a claim to the country. More than any other official, and probably more than was ever justified, Edmunds put the ultimate source of the instability on the Dakota frontier at the feet of Confederate sympathizers. To him the first step toward peace was to prevent "lawbreakers" from entering the territory. In his eyes, the northern prairie was overrun with men from the border states of Missouri, Kentucky, Tennessee, and Kansas, "who take delight in stirring up sedition among the Indians; many of them [are] secessionists or bushwhackers."[70]

Edmunds was not alone in his paranoia about nefarious agents of Dixie hard at work to carry the war to the northern forests and prairies. There was widespread suspicion among Northerners that the leaders of the Confederacy had plotted to incite the Santee uprising in Minnesota in order to draw troops away from the Southern battlefields. No evidence ever surfaced to support these suspicions, but those dark fears of a rebel conspiracy with the Dakota raiders remained with many until long after Appomattox.

Though Edmunds certainly overstated the case, there were indeed a great many men on the prairies from areas "stained" with secessionist fervor. Whether there were many (or any) who were active agents of the Confederacy or whether they were simply men with divided or doubtful loyalties, more obsessed with the various opportunities the frontier might offer than with subversion is debatable. But the governor considered the suppression of these elements, combined with a concerted effort to change the lifestyles of the Indians as the only sure path to peace.

The severe drought of the previous two years was another villain in Edmunds's view of the campaign. It had seriously set back the efforts of Indian agents to encourage their wards into the habits of an agricultural way of life. The governor had called for emergency rations to be issued to feed the treaty Indians so that hunger might not inspire belligerency among formerly peaceful peoples such as the Yanktons. Edmunds advised a policy of placing friendly tribes on protected reservations, where they could be supervised by "loyal and law-abiding citizens."[71]

Commissioner of Indian Affairs William Dole agreed with much of Edmunds's criticism of the military effort against the Sioux and endorsed much of his program of gathering the tribes on reservations defended by the military. He had not expected many positive results from the Sibley-Sully expeditions because of the distances and difficulties of the terrain, the lengthening logistical lines to the supply bases, and the evasive mobility of the Sioux, who were not slowed down by excess baggage and supply trains. Dole did not urge a direct effort to bring the hostiles to battle but rather advocated a containment policy brought about by the establishment of a chain of military posts along the Missouri. The Sioux, in his judgment, could never be brought to their knees by offensive military action but could be so harried and harassed by a tightening constriction resulting from an area studded with frontier forts that they would eventually despair and submit. Only by herding the Indians onto reservations could they be weaned away from their raiding, nomadic lifestyle and at the same time be protected from the many white scoundrels who preyed on them and prodded them into hostility.[72]

Just as with the conflicting casualty counts for the Battle of Whitestone Hill, an accurate judgment of the results of the 1863 campaigns lies somewhere between the ringing endorsements of convincing victory sounded by many military participants and the pessimistic dirges of near total failure by such civilian authorities as Edmunds and Dole.

Many things had been accomplished; many things remained yet incomplete and missions were unfulfilled. Certainly the primary mission of ending the Indian menace to the northern prairies was not accomplished, however good a start to that objective had been made. Sioux pride had been singed by the defeats but not subdued. If the Santee and Yanktonai were largely beaten down and the Yankton still passive, the most important and most numerous branch of the Sioux nation, the Lakota tribes, were now more defiant and stirred up than ever. The large Dakota and Yanktonai camps east of the Missouri were destroyed, however, and their inhabitants scattered to the winds. Many had scooted west across the river, many more had sought refuge in Canada, where a good portion of those refugees remained. Massive war parties no longer threatened the once so vulnerable white settlements in western Minnesota and eastern Dakota. Once panicked white settlers were returning in large numbers to their claims, and the very recent and very real possibility that the whole region might be abandoned by its white civilian population was eliminated for all time.

Sibley and Sully had labored hard at carrying out Pope's strategic design. Perhaps, as Edmunds, Dole, and many other civilians stated, no set of commanders, no matter how tactically blessed and doggedly determined, could have brought Pope's grand plan to total fruition. The obstacles thrown up by climate, distance, and the nomadic enemy were too great to fully realize a strategy of extermination too ambitious to fully implement. Pope had developed a plan that may have been sound on paper but betrayed a hubris that seemed his guiding star and an insufficiency of humility that more experienced frontier army commanders had earned upon embarking on operations against an evasive foe in a generally hostile environment.

The accomplishments of Sibley and Sully were considerable given the burdens they carried and the roadblocks of time and circumstance they encountered on the march. Delayed at the outset and slowed throughout by supply problems, the column commanders had to shape units of largely inexperienced officers and men into capable fighting forces, learning their trade while on the march. While frontier forces could usually at least depend on sufficient forage to feed their livestock while on the march, the Sibley-Sully expeditions generally lacked even that option due to the drought of several years. A campaign plan that depended for its success so much on coordination of units separated by hundreds of miles was fatally hampered from the outset by the almost complete absence of reliable lines of communication between those units. Given all the negatives that weighed down Pope's plan of envelopment, it is remarkable that Sibley and Sully accomplished as much as they did.

Sully, in particular, had to deal with logistical hazards of epic proportions. He was tied to the Missouri River for his supplies. Because of the lack of rainfall, that cord shriveled to an almost unnavigable rivulet. In early July Pope had urged Sully to cut free from the river and strike out overland in order to coordinate with Sibley. Why Sully did not cull his force down to a size that could be supported by the wagons he had and move across the prairie in search of Sibley is unclear. The general left no explanation in the public record to explain his reluctance to separate himself from the river before it was too late to effect a union with Sibley's force.

Perhaps Sully saw danger where Pope espied opportunity. Pope had received reports prior to the 1863 campaign of up to 6,000 hostile warriors awaiting his forces in Dakota. But he had either discounted these figures as exaggerations or had convinced himself, with his usual boundless bravado, that his forces could easily handle any number of belligerent braves—that, in fact, the greater the number to be conquered the greater the glory. Sully, though certainly not lacking in boldness, was through experience and character more appreciative of the fighting potential of his Sioux enemy. He may have decided to err on the side of caution rather than risk catastrophic defeat. The Dakota prairie, filled with unknown numbers of savages ready to fight and unable to support a force large enough to ensure victory, might be a disaster in waiting. The river was his security and his lifeline, and he chose to cling to it until the picture to the east was clear.

At least one military researcher supported this point of view. Major Frederick T. Wilson of the U.S. Army, in an article written in 1894, speculated that Pope in 1863 took as cavalier an attitude about the size and fighting prowess of the Sioux forces as Custer did thirteen years later. Wilson postulated that had Sibley and Sully strictly followed Pope's plans and orders there could have been, instead of an army hammer and anvil crushing the Sioux, an army disaster that would have made the Seventh Cavalry's defeat on the Little Bighorn look like a minor setback. Wilson believed that only a "combination of fortuitous circumstances saved both columns from a crushing defeat."[73]

The danger to the Sibley arm of the campaign expressed by Wilson seems largely unsubstantiated. Given the large size of Sibley's column and its success in late July against the Sioux forces, which seemed more intent on protecting their families than on engaging in heavy combat, Wilson's apprehensions for Sibley's brigade seem considerably exaggerated. However, his fears for Sully's smaller command seem more justified. Had Sully downsized his column (already less than half the size of Sibley's brigade) to a force that his limited wagon-borne supply system could sustain and struck in early July into northeastern Dakota, as Pope directed, he might well have been courting disaster. This could very well have been the motivation that kept Sully close to the river, trusting his instincts and experience more than Pope's orders.

The judgment on Sully's decision rests with history. He was certainly no McClellan on the Missouri, indecisively dallying and fearful of risking his force under any circumstances. Once his supply situation improved and reports of a substantial but not overwhelming force of Indians at Whitestone Hill gave him the opportunity to act, he did so, with rapidity and decisiveness, winning the most substantial victory of the Dakota War as a result. Had Sully thrown caution to the winds à la Pope and struck out across country into the unknown in early July, he might have realized Pope's dream of a Cannae on the prairie, or he might have anticipated by more than a decade Custer's cataclysm under the Montana sky.

10. The Battle
of Killdeer Mountain

Preparations

The degree to which the hostile Sioux had been punished and the 1863 campaign had been successful was debatable, but there was little doubt about the need for further punishment and for another military campaign. Though there were a few dissenting opinions, the need for further action was propounded in all quarters and by many voices, high and low, in and out of uniform. Retribution, fear, and greed worked hand in hand in motivating those voices.

Many of the prime perpetrators of the Minnesota Massacre—the Mdewakantons and other Lower Santees, numbering about 800–1,000—were still at large, mostly concentrated in Canadian territory along the Red River and Assiniboine River, fed by British authorities and supplied with ammunition by Canadian traders who, it was generally believed, encouraged continued hostilities against white America. The Upper Santees were wintering between the Red River and the Missouri River near the Canadian border. Although they had held themselves generally aloof from the 1862 uprising, many vengeful whites of Minnesota considered them guilty by association.

Self-interest drove the impetus for an 1864 campaign as much as vengeance. The Civil War had not much interrupted migration of white settlers into the prairie. The eastern half of Dakota, rich in potentially fertile farmland, beckoned speculators who could enrich themselves on land sales and railroad grants if the Indians were driven safely west of the Missouri. They could also profit in the process of Indian expulsion by securing contracts to supply the troops engaged in that expulsion. Thus, many were doubly motivated to push for a continued military effort against the Sioux. The speculators had a champion in John Hutchinson, the acting territorial governor, who proclaimed, "The hostile tribes must be conquered, and must be compelled to make new treaties [i.e., cede land]."[1]

The Homestead Act, passed in May 1862 to take effect on January 1, 1863, provided another justification for pushing the Indians westward. Particularly in Nebraska, the act produced a flood of new land claims, primarily along the Platte River, and brought in their wake an attendant growth of army posts to protect the new settlements. Those posts, in turn, provided employment for freighters and contractors, as well as markets for hay, beef, and grain. Prosperity beckoned seductively for the territory, but, just as in Dakota, the Indian threat countered with an ever present frown.

It was gold, however, that begat the campaign of 1864 more than anything else. If a hunger for revenge and a cry for security of the eastern Dakota-Minnesota frontier against the eastern Sioux had been the primary catalysts of the 1863 campaign, the protection of the gold strikes in Idaho and Montana and the attendant river and overland business in transportation and supply against the western Sioux was the main impetus of the Sully expedition of 1864. There was now a thriving business on the Missouri, as steamboats paddled up the river to the head of navigation at Fort Benton, Montana, with miners and mining machinery and chugged back down the river with the gold dust that would help the Union finance the Civil War. An overland route was also established by Minnesota political and business leaders, hopeful that a railroad would be established between St. Paul and the gold fields to parallel the overland road and encourage further settlement and further profits. But Indian raids, or the threat of such raids, were at the least a nuisance and, to some eyes, a major deterrent to both routes to the bustling mining towns.

Though Pope and Sibley were in general agreement with the chorus of prospectors, farmers, and speculators calling for another campaign, one important military voice initially spoke against renewed action. Army Chief of Staff Halleck, weighed down by the burden of churning out enough men and supplies to crush the Confederacy, saw another Dakota campaign as an unnecessary diversion of resources to a front where self-interest had replaced security as a reason for further military action. Halleck urged Pope to talk with the Sioux instead of tangling with them, to settle economically by treaty what all other interests seemed to think required the expensive deployment of military force. He understood the motives behind the cynical alarms bleated out by those who saw dollar signs roll by with every army wagon, "If we want war in the spring, a few traders can get one up on the shortest notice."[2]

But even Halleck finally succumbed to the clamoring from the west demanding an Indian campaign after a series of Sioux raids in March and April resulted in horses stolen, a Sixth Iowa Cavalry trooper slain, and three civilians—two trappers and a hunter—killed.[3] Sully also reported a rumor during the winter of 1863/64 that some Tetons had acquired an artillery piece (presumably from Canada) with which they intended to fire on boats on the Missouri.[4] In February, Halleck had already directed Pope to plan a campaign to force the Sioux into submission in 1864. He now authorized the plan's execution.

Sibley had already been composing a scheme for offensive operations in 1864. He planned to reinforce forts Ripley, Abercrombie, and Ridgely and send out from Fort Ridgely an armed expedition that would search the region of the upper Sheyenne River, Devil's Lake, and the Missouri Coteau to "beat up the camps of the prairie Indians."[5]

Pope adopted Sibley's plan and enlarged upon it. The departmental commander proposed a plan that would not only punish the Indians with offensive strikes, but also provide permanent protection for the settlers' river and northern overland routes by erecting a fire line of military posts in the burning heart of Sioux country.

Once again, separate brigades would march into Dakota Territory from Fort Ridgely and Sioux City. The Minnesota brigade would advance from the Minnesota River to the Missouri River against the eastern Sioux. The brigade would also build two forts: one at Devil's Lake, the second on the James River at a point west of the head of the Coteau des Prairies, in order to secure permanently the eastern half of Dakota Territory. The Missouri River brigade would ascend the Missouri against the western Sioux and construct posts near the confluence of the Heart and the Missouri, close to the point the Sibley expedition had reached the year before, and on the Yellowstone. The new forts, plus Fort Sully, built the year before, were specifically planned to guard the settler routes from the upper Mississippi to the Idaho and Montana gold fields. Trails were also to be opened and secured between the new posts.

Pope mapped out a campaign of no more than three months' duration. The high latitude of the region, the immense areas of uninhabited country, and the vast distances from the settled frontier to the theater of campaign all imposed weather and supply constraints that made ninety days the practical limit for troops to be in the field. Pope estimated that up to 6,000 hostile Dakotas and Lakotas would confront his expedition and that they would be extensively armed by the Canadian half-breeds and traders of the Red River region. Given overall field command of the two wings of the "Northwestern Indian Expedition" was Brig. General Sully.[6]

The Minnesota brigade, designated the Second Brigade, was to be commanded this time by Colonel Minor Thomas. General Sibley had apparently had enough of field operations, for he had asked for and obtained permission from Pope to remain in Minnesota.

The primary unit composing the core of the brigade was Lt. Colonel Henry C. Rogers' Eighth Minnesota Infantry Regiment of 1,000 men mounted on Canadian ponies. The Eighth had performed patrol duty in Minnesota in 1863 and had lost six killed in these defensive operations, more than any of the regiments accompanying Sibley into Dakota.[7] Captain McCoy's company of the Eighth Minnesota included forty-nine Confederate deserters (sixteen of whom were later assigned to garrison duty). They had been enrolled in the regiment under the War Department's September 1863 ruling, which stated, "rebel deserters who have been drafted into the U.S. service will be sent to Camp Chase ... and distributed among the regiments in the Department of the Northwest."[8] These former rebels were the first of the "galvanized Yankees" to see active service with Union units. No more would arrive during the ensuing campaign.

The rest of the Second Brigade was made up of 600 men in six companies of Colonel Robert N. McLaren's Second Minnesota Cavalry Regiment; 100 cannoneers in two sections of the Third Minnesota Battery (one section of six-pounder smoothbore guns and one section of twelve-pounder mountain howitzers), commanded by Captain John Jones, the artillery hero of the Battle of Fort Ridgely; 45 scouts; 96 mule teams and their teamsters; and 12 ambulances. Though Colonel Thomas estimated the total force at 2,100 men (as did Sergeant Kingsbury in his memoir of the 1864 expedition), Sibley estimated only 1,550. If the units were at full authorized strength, they would have totaled 1,745. Sibley was left with 700 men to protect Minnesota during the summer.[9]

The First Brigade was to push off from Sioux City. Its biggest unit was Lt. Colonel Samuel M. Pollock's Sixth Iowa Cavalry (of Whitestone Hill experience), with its eleven companies mustering some 880 soldiers. Also attached to the First Brigade was Brackett's Minnesota Battalion of Cavalry, 360 strong in four companies and commanded by Major Alfred B. Brackett. The battalion had been relieved recently from service in the South, where it had fought as part of an Iowa regiment.

The other units comprising the brigade were: three companies, about 240 men, of the Seventh Iowa Cavalry Regiment, commanded by Lt. Colonel John Pattee; two companies of the Dakota Cavalry Regiment, mustering 160 men under the command of Captain Nelson Minor; an 80-man company of "Nebraska Scouts," under the leadership of Captain Christian Stufft; and a "Prairie Battery" of four mountain howitzers, led by Captain Nathaniel Pope, a nephew of General Pope. If all units were at full strength (a doubtful proposition), the personnel of the First Brigade would have totaled 1,780.[10]

The Raiding Season, 1864

As the campaign season opened in June 1864, the Lakotas, Dakotas, and Yanktonais were scattered in camps on the upper Grand and Heart rivers, as well as on the lower Yellowstone, seemingly eager to clash with the soldiers. During the winter the Sioux had relayed bombastic threats through traders and Indians friendly to whites and had carried out sporadic raids on the horse herds at Forts Pierre, Berthold, and Union. But for all their bluster, the Sioux had made few real offensive moves toward breaching the line of white settlement.

In the course of the summer of 1864 a handful of Sioux raiders were able to breach the defenses established by Sibley's regulars and militia companies in Minnesota, but the raids were considerably reduced in scale from those of the previous year and, of course, did not compare with those of the summer of 1862. On August 12, 1864, six to eight Sioux raiders killed one white man, wounded another, and stole their horses ten miles south of Garden City and then managed to escape the pursuing troops. In other raids that summer, two teamsters were killed between Fort Abercrombie and Georgetown, and several Winnebagos, friendly to the whites, were slain south of Sioux City.[11]

The Commencement of the Campaign

Unlike the campaign of 1863, Sully's expedition in 1864 was made up of seasoned campaigners. Both brigades were more mobile than those of the year before, made up almost exclusively of either cavalry or mounted infantry. However, the mounts provided by the government for this second Dakota campaign were not the usual big and strong army horses, but smaller Canadian ponies, thought to be faster and more adaptable to the prairie and its sparse forage. The ponies were unused to the heavy loads of fully equipped soldiers, with their weapons, blankets, haversacks, and other gear, and the initial attempts to break them in resulted in chaos on the drill field. Ponies bolted, troopers were tossed, and equipment was strewn across the prairie. After the loads had been redistributed and lightened, the Canadian mounts eventually settled down, but few of the veteran horse soldiers ever reconciled themselves to the loss of their sturdy old cavalry horses.

As in 1863, Sully relied upon steamboat traffic to provision his force and, again, the Missouri River refused to cooperate, rising too slowly to launch the operation on schedule. The steamers were to ship thousands of tons of supplies for the expedition, including 2,500 uniforms, an equal number of saddles for the ponies recently purchased from Canada for the operation,

10,000 horseshoes and 2,000 muleshoes, four months' rations for 3,500 men, a boatload of corn for the livestock, and seventeen barrels of whiskey.[12]

Thomas's Second Brigade marched out from Fort Ridgely on June 5, proceeding to the tune of "The Girl I Left Behind Me," played by a band mounted on white horses. But the First Brigade did not get underway from Sioux City until June 14. The march for both brigades was leisurely at first. The men rose before dawn to strike camp and travel in formation between ten and twenty-five miles before halting in the early afternoon to pitch camp and graze the pony and cattle herds. The animals were brought into a corral just before sunset, and the soldiers then cooked their evening meal, usually with buffalo chips, which burned quick and hot. Often they also prepared for the next morning's breakfast by placing beans in a fire pit and covering them with hot coals to bake overnight in this "bean hole." On many evenings the band played and Sundays were given over to rest. The weather was generally cooperative, although on June 28 a tornado brushed by Thomas's camp, scattering tents and gear about like feathers.[13]

In this largely uneventful manner the expedition continued on course until June 28, when the First Brigade column neared the mouth of the Little Cheyenne River. The expedition's topographical engineer, Captain John Fielner, was riding some distance ahead of the column, as he often did, to collect geological specimens. Though Sully had offered him a larger escort in his scientific meanderings, Fielner had shrugged off the offer with the joking comment that he doubted that there were any Indians in the whole country. Hence on this day he took only two soldiers with him and found out how tragically wrong he was.

In what is now Potter County, South Dakota, the three men picketed their ponies and strolled toward the river with their canteens. Three warriors concealed in a clump of bushes fired on the trio, and Fielner was mortally wounded by a bullet through the lungs. The hostiles made a lunge for the mounts, but the panicked ponies pulled free from their picket-pins and dashed away. When the two surviving soldiers, one of them wounded, returned to camp to report the slaying, Sully ordered Captain Nelson Minor to mount a patrol of a dozen of his Dakota Cavalrymen (who called themselves the "Coyotes") and pursue the slayers.

After an eight-mile chase, the Coyotes cornered the three killers in a buffalo wallow and, with shouts of "Death to the Murderers," riddled them with some 200 bullets. The patrol returned to camp, bearing the trophies of the Indians' guns and bows and arrows, but Sully wanted more. Returning to the wallow, Sergeant Benjamin Estes decapitated the Sioux with a butcher knife and bundled the heads in a gunny sack. The next morning, a sergeant later recalled, "General Sully directed me to hang the heads on poles on the highest hill as a warning to all Indians who might travel that way."[14]

The news of the triple beheading on the Little Cheyenne stunned and outraged the Sioux. To them the incident was symbolic of the white army's determination to exterminate the Sioux nation. The less stout-hearted counseled flight to remote areas, but many more stalwart bands drifted together into a vast encampment between the Heart and Cannonball rivers. Conspicuously absent from this gathering of the steadfast was Inkpaduta. The old incorrigible was engaged in his favorite pastime, horse thievery, on the Minnesota River. A speedy courier named The Hawk was dispatched to bring Inkpaduta with his fighting skills and fighting spirit to reinforce the assemblage of Sioux soldiers awaiting the invaders.[15]

This time the marches of the two separate brigades were coordinated and well-timed. On June 29 Sully's scouts found Thomas's brigade after it had conducted a largely uneventful march across the James River and eastern Dakota. The Second Brigade was led south to Sully's camp west of Swan Lake (near present-day Akaska, South Dakota). The united brigades rested for a few days while their wagons were sent to the Missouri to resupply from eight steamboats that had arrived. On July 3 the First Brigade broke camp and proceeded north toward the Sioux concentration massing between the Heart and Cannonball rivers. The Second Brigade trailed a day's march behind.

On July 7 Sully laid the groundwork for the first fort to be established by the expedition on the sandstone bluffs on the west bank of the Missouri eight miles above the mouth of the Cannonball River (not the Heart River, as originally planned in Pope's blueprints for the campaign). The new post, 450 miles from Sioux City, was christened Fort Rice. It was to be built and garrisoned by four companies of the Thirtieth Wisconsin Infantry Regiment, commanded by Captain Daniel J. Dill, who had brought his force upriver by steamboat. Sully also dropped off two companies of cavalry to aid in the construction and manning of the post. Fort Rice was to serve as the most forward supply point for the 1864 expedition.[16]

It was now evident to Sully that the hostiles he had hoped to encounter on the east side of the Missouri had crossed the river and, according to his scouts' reports, moved west into an area of rolling hills tucked into the bend of the Little Missouri River 200 miles due west from Fort Rice. This Sioux force was said to be composed of members of several Teton tribes—Hunkpapa, Blackfeet, Miniconjou, and Sans Arc—as well as Yanktonais and some Santees.

One of the general's best informants was the Jesuit missionary, Father Pierre Jean DeSmet. The missionary hooked up with Sully on July 9 as he made his way downriver from Fort Berthold, where he had carried out an unsuccessful peace-making venture sponsored by the Indian Bureau. DeSmet

Fort Rice, Dakota Territory. Established by General Sully in 1864. (From a painting by Seth Eastman, Library of Congress.)

confirmed the concentration of the Sioux in the Little Missouri Badlands, and both he and friendly Yanktonais reported sighting more Teton bands drifting north from the Black Hills toward the area. According to all reports, the Indians were considerably incensed at the approach of the army expedition and enraged at the news of the beheading of the three braves who had killed Captain Fielner. Though many of the Sioux were frightened at the size of the American force headed their way, firebrands like the always belligerent Inkpaduta had stiffened the general resolve and got the Sioux to agree to stand and fight.[17]

Beginning on July 9, 1864, Sully undertook the three-day job of transferring his expedition to the west bank of the Missouri. Carrying two wagons per trip, the steamers ferried 500 army wagons across the river. That mission completed, some of the boats were sent back downstream 200 miles to Farm Island to pick up 1,000 tons of freight, and three were directed upstream to ascend the Yellowstone and meet the expedition at the mouth of the Powder River.[18]

Sully spent a week at the Fort Rice site while hundreds of his men worked alongside the soldiers of the Thirtieth Wisconsin, felling trees and baking bricks for the new fort. By July 18 the general was ready to strike out west toward Rainy Buttes, where he expected to encounter the hostiles. He was encumbered, however, not only by his own train and baggage, but also by an emigrant train of 123 wagons filled with over 200 gold miners and their women and children, whom he had been assigned to protect. The train had accompanied the Minnesota Brigade across eastern Dakota. It was part of an ongoing escort service that Congress had authorized in 1861, encouraging western migration by promising the wagon trains military protection. The same Congressional authorization had provided for volunteer captains, mustered into the Quartermaster Department, to provide paramilitary leadership for the trains. The leader of this train was Thomas A. Holmes, an itinerant frontiersmen and township developer who pestered Sully for protection. Sully was much put out by this assignment, commenting, "I can't send them back, I can't leave them here, for I can't feed them.... Therefore, I am forced to take them with me."[19]

Close behind this train moved a second gold prospecting train that Sully was expected to escort and guard. Sully and his soldiers deeply resented the prospectors and this extra diversion from their primary purpose of fighting Indians. The general looked upon the emigrants as a collection of draft evaders or even rebel sympathizers. Nonetheless, he detailed 400 men from his brigade to escort the wagons as far as the Yellowstone, after which they would be on their own. He announced to the prospectors, "I am damn sorry you are here, but so long as you are, I will do my best to protect you." He also told the emigrants he expected "to jump an Indian camp and give them hell," and advised them to "Keep together for in union there is strength."[20]

The March to Killdeer Mountain

Sully began a five-day march on July 19 with his 3,000 soldiers and emigrants west up the valley of the Cannonball River, following its north branch across the high plains. The noncombatant number in the expedition was increased by one on that first day's march when an emigrant mother gave birth to a daughter, christened "Dakota."

The general's scouts quickly picked up fresh signs of the Sioux trail veering northwest. Certain these were the same Indians he had beaten at Whitestone Hill in 1863 and from whom he had recovered the scalps of fifty white women, Sully turned that direction on July 24 for a day's march that carried him to the Heart River, near present-day Dickinson, North Dakota. The temperature reached 110 degrees that day; water had been scarce all along, and animals and men were exhausted. Twenty-two head of stock died during that sweltering day's march.

The general established a guarded corral there on the Heart River, into which he placed the emigrant train and all of his tents and baggage except for enough food and ammunition for a quick strike. He detached a strong guard of Dakota Cavalry under the command of Captain Tripp to secure the camp. Believing that the Sioux were no more than two days ahead of him, Sully rested his brigade for a day before undertaking the forced march against the Indians. His target was the Knife River, to the northwest, where his scouts reported an enemy village of at least 1,400 lodges.[21]

Sully had intended to march toward the Sioux concentration with his pack mule train loaded with rations and supplies for seven days, as had been recommended to him as a fast-strike option by General Pope. However, upon opening the equipment boxes for the train early on the morning of July 26, the troops found no saddle blankets for the mules. The general solved this snafu by replacing the missing blankets with gunny sacks. But he could not solve the next supply problem, inflicted upon him by the incompetence or corruption of the quartermaster. The cinctures (six- or eight-inch-wide bands that went over the packs and under the mules' bellies) were made not of the correct webbing of several thicknesses of cushioning cloth sewn together, but of three-inch-wide hard leather. Sully considered the cinctures "sheet iron" and so too did the mules. They barely got out of camp before the mules rebelled, rearing and kicking to break the saddles and catapult the packs. The general consequently discarded his pack mule supply system and borrowed from the emigrants forty-five light wagons, each to be pulled by four mules and each loaded with 1,000 pounds of provisions and ammunition. Because of the delay, the column did not depart the Heart River corral until three o'clock in the afternoon.[22]

The 2,200 men that General Sully led eighty miles across the prairie consisted of units from both brigades. From the First Brigade marched eleven companies of Lt. Colonel Pollock's Sixth Iowa Cavalry, three companies of Lt. Colonel Pattee's Seventh Iowa Cavalry, two companies of Captain Minor's Dakota Cavalry, four companies of Brackett's Minnesota Battalion, Captain Pope's two-section prairie battery of four mountain howitzers, and one company of seventy scouts. From Colonel Thomas's Second Brigade marched ten companies of Lt. Colonel Roger's Eighth Minnesota Infantry, six companies of Colonel McLaren's Second Minnesota Cavalry, and two sections of Captain Jones's Third Minnesota Battery with a total of four howitzers. Their prospective opponents, gathered in a camp of up to 1,600 lodges, numbered, according to white estimates, as many as 5,000–6,000 Hunkpapas, Blackfeet, Miniconjous, Sans Arcs, Yanktonais, and Santees, but Sioux participants later insisted that no more than 1,600 warriors had been present at the battle.[23]

The Sioux were waiting for Sully. At the brigade's approach into the Little Missouri region, the village chiefs, at the advice of Inkpaduta, had moved their camp a day's march north to near the Badlands of the Little Missouri River. This area abounded in rugged buttes and ridges, separated by steep-sided ravines and gorges covered with brush and timber. The staircase ridges rose to a dominating mountain mass that served as a natural fortress. A clear flowing spring and the Gros Ventres branch of the Little Missouri made the area well-watered. It was a favorite hunting ground of the Lakotas, who called it Tahchakuty, "the place where they killed the deer." The white men would call it simply Killdeer Mountain.

In this place, with rolling prairie framing it to the front and to the east, the Sioux laid out a four-mile-long camp. According to most later reports of the battle, that camp had been there for some time as the Indians awaited the approaching showdown with considerable confidence. But White Bull, from whose testimony much of the Indian side of the battle is gathered and who was only fourteen years old at the time of Killdeer Mountain, claimed that the Sioux had arrived on site only a day or two before the battle.[24]

In any case, the Sioux were certainly ready and waiting; there was no surprise as at Whitestone Hill. They had at least twenty-four hours notice of Sully's approach, for on July 26 a scouting party of thirty warriors skirmished with Sully's Winnebago and Nebraska scouts sixteen miles from the camp.

The scouts had run into the hostile band near Young Man's Butte, just east of present-day Richardton, North Dakota. In the ensuing exchange of fire, one of the scouts was wounded in the knee and a scout's horse was felled by an arrow. The scouts killed three Indian ponies and captured an Enfield rifle, four buffalo robes, moccasins, and leggings. The captain of the scouting party, having fortified himself with liquid courage, panicked and fled south to report to Sully the annihilation of his entire force. The general disregarded the report, had the drunken captain placed under arrest, and sent Brackett hurrying north to locate the scouts. Having covered ten miles since leaving the Heart River corral, Sully ordered his column into fighting formation, with the wagon train proceeding single file with mounted soldiers riding on both sides.[25]

The brigade continued on for several miles before halting for the night. No fires were permitted; the men chewed on hardtack and lay down fully clothed and armed near their horses picketed on twenty-foot ropes. Nervous sentries and false alarms made for a nearly sleepless night for the expedition.

What little sleep the men managed to get ended shortly after midnight as the brigade prepared for a long march northwest. The first daylight saw the strike force on the road. Thirty-five miles later Sully's men went into bivouac next to a spring near the Knife River. Sleep was again sporadic, for the general had his soldiers saddle up shortly after midnight and go to fifty percent alert status to guard against a possible Indian attack at dawn.[26]

Killdeer Mountain

July 28, 1864, dawned clear and hot, like most days in that summer. The rolling plains south of Killdeer Mountain, over which Sully's brigade approached, had been made almost barren by an implacable sun. The grass was thin, dry, and dusty and interrupted by swatches of prickly pear. The few water holes had been reduced to muddy alkali sinks.

The army troops had been on the Indian trail since before dawn. Six hours of marching brought them a break for coffee and breakfast, but still no sight of the Sioux. Private J. E. Robinson later wrote, "This was the third day out from Heart River and we had all began [sic] to be discouraged; we did not believe there were any Indians in that section of the country."[27]

The column resumed its march and had been on the trail for an hour when interpreter Frank La Framboise and several scouts came racing up to the brigade vanguard to announce the sighting of a huge Sioux camp in the hills ten miles ahead.

The Sioux spotted Sully's scouts at about the same time and confidently prepared for battle. There was no rush to prepare for flight, as at Whitestone Hill, no lodges struck or travois assembled. Quite the contrary, according to most reports the Sioux women and children began to gather on a hillside to witness the impending spectacle. Fanny Kelly, a captive in the camp was the only witness to report that the Sioux noncombatants began moving back into the woods for protection when the soldiers were sighted.

Sully's men also readied themselves for combat. The army scouts scurried to a headquarters wagon to change from native apparel into soldier's uniforms so they would not be mistaken for hostiles in the swirl of battle. Orderlies rushed about with orders and soldiers stocked up on ammunition, and more than a few also on slugs of whiskey. Some of the less hopeful left watches and other valuables with noncombatants and hastily scribbled farewell notes to their families. George Northrup, frontier scout and correspondent for the *St. Paul Press*, turned over his dispatches to a fellow correspondent and, with gallows humor, directed him to, "send these home, and write my obituary when I am dead."[28]

From his own observation and scouting reports, Sully realized that the hilly terrain and deep intersecting timbered ravines ahead made a mounted charge difficult, if not impossible. He thus ordered his cavalry to dismount and formed his brigade into a huge square, a mile and a quarter in length on each side and the soldiers positioned three or four paces apart.

To the front Sully deployed six companies of the Sixth Iowa and three companies of the Seventh Iowa on the right, Pope's battery and two dismounted cavalry companies in the center, and six companies of the Eighth Minnesota on the left. Making up the wings or the flanks of the hollow square were the Second Minnesota Cavalry drawn up by squadrons on the left and Brackett's Minnesota Battalion on the right in similar order. In the middle of the square the general placed Jones's battery and four cavalry companies in reserve, as well as his wagons and the cavalry mounts with their holders (every fourth man holding four ponies). Closing the square was a rear guard of three companies. Thus arrayed, the brigade advanced slowly, with Pattee's Seventh Iowa deployed in an advance line of skirmishers.[29]

The Sioux, armed mostly with bows and only a few rifles, likewise advanced, but in no particular order. Both sides covered about five miles (the soldiers having already marched about twenty miles prior to the scouts' sighting of the Sioux). The soldiers trudging over the dusty ground saw increasing numbers of Indians riding around their flanks and watching them from a distance. Clusters of warriors sat on ponies on every hill and ridge facing the brigade and curled around its flanks. By noon the main Sioux body drew up in a long line facing Sully's square. Generally, the Lakotas, including Sitting Bull and Gall, formed up on the right; the Yanktonais and the Dakotas, led by Inkpaduta, drew up on the left.

There passed an extended period of sizing one another up, during which Sioux braves and Winnebago scouts hurled taunts at each other. Pope later reported to Halleck that Sully talked with the hostile chiefs for an hour and that the Indians were "very defiant and impudent," but Sully made no mention of this in his official report, and the only talk between the two sides may have been the challenges tossed back and forth.[30]

Like two boxers dancing around the ring, each looking for an opening to throw the first punch, the two armies warily moved toward one another. The battle started a little after the noon hour, with an individual challenge as was appropriate for Indian warfare. A young Hunkpapa named Lone Dog rode to a hill within rifle range to flourish his elaborate war club and ridicule the soldiers. The troopers held their fire for some time as Lone Dog galloped across their front. According to White Bull, it was because, "Lone Dog was with a ghost and it was hard to shoot at him—he had a charm."[31]

Apparently, Lone Dog's taunts quickly exhausted the general's patience, for an aide soon rode up to Lt. Colonel Pattee, who commanded the line of skirmishers out front, and announced, "The general sends his compliments and wishes you to kill that Indian for God's sake."[32]

Three sharpshooters took aim and each fired once. Although Sully claimed Lone Dog toppled from his horse, Pattee agreed with the Indians who insisted that the young buck's magic charm held up and the warrior rode unscathed back down the hill.[33]

The battle was thus begun in a desultory fashion, gradually moving five miles north toward the village centered around the spring, which the Indians

Prairie battery at the Battle of Killdeer Mountain. (Courtesy of the State Historical Society of North Dakota.)

called Falling Springs. The Sioux fought with typical Plains Indian tactics, darting on horseback singly or in clusters, probing for weak spots. The Indians rode whooping at Sully's square to fire quick bursts of arrows or fur-trade musket balls, then dashed back out of range. Once in a while larger groups gathered to rapidly thrust at the brigade in an attempt to pierce Sully's lines. The soldiers advanced steadily in a skirmish line at close intervals, but the Sioux resistance became more vigorous as the terrain grew more rugged. "The ground over which we advanced," reported one battalion commander, "was very uneven, and the Indians would gather behind knolls and in ravines on our front and fire upon us and scatter away on their swift-footed ponies."[34]

Bands of warriors probed the flanks, first on the left, then on the right. Artillery fire harried the Indians, while the Second Cavalry on the left and Brackett's Battalion on the right easily parried the Sioux thrusts. The battle line extended in a circle three miles in length as a batch of braves assembled for an attack on Brackett's Battalion, which had, in its clearing of the right flank, become somewhat isolated from the rest of Sully's square. A few well-placed canister rounds from Jones's battery, however, scattered this group. Several Indians were catapulted from their saddles by shot and shell, but were invariably scooped up by other warriors racing to their rescue at full gallop.

As the running battle sputtered across the dusty prairie, the only serious threat of the day to the integrity of Sully's formation came from the rear. A party of 100 or more Sioux (some reports claimed as many as 500), who had ridden off from the camp earlier in the day in search of Sully's

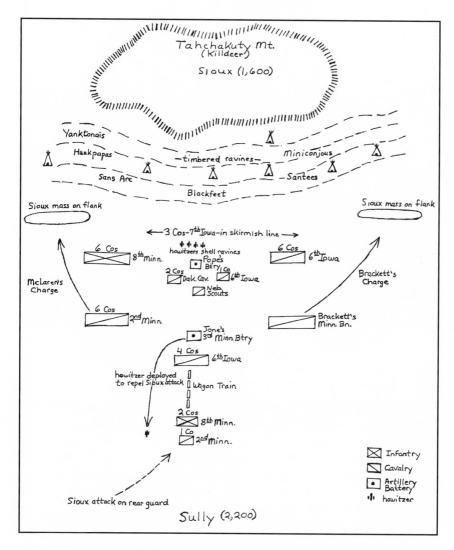

Killdeer Mountain, July 28, 1864.

brigade, blundered into their quarry's rear as they returned from their so far unsuccessful sweep. Alerted to this sudden threat to his wagon train and cavalry horses, Sully ordered one howitzer from Jones's battery to reinforce the rear guard. The cannoneers galloped to the rear with their gun. A single round exploded among the attackers, killing six warriors and five horses. The rest of the warriors in this group quickly scattered.[35]

It was by now obvious to the Indians that despite their numbers and boldness, they could not prevail with their largely primitive arms against

**"The Eighth Minnesota Infantry (Mounted) in the Battle of Ta-Ha-Kouty."
Carl L. Boeckmann, oil on canvas, ca. 1910. Original in the collections of the
Minnesota Historical Society. (Courtesy of the Minnesota Historical Society.)**

the disciplined volley fire and the artillery of the white soldiers. With their
speed, agility, and reluctance to mass in large groups for very long, the Sioux
had suffered relatively few casualties so far, but their pinprick attacks could
not penetrate the soldiers' lines. In fact, because of the Indians' unwilling-
ness to close with the enemy in a real slugging match, the soldiers had so
far not suffered any casualties. The Sioux's top priority now was to evacuate their camp and save their families.

By late afternoon the Indians had fallen back to the edges of their
camp, posting themselves in the woody ravines that cut across the first slopes
of the Killdeer Mountain mass. Some of the squaws and old men had been
observing the battle from a high hill called Crosby Butte until a round from
one of Pope's howitzers exploded among them. However, most of the village's noncombatants were busy striking the tepees and preparing for flight
while the warriors broke into small groups and opened fire from the concealment of rocks and trees.[36]

It was at this point that the heaviest action of the day occurred. Prob-
ably to cover the evacuation of the village, Inkpaduta concentrated his
Dakotas and Yanktonais for a lunge at Sully's right. The general ordered
Major Brackett to mount his battalion, draw sabers, and charge Inkpaduta's

force. The Minnesota troopers galloped down one slope, across a rocky ravine, and then up the opposite slope into the Indian mass. Fighting at close quarters ensued, saber against tomahawk, before the Indians broke away. They fell back into the brush to shoot cascades of arrows at the cavalrymen, then staged a fighting withdrawal one and a half miles to the timbered ravines at the foot of Killdeer Mountain. As fighting intensified at the base of the steep bluff, Brackett's men dismounted to direct heavy carbine fire against the Indians. When the Sioux were apparently trying to organize a counterattack, Jones's howitzers were unlimbered to place well-aimed rounds into the timber. After this, the Sioux facing Brackett's Battalion finally broke away and scattered.[37]

Brackett's men accounted for at least twenty-seven Sioux dead in the course of the battle. Thirteen of those dead, including ten slain by sabers, fell during the battalion's mounted charge. The Minnesota cavalrymen lost eight men wounded in their charge and one man killed. The fatality was George Northrup. Often called the "Kit Carson of the Northwest," Northrup, in addition to his exploits on the Indian frontier, had enlisted in the war against the Confederacy and had carried out a daring scouting expedition 100 miles behind the lines in North Carolina. When Northrup was reassigned from the South to Sully's expedition, he wrote prophetically to his sister, "If I scout as much here as I did south, it may become a pleasant duty to relate or rather narrate, some very difficult scouts with 'hair-breadth escapes,' or the unpleasant duty of comrades to chronicle the loss of my hair and inform you of the demise of your friend.[38]

When Brackett had launched his mounted charge, the dashing twenty-seven-year-old took the lead of his unit, Company C, to shout challenges at the Sioux, who years before had captured and robbed him when he guided some Englishmen on a hunting trip near Devil's Lake in 1861. At Killdeer Mountain Northrup shot down three warriors before he was struck by a bullet and three arrows. The Sioux rushed for his body with scalping knives, but a corporal, under orders from Brackett to recover the corpse "if it costs the life of every man in your squad," reached Northrup's lifeless form first and dragged it away. Brackett's Battalion suffered one other combat death that day when Horatio Austin of Company D fell with a bullet between the eyes as the Minnesota men drove the Sioux up the precipitous slopes of the butte. The two dead of Brackett's Battalion were buried that night without the drum or bugle of "Taps" to honor them, and horses were picketed over their unmarked graves to obliterate any signs that might guide mutilation-minded Indians to the site.[39]

Meanwhile, on the western flank of the battlefield, where the soldiers faced mostly Lakota warriors, Sully swung his left around the Sioux right wing in an arc aimed directly at the village. Pope's guns and two companies of Dakota Cavalry pushed forward, with the artillery clearing the hilltops and firing explosive rounds that burst eighty feet above the ravines packed with Indians seeking cover. It was in those ravines and under that artillery fire that the majority of the Indian casualties at Killdeer Mountain occurred. Some of the Lakota Sioux, under indirect howitzer fire for the first time, fired into the air in a desperate attempt to shoot down the invisible terror that was killing their families.

With Jones's battery and Brackett's Battalion advancing on the right, the whole U.S. line surged forward at the same time. Before the soldiers could plunge deeper into the timber hugging the base of the butte, Sully, rather than risk his men in the fading light and thick foliage, halted his advance and determined to let his howitzers finish the job.[40]

Most of the Sioux fled over the mountaintop, with howitzer rounds bursting in their midst, but a few remained in the village. One of them was Bear's Heart (also called Man-Who-Never-Walked), a forty-year-old cripple. As the soldiers moved into the camp, a Hunkpapa emerged singing and leading a horse that pulled a travois holding the crippled Indian. Bear's Heart had told his people that he was tired of being useless all his life in a culture that had no real place for the physically disabled and that he wanted to die in battle. He got his wish. The chanting Hunkpapa pointed the horse toward the soldiers and lashed it into a run. Rifle fire brought down the horse, the drag collapsed, and Bear's Heart finally found his place in the warrior culture of the Sioux as bullets ended his life.[41]

Fighting among the Tetons on the western flank that day was Sitting Bull. Mounted on a fast sorrel and armed with a musket and bow and arrows, he fought until, during the final army assault on the village, he witnessed his uncle, Chief Four Horns, struck in the back by a rifle bullet. Rushing to his uncle's side, Sitting Bull grasped the bridle of the chief's horse and, with White Bull steadying the wounded warrior, he led him to the concealment of a thicket. There Sitting Bull and White Bull applied medicine and bandages to the wound. The chief survived the day and recovered from his wound, later claiming that the bullet dropped into his stomach and never bothered him again.[42]

Just before dusk, as the artillery continued to pound the buttes of Killdeer Mountain, a group of 250–300 Indians appeared on the mountaintop over which they had previously fled. Sully sent Major George Camp with four companies of the Eighth Minnesota to climb the slopes and scatter this force, whose mission seemed to have been one of delaying the soldiers while their women and children escaped up Dead Man's Gulch and other ravines that led to the far side of the mountain. Camp's companies quickly dispersed the Sioux, killing twelve and wounding many more. At the same time other units were sent into the woods and ravines at the base

George Northrup. (Courtesy of the State Historical Society of North Dakota.)

of the mountain to search for and kill stragglers. Captain Stufft's Indian scouts found three Sioux whom, in his words, "my Winnebago boys afterwards killed, scalped and beheaded."[43]

By sunset no live Indians remained on the soldiers' side of Killdeer Mountain. The victorious troops settled down to sleep on the battlefield. Having marched and fought all day without food or water, the soldiers that night finally found a water hole a half a mile from camp and, with three picket lines established to protect the bivouac, the men finally settled down around midnight to consume their hardtack and coffee after twenty hours of fasting and five hours of battle.[44]

Before sunrise of the following day, Sully, after leaving Colonel McLaren and 700 men of the Second Minnesota Cavalry behind to destroy the Indian village, began his march around Killdeer Mountain in pursuit of the Sioux. Unable to climb over the mountain as the retreating Indians had done, because of his wagons and artillery, Sully worked his way six miles around the southwest spur of the mountain mass until he came in sight of a trail leading northwest on the other side. Though this was obviously the trail the Sioux had taken in their flight, Sully was not able to get to it because of the wooded, broken nature of the intervening ground. Taking a pair of binoculars, the general climbed a nearby hill to survey the countryside. He was confronted with an intimidating view of the Little Badlands, thirty miles of rugged country slashed by timbered ravines, some of them 100 feet deep with almost perpendicular banks. Convinced that continued pursuit of the Indians through such terrain was hopeless, Sully ordered a return to the abandoned Sioux camp at Killdeer.[45]

The work of destruction there at the camp had continued apace. The fleeing Indian noncombatants had been able to disassemble and pack a few of their 1,500 plus lodges and had tossed some of their dried meat into ravines with the hope of later returning and recovering it. But most of their buffalo and elkskin tepees, their supplies and livelihood, had been left behind, including even their dogs and ponies tied to pickets. McLaren's soldiers spent the day torching tepees, forty tons of pemmican (dried buffalo meat packed in buffalo skins), dried berries, tanned buffalo, elk, and antelope hides, brass and copper kettles and mess pans, saddles, travois, and lodge poles. Even the surrounding woods were set afire. So massive was the job of destruction that McLaren had to request another 500 men from the brigade, after it had returned from its morning reconnaissance mission, to complete the task. Though the number of Indians killed at Killdeer Mountain was in dispute, there was no disputing the extent of the materiel damage inflicted on the Sioux. Such a vast loss of stores was certainly as damaging as any loss of warriors. Sully certainly thought so, "I would rather destroy their supplies than kill fifty of their warriors."[46]

Among the tasks of obliteration was the shooting of the many dogs left behind by the Indians. The crack of rifles and the howl of dying dogs resounded across the village all day long as up to 3,000 dogs were executed. Also executed were a few Indians left behind by the fleeing Sioux. Sully had ordered all wounded warriors found by the searching soldiers to be treated as prisoners of war, but the only brave discovered panicked and fired at a soldier and paid for it dearly. Minor's Dakota Coyotes hauled him to the edge of the village, made a single file on horseback, and then shredded his body with bullets as they rode by.[47]

A worse atrocity occurred when soldiers found two papooses in one of the abandoned lodges. The boys were placed on a buffalo robe and given hardtack to eat. The soldiers' compassion was supplanted by savagery when

Winnebago scouts made moot the men's discussion about what to do with the papooses by bashing in their skulls with tomahawks. The scouts' explanation for their act was, "Nits make lice!"[48]

Most of the Indians had scattered sixty miles southwest across the Little Missouri to the western edge of the Badlands, where they were reinforced by Miniconjous, Sans Arcs, Brules, and some Cheyenne coming north from the Black Hills. But some Indians lingered in the vicinity of the battlefield. After Sully had returned to the Sioux village at Killdeer Mountain, a group of Indians appeared on a bluff overlooking the camp and planted a white flag on the hillside. Before Sully could respond to this offer of surrender, or at least negotiations, overly enthusiastic soldiers fired on the Indians and they fled.[49]

Their work of ruin accomplished, Sully's soldiers left the ashes of the camp behind them late in the afternoon and plodded six miles southeast to bivouac on Spring Creek, west of the present-day town of Killdeer. The soldiers, having marched 160 miles, fought a pitched battle, and destroyed a huge camp, all on very little food, water, or rest, hoped for a quiet night, but those hopes died with three of their comrades.

As usual, a picket line was posted on the highest ground available to guard the camp and the grazing ponies and mules. Set into the foothills some four miles from the brigade bivouac, fifteen posts of three men each were stationed at regular intervals to give warning of an enemy approach. The pickets were manned largely by Company D of the Second Minnesota Cavalry and placed under the overall charge of Sergeant William M. Campbell, a former United States marshal. The picket line was to be pulled in closer to the camp perimeter after the herd had been grazed.

From concealed positions in the hills some fifty hostiles observed the pickets. Just as the sun disappeared behind the hills, the war party dashed for the herd. They rode past one picket post that did not fire upon the raiders because the guards took them for their own Indian scouts. A second Company D post received the full brunt of the Sioux attack. One of the trio of cavalrymen tried to flee, but his horse went down under a shower of arrows and he was wounded. In the gathering darkness, the soldier slithered to safety and spread the alarm, but his comrades were not so fortunate. Though they resisted stoutly, both men, David La Plant and Anton Holzgen, were killed. One of the privates was found the following morning pinioned with fifteen arrows, the second with nine.

The raiders stripped the horse soldiers of their guns and sabers and rode off with their ponies. Other raiders stampeded a few of the grazing animals, but the herdsmen managed to round up most of the livestock and bring them safely back to camp. The brigade interrupted its preparations for supper to go on full alert and maintain a vigil throughout the night.[50]

Meanwhile, Sergeant Campbell, fearful that his picket posts would be cut off one by one and eliminated in the darkening hills, rode the picket line to gather in his sentries and lead them down into the open plain. Darkness had descended by the time the sergeant had consolidated his posts, and the brigade camp, all lights now extinguished because of the Sioux probe, was four miles distant. Fearful of being hit by friendly fire or ambushed by the raiders, the picket detail stumbled in the dark until it finally reached the brigade perimeter between one and two o'clock in the morning.[51]

Though Campbell's men made it to safety without falling victim to friendly fire, the anxiety-ridden night did claim another victim. With Indians howling and nerves on knife's edge, a perimeter guard from Company G of the Sixth Iowa Cavalry mistook his sergeant, Isaac Winget, for a sneaking Sioux raider and, without bothering to shout a challenge, shot him to death.

The hostiles maintained their howling harassment throughout the night. They shouted to the Indian scouts that Killdeer Mountain had not been a fair fight because so many of their warriors had been absent looking for Sully's column. They demanded a rematch. The scouts shouted back that a second battle was all they desired and that if the hostiles would stand their ground and fight instead of fleeing the bluecoats would kill them all.[52]

In the morning Sully headed back toward the corral on the Heart River. A two-day forced march of sixty-six miles carried the brigade under a driving rain into the Heart River corral. The weary soldiers hoped finally for rest, but once again their hopes were dashed. Wolf howls set off a staccato of gunshots by picket sentries, and the night of July 31 passed in fear and apprehension. The troops and emigrants left behind in the Heart River corral were vastly relieved to witness the return of Sully's strike force. They had passed five anxious days, certain that the Sioux army would simply skip around Sully's column and descend upon the corral. Many more rifle pits had been excavated and a large log had been hollowed out and reinforced with iron bands to build a "Quaker" cannon with which to intimidate any attackers.[53]

With all elements of his expedition safely reunited at the Heart River base, Sully could now evaluate his victory. He had accomplished much. Besides all the stores destroyed, the brigade had inflicted heavy casualties on the Sioux. The general claimed a body count of 100 (which Pope enlarged to 125). Because his troops saw many Indian casualties carried off, Sully estimated the total Indian dead at 150. He claimed that only the strong positions the Sioux occupied and the broken terrain over which they fled prevented an even larger Indian casualty toll. The Sioux themselves admitted to only thirty-one dead, but Sully's estimate was probably more accurate.[54]

Whatever the toll, the Indians killed at Killdeer Mountain, unlike those at Whitestone Hill, were almost exclusively warriors. The Sioux women and children, though they had to make a hasty evacuation of the village after their warriors failed to stop the soldiers' advance, were not caught in the crossfire of a surprise army attack, as they had been at Whitestone Hill. Thus, only a small number of noncombatants were killed and most of these were slain by stray artillery rounds.

Sully's casualties were also far less than at Whitestone Hill, mostly due to his tight tactical square formation in the approach to Killdeer Mountain and to his judicious reliance on his howitzers to pry the Indians from positions in the wooded ravines at the camp, instead of employing infantrymen or cavalrymen to accomplish that task. The general's total loss, including the three men killed on the night following the main battle, was five killed and ten wounded, distributed thus: Brackett's Battalion: two killed, eight wounded (plus twenty-two horses killed); Sixth Iowa Cavalry: one killed (the friendly fire fatality), one wounded; Second Minnesota Cavalry: two killed (the picket guards slain on the night of July 29); First Battalion of Dakota Cavalry: one wounded. Almost all of Sully's casualties during the battle on July 28 occurred in the one significant cavalry charge of the day— Brackett's Battalion's saber-swinging assault on the right wing of the action.[55]

11. The Battle of the Badlands

Given the scope of the victory at Killdeer Mountain and the challenge posed by nature in the Badlands, Sully might well have been content to rest on his laurels. But of Pope's initial reservations and complaints about him notwithstanding, Sully had shown himself to be a hard-core campaigner. His primary mission had been to defeat the Sioux. He had certainly punished them, but he had not completely defeated them. Also driving the general onward were the secondary goals of the expedition—escorting the emigrant train to the Yellowstone and erecting a fort there on that river. The Badlands ahead of his column were indeed daunting, but General Sully was determined to find a way through them.

With only enough rations on hand for six days, Sully needed to reach a post on the Yellowstone called Brazeau's Houses by the most direct route. There he was to rendezvous with two steamers in early August. Consulting with his Indian and half-breed guides about the best course to take, Sully learned that it was impossible for the wagons to traverse the Little Missouri area unless they detoured south back to the route the general had been on before the reports of the Sioux concentration on the Knife River caused him to turn his column north. However, following that course, the expedition would not reach the Yellowstone near its junction with the Powder River for two or three weeks and would miss the steamboats.[1]

Fortunately, a Blackfoot scout rendered a more optimistic appraisal of the route ahead. He claimed that he had completed frequent trips across this country in war parties and hunting parties, and he thought that the wagons could get through one particular pass with some digging and leveling of the hills that pinched and crowded the passage. Cutting bread rations by one-third and all other provisions, except meat, by one-half, Sully rolled out his column, after two days rest, to follow the Blackfoot guide for three days west along the Heart River.[2]

Aside from a patch ravaged by locust swarms that left not one green

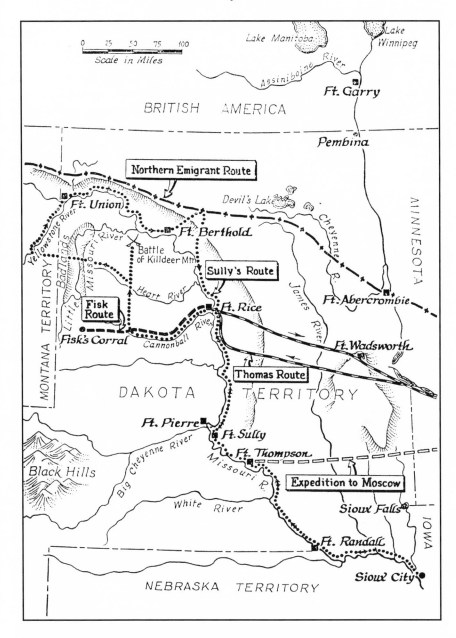

The Badlands Campaign, 1864. (From *The Civil War in the Northwest* by Robert
H. Jones. Courtesy of Robert H. Jones.)

stalk standing except for a few hardy cactus blooms, grass and water were plentiful along this route, though timber was scarce. Sully, always the explorer as well as the soldier, noted extensive coal deposits in this area, with some of the veins ten feet thick. The general was convinced that the whole region from the Missouri to the Yellowstone was good coal country. Though sympathetic to the Indians, Sully was also a man of his time, seeing the land as an exploitable resource for the advancement of a progressive civilization and the nomadic tribesmen as impediments to that advancement.

With the exception of sighting a scouting party of twenty to thirty Sioux riding far ahead of the column, the march was uneventful until the afternoon of August 5. The gently rolling hills that seemed to go on forever suddenly gave way to a monumental chasm that extended along the Little Missouri River on both sides with a width of more than twenty miles. What Sully sighted from the top of the tableland across which his column had marched, he later described as "hell with the fire out."[3]

Soldiers crowded the rim of what became known as Cedar Canyon of the Badlands to view deep gorges brooded over by buttes up to 300 feet high, some sharp-pointed, some chimney-like, in formations that looked like the ruins of a Norman castle, a castle formed by burning coal deposits and erosion. The hillsides were steep, the gullies deep, and the whole area was crisscrossed by brushy ravines and dry streambeds.

The explorer-general later rendered a vivid description of the Badlands.

> It was grand, dismal and majestic. You can imagine a deep basin, 600 feet deep and twenty-five miles in diameter, filled with a number of cones and oven-shaped knolls of all sizes from twenty feet to several hundred feet high, sometimes by themselves, sometimes piled large heaps one on top of another, in all conceivable shapes and confusion. Most of these hills were of a gray clay, but many of a light brick color, of burnt clay; little or no vegetation. Some of the sides of the hills, however, were covered with a few scrub cedars. Viewed in the distance at sunset it looked exactly like the ruins of an ancient city. ... It was covered with pieces of petrified wood, and on the tops of some of the hills we found petrified stumps of trees, the remains of a great forest. In some cases these trees were sixteen to eighteen feet in diameter. Large quantities of iron ore, lava, and impressions of leaves in the rocks of a size and shape not known to any of us.[4]

Sully's initial impression of the Badlands filled him with alarm, and he despaired of successfully crossing it. He might have turned back, had not the miscalculations of his commissary back at Fort Rice left the brigade with too few rations for a return march to the base. They had only enough supplies to proceed on toward the hoped-for rendezvous with the steamers on the Yellowstone. The brigade settled in for the night at the desolate site on the promontory, almost bereft of grass for the animals and with only a few holes containing muddy rainwater to drink. Three cavalrymen, blinded by the glare of a campfire, tumbled over the edge of the bluff and suffered serious injuries on the rocks below.

With this accident hanging like an omen over the camp, pessimism prevailed. Only a few of the Indian scouts seemed confident. The Blackfoot guide, one of the youngest, tried to reassure the general with a confident forecast that he would find his way through the maze on the morrow. The oldest, a man named Fool Dog, predicted that the expedition would "smell the blood of his enemies within two days."[5]

The work of passage began the morning of August 6. The column wound its way through choking dust along a narrow serpentine route, in places barely wide enough for the wagons to pass. The emigrant wagons, pulled by oxen, seriously slowed down the march and caused the column to string out for a distance of three to four miles. Sully had to deploy a double line of guards to protect his train against the Indians he knew would be lurking behind the buttes and bluffs. Working parties were sent out to widen and level the route to the Little Missouri. Gullies had to be filled in and wagons lowered in places with ropes. Several wagons slid down slopes of black vitreous slag and were wrecked. By dusk, however, the column had dug its way twelve miles to the banks of the Little Missouri, thickly timbered with cottonwood trees, near the site of present-day Medora ("where the hills look at each other"). Having scraped and shoveled its way to the middle of the Badlands, the brigade now faced the task of digging its way out to the other side.

The general decided to rest his men in camp on Sunday, August 7, while the animals foraged in the good grass of the Little Missouri bottomlands. A strong working detail of 150 men was sent out the next morning to continue the work of filling in defiles and leveling slopes along a looping stretch of the river that would require a double crossing of the 100-foot-wide Little Missouri. The men were accompanied by a guard detail of seven companies under Seventh Iowa Cavalry commander, Lt. Colonel Pattee.

Around nine o'clock that morning several men disregarded orders and led their horses beyond the camp's picket line in search of better forage. They compounded their delinquency by foolishly leaving both saddles and arms behind in the bivouac. A small party of Sioux made the soldiers pay for their irresponsibility by creeping up to the foragers, opening fire, and stampeding the horses. Most of the soldiers fled, content to lose the horses and escape with their lives. All of the armed guards on the picket line also took to their heels, except for Private John Beltz, who single-handedly repelled the raiders with rapid fire from his carbine and revolver. Three or four soldiers mounted horses bareback and chased after the Indians and their stampeding mounts.

The soldiers managed to recover all but a couple of the horses. A cavalry company was then sent in pursuit of the raiders, but the Indians escaped through the ravines and into the cottonwoods fringing the river.[6]

The rest of the brigade, upon hearing the gunfire of the raid had saddled up and hitched the wagons to their teams. With his men thus mobilized by the alarm, Sully decided to take advantage of the situation by directing his column three miles upriver in search of better grass. The morning work and scouting party was ordered to rejoin the main column after having engineered another three miles of route into this devil's amphitheater.

Unfortunately, Company K of the Seventh Iowa Cavalry, which was part of the work detail, did not receive notice of the pull-out and was left behind. Numerous warriors quickly surrounded the isolated company and threatened to cut it off from the rest of the brigade. Realizing their peril, the soldier-laborers beat a hasty retreat through a deep fissure in the valley where a section of the road the brigade was to follow had just been cut. The Sioux braves pursued, firing from the hilltops and buttes. They persisted in that pursuit all the way to the river. The company paused in its flight to turn about, form a line, and fire a volley, which emptied two Indian saddles. Then Company K wheeled about and rushed for the river to cross into Sully's new camp on a sandy flat on the east side.[7]

As sundown purpled the buttes of the Badlands, up to 1,000 warriors appeared on the 500-foot-high bluff across the river from Sully's bivouac. Safely out of rifle range, they began a verbal assault on the troops, claiming that the addition of 500 more lodges since the Killdeer battle had increased their number to 10,000 braves. They boasted of a captive white woman—Fanny Kelly—in their camp and dared the soldiers to attempt a rescue. They promised a morning of massacre and vowed that soldiers taken captive would be forced to eat one another.

The soldiers' reply was a round from a brass howitzer. That round and a second were solid shot to fix the range. When the balls bounced harmlessly against the bluff, the Indians, who had scattered at the initial report, regained their courage. Several braves boldly ran up to a still rolling third howitzer ball. But this round was an explosive shell and its detonation killed several of these reckless warriors and dispersed the rest.[8]

The howitzer fire may have momentarily scattered the Sioux, but it did not guarantee a quiet night. Both wolves and warriors circled the camp with a howling choir. The reinforced perimeter guards and the Idaho-bound emigrants nervously shot some 3,000 rounds into the darkness to keep their fears and their foes at bay. So trigger-happy were the gold-seekers, blasting bullets from their wagons into the perimeter line every time the guard was changed, that Sully had to threaten them with shell fire from his howitzers in order to stop their shooting at the sentries.[9]

The Battle of the Badlands kicked into full swing on August 8. Sully, laid low with rheumatism and dysentery, realized that he had definitely overtaken the Indians he had grappled with at Killdeer Mountain and that he had to deal with them now in the worst possible terrain of the Dakota Territory. The general had called Colonel Thomas to his tent the evening before and passed on the tactical command of the expedition for August 8. He directed Thomas to "Have everything ready to move at six o'clock in the morning, in perfect fighting order.... You will meet them at the head of the ravine, and have the biggest Indian fight that ever will happen on this continent."[10]

The column inched forward without water on a burning day, the dust gagging horses and men. As Colonel Thomas's Minnesota Brigade took the lead, Sully peered from his ambulance at the forming ranks of his soldiers to exclaim, "Those fellows can whip the devil and all his angels." To Thomas the general exhorted, "You must make some history today."[11]

The column line stretched for three to four miles as the expedition crossed the Little Missouri for the third time, with the troops strung out in a column of twos and the wagons following one behind the other. The heavily loaded emigrant train, pulled by ox teams, reduced progress to a snail's pace. The many women and children aboard the miners' train gave Sully more anxiety than the well-being of the troops of his command.

The route ahead, up the dry bed of a winding creek, led through a series of mountain-rimmed gorges, deep funnels with perpendicular bluffs, so narrow that only a single wagon at a time could pass through. Intersecting ravines ran into the line of march, and from those ravines Indians could hurl themselves against the wagon train at any moment. Sully and Thomas did their best to protect the train, deploying troops all along the flanks of the rolling wagons and posting a strong rear guard that included Pope's four howitzers. Protective companies of troops were ordered to dismount and climb the heights at particularly dangerous points, remaining there until the next company in the line of march could relieve them. In order to diminish the vulnerability of the long, strung-out column, Sully had ordered that at every possible point in the march route where the terrain allowed it the wagons were to double up side-by-side and that each team should follow one another as closely as possible to shorten the column and close up the rear.[12]

The order of march had three companies from the Minnesota Second Brigade in the vanguard, along with the pioneer company. In the center Jones's battery and Colonel Thomas with the rest of the Second Brigade covered the flanks of the miners' train. The First Brigade made up the rear guard and protected the rest of the train. Sully's ambulance rolled along with the advance brigade.[13]

After having covered about three miles, the column encountered Sioux warriors in large numbers—Sully estimated about 1,000 or more—in front and flanks, as the expedition started through a deep pass with steep, rocky slopes. First to encounter the hostiles as the column emerged from the dry creek were the scouts, who broke and ran. A soldier in the vanguard snapped the scouts out of their panic by threatening to shoot the chief scout if he did not get his men under control.[14] The Blackfoot guide took a bullet in the breast and went into shock. Without his guidance, the column wandered in some confusion for a while before he could recover enough to point out the route from his perch in an ambulance.[15]

The Indians were rapidly dislodged from their first positions by shells from Jones's battery, and the column pushed on, with the pioneer company forging a road through the wilderness as they marched. The Sioux continued to appear on the buttes and bluffs on both sides of the column, but skirmishers and artillery kept the Indians beyond the range of their muskets and bows. Most of the Dakota, Lakota, and Yanktonai braves, short of ammunition and hungry because they had lost all their stores at Killdeer Mountain, showed little heart for narrowing the range and closing in on the enemy. They carried off most of their dead, but proof of their casualties came in the form of several Indian ponies that trotted into the white lines bearing the bloodstains of their absent riders.

The battle sputtered along as the blue-jacketed laborers continued to carve out a road. Several more wagons were disabled along the rugged trail and they were burned by the rear guard, which also killed all the animals that had collapsed under the twin tortures of heat and thirst. Several hundred Sioux lunged at the two companies of the Sixth Iowa protecting the rear of the wagon train, but a charge by Company A of the Dakota Cavalry threw them back and blasted two Indian riders off the backs of their ponies. As the Sioux formed for a second try at the train, Lt. Colonel Pattee deployed dismounted men from his Seventh Iowa in concealed positions across the rear of the wagon train. The Indian assault got to within twenty yards of the hidden troops before the soldiers opened fire and bowled two of the attackers off their horses, stopping the charge in its tracks.[16]

While the rear was thus engaged, the advance guard reached a pond of rainwater in a basin on the northeast side of Flat Top Butte, some nine hours and ten miles distant from where the day's march had begun. Men and animals driven almost mad from thirst quickly churned the little lake into a mud hole. Thirsty soldiers and emigrants coming up later from the rear of the column to the nearly drained pool desperately offered a dollar or more for a canteen full of the muddy broth.[17]

The Sioux continued their resistance, appearing in great numbers around the basin. Colonel McLaren's Second Minnesota fanned out to clear a perimeter around the lake so that the expedition could make camp. In the course of the deployment, one of the regiment's companies found itself cut off and surrounded by hundreds of Sioux warriors. The company formed a circle in a rocky hollow and held the hostiles at bay until it was relieved by several more companies sent to its rescue by Colonel Thomas. For all the peril of its situation, the cavalry company suffered only slight losses—only a few men were wounded by arrows.

As the column set up camp under a setting sun, the Sioux made one last swipe at the expedition. Several hundred braves surged down from the ridge surrounding the basin to panic the emigrants and send the soldiers to their rifles and howitzers, with which they quickly repulsed the attack. The combat for the day was ended, and despite the long hours of battle and heavy fire exchanged, the soldiers had escaped with only six men wounded, five of them by arrows. The most serious casualty in terms of the continuation of the passage through the Badlands was the most important man in the expedition, the young Blackfoot guide. Though there was no way to calculate accurately the Indian losses of the day, Sully estimated them at about 100 killed or wounded.[18]

The campsite was generally quiet that night, though the fear of lurking Indians required that every soldier who was not sick or wounded serve a stint of guard duty. The advance continued the next morning, August 9, once again with approximately 1,000 Indians to the expedition's front prepared to give battle. The deployment for this third day in the Badlands saw Major House with two companies of the Sixth Iowa and Captain Tripp's Dakota Cavalry taking the lead. Directly behind the vanguard rode Major Brackett with a company of his battalion and Pope's four howitzers. Once again, Sully sent dismounted units to cover the flanks of the marching column: Lt. Colonel Pollock with the rest of the Sixth Iowa on the right and Lt. Colonel Pattee with three companies of the Seventh Iowa on the left. The flanking companies pushed out on the wings to clear the multicolored cones framing the route of march through two large canyons winding past the north slopes of Flat Top Butte. Jones's battery accompanied the wagon trains, and Colonel Thomas's Minnesota Brigade brought up the rear.[19]

The Indians on the heights along the path of the column seemed dispirited and exhibited little of the spirit and audacity that had marked moments of the Battle of Killdeer Mountain. They talked a better fight than they displayed. Among all the taunts and challenges the Sioux hurled from the buttes at the column, White Bull remembered the following exchange between Sully's Indian scouts and Sitting Bull, though it is not clear whether this exchange took place on August 8 or August 9:

> One of the Yankton guides called out, "We are thirsty to death and want to know what Indians you are."

Sitting Bull answered, "Hunkpapas, Sans Arc, Miniconjou, Yanktonai, and others. Who are you?"

The scout shouted back, "Some Indians with the soldiers."

Sitting Bull's reply was, "You have no business with the soldiers. The Indians here have no fight with the whites. Why is it the whites come to fight the Indians? Now we have to kill you, too, and let you thirst to death."[20]

It was rather disingenuous of Sitting Bull by now, after Teton involvement at both Whitestone Hill and Killdeer Mountain, to suggest that the Lakota tribes had no quarrel with the invading whites. And his boasts of killing the Indian scouts and their accompanying soldiers proved to be idle threats. The fight was pretty much gone from the Sioux by now, regardless of their boasts. The soldiers' advance proceeded with little trouble. Light skirmishing flared to the front, and the hostiles mounted a semi-serious attack on the expedition's rear, but at all points and at all times the Indians were easily repelled.

Colonel Thomas described the action on August 9 as follows: "The Indian shotguns and bows and arrows were no match for the accurate aim and long range of our rifles and carbines, and when the artillery sent shells into their assemblies on the hills and into their retreats in the ravines, the cowardly rascals soon learned that they were no match for soldiers that had come 1,000 miles to fight them."[21]

As the Indians became increasingly reluctant to close to within artillery and long-range rifle fire of the soldiers, Sully's subordinate commanders demonstrated their ingenuity and earned the praise of their general by adapting the Plains Indians' own tactics to the situation. While platoons of soldiers crawled into concealed positions behind the hills, a small mounted force rode against the Indians, fired and retreated, as if in disorder, to draw the Sioux into the enfilade of the hidden marksmen. The success of these tactics smothered what little fighting spirit remained in the Sioux on that August day. After a few more miles of advance against ever lessening Indian resistance, the Sully column finally broke through into open country to witness a huge cloud of dust about six miles distant, behind which the Sioux fled. The Battle of the Badlands, a battle as much against nature as against the Indians, was over.[22]

The casualties in the three days of fighting that fluctuated from intense to lackadaisical were even more a matter of dispute than those of the previous battles of the Dakota War. Because most of the fighting was done at long range, because the Indians carried off most of their fallen, and because the rugged terrain of the Badlands made body counting extremely difficult, the losses inflicted on the hostiles could not be estimated with accuracy. Sully estimated 100 Indians killed in the Badlands, while some of his officers pumped up the total to two or three times that figure.[23] Given the natural protection afforded the Indians by the turrets and buttes of the Badlands and the infrequency and brevity of any combat at close quarters during the battle, even Sully's figure was probably too high. Colonel Thomas, in attempting to inflate the size and importance of the battle, even claimed the ridiculous figures of 311 Indians killed and between 600 and 700 wounded, out of 8,000 engaged (figures that would have made the Badlands the biggest and bloodiest battle for the American Indians west of the Mississippi). Thomas also placed army casualties at 9 killed and 100 wounded.[24] No other officer, diarist, or reporter even mentions a single U.S. Army fatality. In actuality, the only serious casualty among Sully's ranks seems to have been the Blackfoot scout who had led the column into this purgatory of the plains. In addition, about a dozen of Sully's soldiers were more lightly wounded, and one of Sully's Indian guides was killed near the end of the crossing of the Badlands when he carelessly wandered away from the main scouting party.

The Return March

By noon on August 9 the last of the Indians had disappeared. Sully's Indian guides claimed, based on their debates at a distance with the hostiles, that the Indian combatants in the Badlands had been the same Indians who had fought the U.S. expedition at Killdeer Mountain, plus Cheyenne, Brules, Miniconjous, and others who had ridden up from the south. Sully wanted to pursue the fleeing hostiles and felt certain he could have overtaken them if he'd had sufficient rations remaining, if his ponies and mules were not so worn down by a lack of forage, and if he had not been encumbered by the emigrant wagon train.

After a further three-mile march west, the expedition reached the main Indian camp, about five miles southeast of the present-day town of Sentinel Butte. The camp was one mile by one-half mile in area and smaller camps close by increased the area occupied by the Indians to three miles long by three-quarters of a mile wide. By its size, Sully estimated that all the Indians in the region had camped there, though apparently no lodges had been erected (most of those had been destroyed at Killdeer Mountain).

One army officer reported, "Their fires were yet burning and many of their effects, including the undisposed bodies of dead warriors, were left in camp to tell of the hasty and unexpected flight."[25]

The Indian trails from the campsite led both southwest and northeast, back in the direction of Killdeer Mountain. Many of the Indians recrossed the Little Missouri and headed east before breaking up into smaller bands and scattering. Sitting Bull, for example, with Four Horns' band and other Hunkpapa bands, drifted southeast in search of buffalo herds.

Sully continued west and north toward the Yellowstone. The country-side was stripped almost bare of vegetation by grasshoppers, rations dwindled, and water holes were few and alkaline. The expedition's animals starved all the way to the Yellowstone and many of them had to be shot. On August 11 alone, as the column staggered twenty-eight and a half miles across the barren terrain, some $30,000 worth of stock died or were put out of their misery by a bullet.[26]

Reduced to a ration of two hardtack biscuits, a small slab of pork belly, and a pint of rancid-tasting coffee a day, with tongues so swollen from heat and thirst that many men could not talk, the expedition witnessed its first hopeful sight in three days when, on August 12, a scout galloped up to General Sully to enthusiastically hand him a chip of wood. Scooped out of the Yellowstone, the freshly cut wood chip was taken as evidence that the life-saving steamboats were nearby. An orderly rode with the chip down the straggling, dispirited column line to instantly revive morale and re-energize the weary troops.[27]

The howitzers fired signal shells into the sky and answering shots echoed upstream from two stern-wheelers, the *Chippewa Falls* and the *Alone*, the first steamboats to ascend the Yellowstone. They had been scheduled to meet the expedition at Brazeau's Houses, five miles further south along the river, but low water had prevented them from proceeding on upstream. The delirious condition of the wounded Blackfoot guide had caused the column to veer from its intended route to the Yellowstone, and thus, providentially, steamboats and soldiers united below the original link-up site, at a point on the river some fifteen miles south of present-day Sidney, Montana. Each of the boats carried fifty tons of freight, but little corn for the expedition's animals. Most of the corn had been aboard a third steamer, the *Island City*, which had struck a snag in the Missouri River near Fort Union and sunk.[28]

The men of Sully's column reached the Yellowstone by early afternoon, joyfully broke ranks, and rushed into the river to drink their full. The stock was herded into the bottoms to graze on rushes and rosebuds, while hunting parties harvested elk and black-tailed deer, and another detail gathered berries and choke cherries for the many men wracked with dysentery. As the ribs and steaks from the afternoon's bountiful hunt roasted over campfires, the steamboats floated downstream to tie up at the brigade camp-site. The steamboat sailors further boosted the soaring spirits of the soldiers by reporting, more than seven months prematurely, the fall of Richmond to Union forces, and the regimental bands celebrated this false sunrise in Virginia and the real salvation on the Yellowstone with an evening concert.[29]

Sully had tangled twice with the Sioux and he had spun plans to take them on a third time by sending part of his expedition to pursue the Indians into their haunts northeast of the Yellowstone. But no grass and no grain forced a change of plans. Included in this change of plans was his decision not to build the projected post at the confluence of the Yellowstone and Powder rivers. The loss of the *Island City*, the impossibility of steaming more boats up the rapidly falling river, and the sparseness of grass, which would preclude wagons from hauling freight the necessary several hundred miles upriver in place of the steamboats, all conspired to make the construction of a fort on the Powder River impracticable. Consequently, the expedition's commander decided to return down the Yellowstone to its mouth, then cross the Missouri to Fort Union and from there go on to Fort Berthold, where good grass and an easier path would smooth the way.

The expedition forded the Yellowstone on August 14 to the tableland on the western side. The steamboats ferried the heavier freight across, while the soldiers and emigrants floated their wagons and swam their animals over with guide ropes. At least two gold-seekers and one soldier as well as thirty or more mules were caught in the river's swirling current and drowned and some reports even claimed as many as nine gold-seekers drowned.[30]

Proceeding downriver on August 15 toward Fort Union, thirty-five miles distant, the lack of grass, almost nonexistent in that unusual year because of no winter snows and rains that arrived too late, required Sully to fragment his command over a large area to find forage. The country was so sere it appeared burned over. The hostiles added to the column's discomfort by setting fire to a patch of woods lying in the path of the expedition.[31]

The boats had so much trouble getting downriver over the rapids and sandbars that Sully had to unload his wagons so that the freight could be transferred from the boats. The lightened steamers then were able to float free of the river shoals and finally reached Fort Union on August 17.

Reaching the junction of the Yellowstone with the Missouri, the expedition now faced the hurdle of quicksand obstructing its passage across the Missouri. The laborious process of unloading the wagons, taking them apart, and then loading them and their baggage on the now freed-up boats had to be undertaken before the brigade could get across the river. The crossing was completed by August 20, but not before a man from Company L, Seventh Iowa and three animals were drowned and two wagons lost. It was now one month and 460 miles since the expedition had left Fort Rice.[32]

The first night after the crossing a party of Crows cantered into camp to report that a Sioux contingent had stampeded all but two of Fort Union's horse herd and had killed six friendly Indians near the post. Brackett's Battalion, with Pope's guns in consort, was sent out to track the war party, but the military posse found no trace of the raiders.[33]

Though the Crows seemed most amiable and urged Sully to stay in the area so that the entire tribe could gather to parley with the white general, the traders at Fort Union claimed the Crows, apparently upset over the paucity of the annuities, had been troublesome and even truculent prior to the arrival of the expedition. *Assiniboine* had also been at Fort Union a few days before to receive an annuity distribution from the post commander, having missed the agent for the Upper Bands who had passed through the area weeks before. Sully had nothing but contempt for the government's program of purchasing the good behavior of the Indians with annuity bribes. In his opinion, "the system of issuing annuity goods is one grand humbug."[34]

Though plans for the Powder River post had been abandoned, Sully judged that a fort lower down the Yellowstone, at the confluence of that river with the Missouri, would serve the army's strategic purposes best. The stores for the projected Yellowstone-Powder River fort had been deposited at Fort Union under guard of a company of the Thirtieth Wisconsin Regiment since June 13. The general had a site several miles downstream from Fort Union surveyed for a military post by topographical engineer Captain H. von Minden. It was on that site that Fort Buford was built in 1866. This post plus Fort Berthold and Fort Rice, were thus intended to form a chain to keep the Missouri River open, secure travel both by way of the river and overland, and prevent the separated Indian tribes from combining to campaign against the whites.[35]

Sully was finally able to free his column of the burden of the miners' train at Fort Union. The emigrants hired a half-breed scout to guide them the rest of the way to Fort Benton and the Montana mines. When they departed westward from Fort Union on August 19, they took with them a considerable amount of U.S. Army property, including horses, mules, and oxen, as well as arms and ammunition—mostly procured from Sully's soldiers, who had been plied liberally with whiskey. Also leaving with the miners were about forty soldiers and mule skinners from the expedition, who had decided that panning for gold held more attraction for them than fighting the Sioux. Sully "sent a force after the Idaho gentlemen," but the deserters galloped away from the easily overtaken wagon train and managed to evade the posse. Before they could rejoin the emigrant train, however, the party of deserters encountered a group of Sioux warriors and one of the soldiers paid for his gold greed with his life.[36]

Sully spent a few days at Fort Union, grazing his half-starved stock and resting his troops, who feasted on the apple pies baked by the garrison and sold for fifty cents each. Leaving the Thirtieth Wisconsin to protect the stores at Fort Union during the coming winter, the general headed his column east down the north bank of the Missouri on August 21 toward Fort

Rice. On August 28, after a march of 140 miles, the column paused in its return march at Nishu, five miles west of the old trading post of Fort Berthold. The post was the home of the smallpox-ravaged Mandan, Arikara, and Hidasta (or Gros Ventres) tribes, all together numbering about 2,500. Blood enemies of the Sioux but too weak to fight from the effects of diseases and temptations brought by the whites, the tribal remnants begged Sully for protection. The general acceded, leaving a company of the Sixth Iowa under Captain Mooreland to protect the tribes and establish a communication link between Fort Rice and Fort Union.[37]

12. The Siege of Fort Dilts

Sully passed by Fort Berthold on August 30, anxious to lead his men away from the temptations of the whiskey-besotted trade Indians and their squaws, and camped five miles to the east of the post. During the night several soldiers sneaked past the guards to return to the fort and join the Indians in a drunken debauch, the distilled spirits for which were provided by Canadian half-breeds.[1]

A report that Inkpaduta and a band of Santees was sighted in the vicinity of Dog Den Butte at the southern edge of the Mouse River Valley caused Sully to veer to the northeast to undertake one last effort to bring the old incorrigible to justice. Leaving his trains at Snake Creek, where the Missouri turns sharply to the south, Sully made a quick march sixty miles to the northeast on September 1. Along the way the soldiers encountered thousands of buffalo, and a shooting party quickly left the prairie strewn with more than fifty bison carcasses.

Sully silenced the shooters on September 2 as he approached Dog Den Butte, but "Inky" slipped away again, and the general's scouts found only his still warm campfires. Realizing that he could not catch Inkpaduta before he gained British territory, Sully turned his troops back around to rejoin his supply trains on the Missouri.[2]

The last skirmish of Sully's 1864 campaign took place at this point. Two of the expedition's officers, Major Robert Rose and Captain James Paine, were allowed to remain in the rear of Sully's departing column to hunt buffalo. Each had killed a bull, and they were cutting out the tongues when they were attacked by some twenty warriors of Inkpaduta's rear guard. The officers spun two Santees out of their saddles with carbine shots and then mounted up to race their horses over the open plains with the hostiles in hot pursuit. Captain P. B. Davy of Company H, Second Minnesota Cavalry, in command of Sully's rear guard some ten miles distant, heard the firing and took one company of mounted troops with him to rescue the officers and repel the Indians.[3]

The column resumed its progress down the Missouri toward Fort Rice, continuing to encounter huge buffalo herds that, at least on one occasion stampeded through the expedition's campsite, threatening to wreck wagons and trample soldiers. An all-day chilling rain added to the catalogue of miseries endured by the Sully Expedition. Fifty horses died in one day as a result of months of exhaustion and hunger.

The column reached Apple River on September 7, near where General Sibley had camped in 1863. The grave of Sibley's aide, Lieutenant Beaver, was located and marked. In 1873 his remains were disinterred and boxed up for reburial beyond the Great Plains.[4]

The column finally caught sight of Fort Rice, across the Missouri River, on September 8, and the weary soldiers received their first mail since departing from that post on July 19. The general was pleased by the appearance of the post and praised the garrison of Colonel Daniel J. Dill's Thirtieth Wisconsin Regiment, which had "done an immense amount of labor in the last two months." Sully predicted that "the post when finished will be one of the best posts in the West."[5]

The general was far less pleased to hear that Captain James Fisk's so-called Montana and Idaho Expedition had passed through Fort Rice on August 23 with 200 emigrants in eighty-eight wagons headed for the gold mines. Fisk had tapped his political connections in order to procure an official commission to open overland routes to the mines and authorization to secure military protection for his expedition. He had consequently managed to wheedle an escort of forty-seven soldiers, led by Lieutenant Smith of Company A, Dakota Cavalry, out of the Fort Rice garrison as he proceeded westward.[6]

Having just freed himself of one train of "draft dodging" miners that he had been forced to protect, Sully now found himself responsible for a second group. He was incensed. In a missive to Pope, Sully complained, "They can't go forward on their trail; there is no grass and very little water. Fisk was told of this before he started from here, but he, though he had never been over the country, knew better." Fisk's attitude, according to Sully, was that the warning of inhospitable terrain before him "was a damned trick of the traders; they wanted him to go ninety miles out of his way, by Berthold, to get money out of his men."[7] Instead of proceeding along the Missouri, then, Fisk had stubbornly cut across country, where Sully knew he would run into trouble and need rescue. And so he did.

Fisk's misfortune and the last significant battle of the Dakota War began on September 2, 1864, 160 miles west of Fort Rice and 22 miles east of the Badlands (near present-day Dickinson, North Dakota). As the miners' train descended toward Deep Creek, the emigrants encountered the obstacle of a deep gulch in their path. Though the miners shoveled away at the banks to improve the passage, a wagon overturned while trying to thread the defile. A second wagon pulled out of line to assist, and two emigrants set about the task of helping the driver repair his disabled wagon, while nine soldiers remained behind to guard them. The rest of the train rolled on, though one other civilian rode back to the gulch to look for the revolver he had lost. The train had covered one more mile toward its destination in the distant gilded mountains, when the rumble of gunfire alerted Fisk's outfit that the party left behind was under attack. The wagons quickly circled in a corral and fifty soldiers and citizens formed up to hasten back to their compatriots' rescue.

The pair of wagons left behind had been assaulted by a party of 100 Hunkpapas led by Sitting Bull. The future leader of the Tetons galloped toward the isolated wagons in front of his warriors and rode into the whites to grapple in hand-to-hand combat with one of the soldiers. The soldier managed to pull out his revolver and shoot a bullet into Sitting Bull's left hip, the bullet exiting out the small of his back. The young chief slid over to the opposite side of his horse to protect himself from further wounds and rode off, with White Bull, Jumping Bull, and a third warrior escorting him to safety. Once they were out of the solders' rifle range, Jumping Bull attended to Sitting Bull's wound, managed to stop the bleeding, and bandaged him. The Tetons then remounted and led the wounded warrior to a Sioux village six miles away to recuperate.[8]

Meanwhile, in close-quarters combat around the two wagons, the Hunkpapas cut down most of the whites with arrows, tomahawks, and knives, although one man did escape to warn the wagon train up ahead. The rescue party had already been dispatched, of course, at the first shots.

A scout named Jefferson Dilts rode in the forefront, considerably ahead of the others, who were mostly on foot. Dilts recklessly charged the Tetons single-handedly, catching them by surprise as they were looting the captured wagons. Opening up with his carbine and six-shooter, the scout cut down at least six of the Hunkpapas (some veterans of the battle claimed an unlikely total of eleven Indians killed or mortally wounded by the deadeye Dilts). Then, possibly realizing the foolhardiness of his one-man attack, Dilts reined his horse around and headed back to white lines. He could not ride fast enough, however. Three arrows penetrated his back, fatally wounding the fearless scout.[9]

The men coming up behind Dilts then ran squarely into the Hunkpapa line and had to fight until sunset to extricate themselves from an untenable situation. By the time the rescue party had rescued themselves and returned to the corral, the white toll for the day amounted to six soldiers and two teamsters killed and four more soldiers mortally wounded. Although the train had circled in a vulnerable position on low ground ringed by heights, the Tetons chose not to attack again that night. After dark a burial party left the corral to carefully maneuver its way back to the scene of the skirmish and locate and bury six of the dead by lantern light. The soldiers and civilians of the Fisk expedition then passed a largely sleepless night, made more miserable by a late evening thunderstorm that filled the low-lying camp with up to three inches of water by morning.[10]

One of the wagons captured by the Hunkpapas contained 4,000 bullets and several carbines and muskets. The other was full of liquor and cigars. Also taken by the Indians, according to later stories about the Battle of Red Buttes, as it was called, was a box of hard bread that had been poisoned and had been intended to be discarded along the trail as a deadly treat to passing Indians. Though there were no verified reports of Indians partaking of the toxic bread, the Lakotas shadowing the Fisk train certainly indulged in the hard spirits and tobacco they had captured. As the train moved out from its overnight corral on the morning of September 3, drunken Tetons, puffing on cheroots, hung about its flanks, some of them dashing wagonward in inebriated sallies to shoot arrows or carbine rounds at the wagon line. The train, under harassment by firewater-fueled Lakotas all day, moved only two miles before it again corralled.[11]

Fisk had his train on the move the next morning, but the hostiles soon reappeared; this time in much stronger numbers and in more determined temperament. After enduring hours of probing attacks on both sides of the train, Fisk despaired of further progress, looked for suitable ground, and then corralled, at a site a few miles east of the Little Missouri River (not far from present-day Marmarth, North Dakota). The Lakota attacks having escalated far beyond harassment, Fisk knew that he would have to endure a siege, and he fortified accordingly. He had his men put up a breastworks of sod six feet high to enclose the corral and scooped out embrasures to position the mountain howitzer carried by the emigrants. The hastily erected fortification was named Fort Dilts in honor of the valiant scout killed in the skirmish of September 2.

All day on September 5 some 300 to 500 Lakotas probed the sod earthworks of Fort Dilts, but once again the sturdy little mountain howitzer was the equalizer, keeping the Indians at bay. Though the Teton fire was heavy at times, it was all long-range and the Fisk party, secure behind the ramparts of prairie earth, suffered no casualties.

That night, Lieutenant Smith and thirteen of his men easily slipped out of the fortified corral and headed for Fort Rice to get help. The men they left behind were in no great danger as long as they stayed behind their fortifications and their howitzer. A spring near the corral provided plenty of water and the wagons were loaded with provisions. But the hundreds of Indians lurking about (Fisk would later claim the preposterous total of 3,000 besieging braves) made it impossible for the emigrants to move out of their corral and resume their journey. Until rescue came from Fort Rice, the miners were stuck. The siege of Fort Dilts continued for sixteen days.[12]

The Lakotas interrupted the boring stalemate of the siege by opening negotiations. Their agent for these talks was a white woman captive named Fanny Kelly, from Geneva, Kansas. She had been abducted during a July 12 Oglala raid on a wagon train on the Platte River near Fort Laramie. Carried away to the north, Kelly had been traded by her original captors to a Hunkpapa named Brings Plenty on the eve of Killdeer Mountain. Now the Indians forced her to write a message to the men of Fort Dilts, using the point of a lead bullet to etch on paper an offer to trade the captive for booty. Under a white flag, a warrior named Porcupine and two other Hunkpapas carried the message to a hillside in view of the corral and staked the paper to the ground.

Fisk tried to win Kelly's freedom with an offer of three horses, plus flour, coffee, and sugar, but the Lakotas demanded forty head of cattle and four wagons. The negotiating mood of the Indians was not improved when, according to Kelly's later testimony, several Lakotas died from eating the poisoned bread taken from the two wagons captured during the September 2 firefight. However, Kelly's poisoned bread stories, like many of the episodes she described in her memoir, may have been apocryphal and were not confirmed by any other reliable report. In any case, negotiations broke off, and Fanny Kelly had to endure several more months of Indian captivity.[13]

Two weeks into the siege, most of the Lakotas had become tired of the tedium and left to hunt the buffalo driven away from the area by the sound of the howitzer discharging. Lieutenant Smith's courier party, which had wriggled out of Fort Dilts during the stormy night of September 5, had reached Fort Rice after covering 175 miles in fifty-six hours. Sully, with no great enthusiasm, organized a relief expedition consisting of 300 men of the Thirtieth Wisconsin, 200 of the Eighth Minnesota, and 100 of the Seventh Iowa, all dismounted, as well as 100 mounted men each from Brackett's Battalion, the Second Minnesota, and the Sixth Iowa, all under the command of Colonel Dill. This rescue column of 900 left Fort Rice on September 18, and two days later the cavalry vanguard of the column reached the corral and ended the siege of Fort Dilts. Except for an early morning horse-stealing raid by about thirty hostiles that netted them fourteen Sixth Iowa Cavalry mounts, the Sioux did not resist the relief expedition.

Fisk was pleased to see the Fort Rice column, but he was subsequently enraged at Sully when informed that the rescue column would escort the emigrants back to Fort Rice, but not on to the Yellowstone, as Fisk had demanded. Most of the emigrants took Dill up on his offer, and from Fort Rice journeyed on back to Minnesota. A few of the more daring, their greed surmounting their fear, continued the trek toward the Montana gold fields.

The rescue force returned with the emigrant train on September 30, having lost one man who straggled from the rear and was not seen again, most likely a victim to the Indians, the wolves, or his own greed.[14]

The Conclusion of the Campaign

Back at Fort Rice, the Second Minnesota Brigade was relieved of further participation in the campaign. The brigade returned overland to Fort Ridgely, which it reached on October 8, having marched a total of 1,625 miles in four months and three days of campaigning.

The infantry units of the Minnesota Brigade were sent south to fight the Confederacy. The Second Minnesota Cavalry Regiment, which had lost two men killed in action and five dead of disease during the 1864 campaign, remained in Minnesota for patrol duty on the northern and western borders of the state until the end of the Civil War. The regiment lost another man, Private Jolly of Company F, to marauding Santees on May 7, 1865, and Captain Field and three enlisted men froze to death in a blizzard between Forts Wadsworth and Abercrombie on February 14, 1866.[15]

Brackett's Battalion served again in Sully's district from the spring of 1865 to the following spring, patrolling the prairies from the Missouri River to Devil's Lake. The Third Battery of Light Artillery was posted to the three Minnesota forts for the winter, and in the summer of 1865 three sections, led by Captain Jones, made an eventless excursion to the Devil's Lake area to check out false reports of hostile Yanktonais. The battery was mustered out of service in February 1866.[16]

Leaving Fort Rice well garrisoned, Sully relieved the Thirtieth Wisconsin of their garrison duty there and sent the regiment on its way toward the Mississippi and eventual assignment with Sherman in Georgia. Then Sully left with his First Brigade and slowly proceeded back down the Missouri toward Yankton and Sioux City. Lt. Colonel Pattee was put in charge of a boat-building detail that constructed eight barges, aboard which 411 men who had lost their horses during the summer campaign floated down the river 1,000 miles to Sioux City. Pattee's Seventh Iowa Cavalry went into winter quarters there and recommenced defensive patrol duty on the frontier. The only incident of note that fall and winter occurred in November when Pattee led a patrol of fifty-five men up the Big Sioux River in search of a Santee horse-thieving band. Pattee failed to find the raiders but did come across the remains of his brother, Frederick, and another man, killed by Santees while canoeing the river on April 9, 1864.[17]

As Sully's expedition returned to bases in Minnesota and the far southeastern edge of Dakota Territory, it left garrisons planted deep in Sioux country. Although supply difficulties had kept him from erecting a post on the lower Yellowstone, Sully had deposited units at the old trading posts of Fort Union and Fort Berthold and had installed a large permanent garrison at Fort Rice on the west bank of the Missouri, ten miles above the mouth of the Cannonball. Pope's planned fort at Devil's Lake had not been established, but Sibley, acting on his own discretion, had sent out a detachment of Wisconsin infantry to put up a fortification west of the head of the Coteau des Prairies, midway between Lake Traverse and the James River. The new post was named Fort Wadsworth (later called Fort Sisseton), and it was constructed on a site more defensible and with more accessible wood than the fort originally planned by Pope. It also protected friendly Sissetons from the remaining hostile Dakota bands.

Forts Sully and Rice had established the U.S. Army solidly along the Missouri as far north and west as the Cannonball, and the companies at Bertold and Union had begun the effective military penetration of the white race toward the mouth of the Yellowstone. From Fort Sully, established one year earlier, the military frontier had thus leaped 300 miles up the Missouri to the mouth of the Yellowstone.[18]

The new forts demonstrated the mounting importance of the Missouri as an avenue to Montana (organized as a territory in 1864 as new gold strikes attracted new emigrants). The Missouri, navigable each summer as far as Fort Benton, was now a vital link to Montana and Idaho, and the new military posts greatly increased the security of that link. At the same time, the northern overland routes were becoming less important, even though Fisk would undertake two more Conestoga trips across the Dakota and Montana prairies in 1865 and 1866. The Platte River Road, to the south, which eventually linked with the northern trails near the Great Salt Lake—due to better weather, water, terrain, and fewer Indians—proved to be the best if not the shortest overland route to Montana and Idaho.[19]

To help garrison the posts on the Missouri and the Minnesota-Dakota borderlands in the fall of 1864, the First U.S. Volunteers, the first of six regiments of former Confederate POWs, arrived in Chicago to be dispatched to forts on the frontier. These "galvanized Yankees," unused to these northern climes, would suffer extreme hardships that winter of 1864/65 as frigid winds and blizzards blew across the Dakota prairies.

Six companies of the regiment, led by Colonel Charles A. R. Dimon, a brash and rash young protégé of the political general, Ben Butler, were assigned to relieve the Thirtieth Wisconsin at Fort Rice so that the Wisconsin infantrymen could head south to share in the coming victory over the secession. Raided by the Sioux and ravaged by disease and abominable weather, ten percent of the garrison's personnel died from scurvy, dysentery, and other diseases by the spring of 1865.[20]

In addition to the string of forts, Sully had also left behind a Sioux nation that was not subdued, certainly, but sobered. The campaigns of 1863–64 had been intended to punish the Dakotas and intimidate the Lakotas, and to a certain extent those objectives were met. On the other hand, Teton tribes, nominally still at peace with the U.S. government prior to the Sibley-Sully campaigns, were now fully engaged in active warfare against white America, and the theater of war had moved hundreds of miles west across the northern plains. There was no denying, however, that a good many Sioux chieftains and warriors, once so certain of their martial superiority, now had a healthy respect for the whites and their army and had at least begun the process of reconciling themselves to the inevitable domination of their homelands by the white citizens of the United States.

The fall of 1864 witnessed several chiefs of Sioux tribes traveling to Forts Randall and Pierre to sue for peace. Once they were told that the only conditions for peace, at least initially, were the end of attacks on white settlers and the suspension of hostilities against the U.S. Army, the chiefs were surprised and relieved at the easy terms and left to bring their principal spokesmen to talk with Sully at Fort Randall.

Upon hearing of this, Pope expressed his expectations to Halleck that most of the tribes west of the Missouri would agree to peace that winter, and that it would be a peace based solely on trust and good behavior, not the bribed peace of annuity distributions. The departmental commander was only pessimistic about those Yanktonais who had fled northeast of the Missouri toward Canada, from whence, with British and half-breed backing, they might continue hostilities. Pope now felt that the Minnesota frontier was secure, his campaigns of the last two years having established a barrier of a vast, largely barren prairie separating by hundreds of miles the hostiles from the line of white settlement. Now there should be nothing to fear from the Indians, except for the occasional nuisance of small thieving bands.[21]

Further indications of a more conciliatory Sioux attitude occurred on October 23, 1864, when some 200 Hunkpapas and Blackfeet, led by Bear's Rib, arrived at Fort Sully to parley with Sully's adjutant-general, Captain John H. Pell. Bear's Rib expressed the Tetons' lesson in humility:

> We used to laugh when they said the whites were going to try and go through our country to fight us. [But after Sibley and Sully,] we realize that the whites go wherever they want to, that nothing can stop them. That where they want to stay we can no more drive them away than we can a wall of solid rock.[22]

Pell pressed his advantage, warning of more expeditions and demanding the release of Fanny Kelly before the army would stop its war against the Lakotas. Six chiefs promised to work for her release, but her captor (and owner), Brings Plenty, stubbornly refused an offer of horses in exchange for

Kelly. Twice the influential Sitting Bull pressed Brings Plenty to free his captive, but the warrior remained adamant. Finally, Sitting Bull, more because his sense of honor had been pricked than because he desired peace with the whites, confronted Brings Plenty in his tepee. With the warrior Crawler at his side, Sitting Bull declaimed, "My friend, I sent for this woman to be brought to me at my tepee and you would not give her up."[23]

Brings Plenty at this point backed down in the face of the formidable, if still controlled, fury of Sitting Bull. Crawler motioned to Kelly, standing apprehensively nearby, and the three walked out of the tepee. On December 9, 1864, a delegation of Blackfeet Sioux rode to Fort Sully to deliver the white woman, wrapped in buffalo robes, to the army. As the gate of the fort closed behind her, Miss Kelly, after four months of captivity, joyously exclaimed, "My God, am I a free woman!"[24]

The Dakota expeditions of the previous two years had certainly been costly in blood, particularly for the Indians. But a good many white critics seemed to believe that the heaviest costs of the campaigns were those borne by the government's pocketbook. They offered the opinion that the money spent fighting Indians might have been more profitably spent buying the Sioux's submission with annual installments, thus avoiding the diversion of so much military effort and so many resources away from the vital Civil War fronts.

But the events of 1862 had demanded retribution; a certain number of dead Indians had to be counted to assuage the many who demanded revenge. Further motivating this urge for revenge were the ambitions of politicians and the greed of army contractors who saw advancement and profit in campaigns against the Sioux. A good many Minnesota soldiers were themselves enthusiastic for the expeditions, not only to get even for August 1862, but also to avoid service on far bloodier battlefields south of the Ohio.

In any case, few people at the highest reaches of regional politics and military power were receptive to those who called for purchasing the Sioux's submission. Pope, in particular, was fervent in his opposition to the whole concept of annuities, trade, and, in general, to much of any white civilian contact with the Indians. In his correspondence with Halleck, the departmental commander complained about half-breeds and other British subjects filtering into U.S. territory to incite the Indians to hostilities and to arm and supply them in their depredations. Pope held the Canadians responsible for much of the trouble with the Sioux because of their refusal to control them after granting them refuge in Canadian territory and because they refused requests from the U.S. Army to continue pursuit of hostile bands across the border. As an example, Pope pointed to the Yanktonais beaten by Sully at Killdeer Mountain who then fled northeast to safety in Canada.[25]

Canadians were not the only whites guilty of complicity in the Indian troubles in Pope's view. He pointed to wagon trains like Fisk's, that violated the Sioux's territory in their lust for gold, and to Fisk in particular for his recklessness and ignorance that put soldiers at risk, as well as for his arrogant disrespect shown to Sibley and Sully. Pope railed against the swarms of grasping, dishonest traders swilling Indians with whiskey and swelling their resentments with their cheating commerce. Pope urged the forcing of all traders to locate their stores at military posts, where they could be closely monitored.

With dishonest traders sent packing, Pope hoped to induce many Indians to make their permanent homes—except for the summer hunt, of course—adjacent to army forts, where they could trade without being cheated and where they would be protected by the military from other unscrupulous whites. "If there be no other places to trade except the military posts the Indians will necessarily resort to them, and will there remain.... If fair dealing with the Indians can be enforced there never will be danger of any Indian wars."[26]

Pope expanded on his vision of a permanent peace with the Plains Indians by urging that the only white men, other than the military and army-supervised traders, allowed to communicate with the Indians should be missionaries. The missionaries should, in his view, teach their nomadic parishioners practical skills in agriculture and carpentry first, then give them religious instructions (not the other way around, which Pope thought often resulted in Indians acquiring a dependence on heavenly rewards and neglecting earthly duties). One small missionary family should be assigned to every small post, two to larger installations.

Pope planned to establish the first mission-trading post-fort in the spring of 1865 to begin the peace process. In the meantime, he instructed Sibley and Sully to offer peace terms to the Sioux based solely on non-molestation by both parties. He firmly believed that annuities only encouraged fraud and Indian hostilities, because the disbursements were considered by the tribesmen as bribes to be on their best behavior. Pope pointed out to Halleck a truism among the Sioux: that when they required powder, blankets, and other supplies, they needed only to raid the overland wagon routes and kill a few whites so that the U.S. government would offer another annuity treaty. Pope planned to do away with the annuity peace process.

He asked the chief of staff for complete military control and no civilian Indian agents in the Sioux territory. Once these conditions were granted and he had his peace program in place, Pope guaranteed tranquility and security on the northern plains, with only a small military force necessary to enforce that peace. Pope was never less than grand in his ambitions, whether the arena for those ambitions was war or peace. Unfortunately, on the northern prairies, just as on the Virginia battlefields, his reach proved to be greater than his grasp.[27]

13. The Last
Dakota Campaign

Sand Creek and the Powder River Expedition

In 1865 the Dakota War merged fully with the conflict that had broken out on the southern prairies in November 1864, often called the Cheyenne-Arapaho War although it involved the Kiowa, Comanche, and Teton Sioux as well. The merging conflicts on the northern and southern plains could be properly called a general Plains Indian War. From Dakota and Montana, through Wyoming, Nebraska, Kansas, and Colorado, to Texas and the Indian Territory, the prairies thundered with war in 1865. It was the most widespread conflict and involved the greatest number of combatants on either side of any of the Plains Indian wars.

Just as massacre in Minnesota begat war in Dakota, so too did a slaughter of the innocents set soldier and brave at saber and lance point in 1865. White retaliation stomped heavily on the heels of Indian depredation in a dance of death across the southern plains in the summer and early fall of 1864. Firefights flickered and several fair-sized operations were launched against the Plains tribes.

On November 25, 1864, the old mountain man and frontier legend, Kit Carson, fresh from his conquest of the Navaho, commanded a force of 335 soldiers and 72 Ute scouts that collided with up to 1,000 Kiowa, Comanche, and Southern Cheyenne at Adobe Walls in north Texas. The fire of Carson's two twelve-pounder mountain howitzers helped greatly in resisting the Indian attacks. Kit and his command lost two killed, three dead of wounds, and eighteen wounded, as well as one Ute scout slain, while claiming sixty hostiles killed or wounded.[1]

Just four days later, near Fort Lyon, Colorado, the American army got in a much harder blow, both to the Plains Indians and to national honor. Colonel John M. Chivington, a harsh man with an Old Testament thirst for vengeance, led his 700 scruffy volunteers and four mountain howitzers

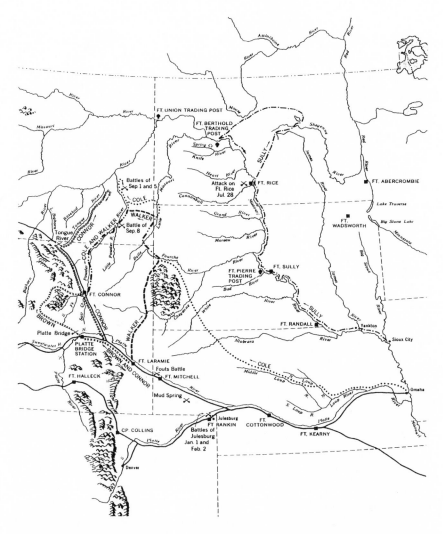

Operations in the northern plains, 1865. (From *Frontiersmen in Blue: The United States Army and the Indian, 1846–1865* **by Robert M. Utley. Courtesy of Robert M. Utley.)**

of the First and Third Colorado Cavalry regiments into a descent onto the Southern Cheyenne village of Chief Black Kettle at Sand Creek. The 100-lodge camp, inhabited by 500 men, women, and children, had been located at that site at the behest of the local army commander, who had promised the Cheyenne protection if they would gather peacefully there and cease any further participation in the raids that had harassed Colorado that summer and fall. The presence of a large American flag flying over the camp did not deter the charging Colorado cavalrymen, however. Black Kettle escaped (only to die four winters later when Custer emulated Chivington by rushing another sleeping Cheyenne camp on the banks of the Washita), but at least 163 of his fellow Cheyenne and Arapaho, 110 of them women and children, did not. The Colorado column rode back into Denver several days later, bearing and boasting of 100 Cheyenne scalps and escorting only five prisoners—two women and three children. Fourteen of the soldiers were killed or died of wounds at Sand Creek and thirty-nine were wounded, but many of the white casualties were inflicted by their own weapons as the undisciplined and, in many cases, drunken slaughterers were caught in their own crossfire.[2] The Sand Creek episode was the bloodiest atrocity committed by an American military unit in the republic's history; in fact, the record would stand more than one hundred years, until the My Lai Massacre in Vietnam in March 1968.

The incident at Sand Creek set the plains afire. Raiding parties struck in retaliation from Montana to north Texas in the first months of 1865. In Colorado alone more than fifty whites were killed by hostiles in January and February. The town of Julesburg was sacked and torched. A fifty-man cavalry unit was enticed out of Fort Rankin by Indian decoys on January 7 and led into an ambush hiding up to 1,000 warriors. Fourteen soldiers and four civilian volunteers were killed.[3]

The raids continued into the spring and summer and the two sides continued to thrust and parry as the U.S. Army prepared major converging campaigns to force the hostiles to a powwow. The biggest battle prior to the American offensive took place on July 26, 1865, at the Platte River Bridge, 136 miles west of Fort Laramie. When a military wagon train manned and escorted by twenty-five soldiers and teamsters came under attack by up to 2,000 warriors led by the Southern Cheyenne war chief, Roman Nose, a hopelessly inadequate relief force of twenty soldiers under Lieutenant Casper Collins was dispatched in a vain rescue attempt that could do little but add victims to the slaughter. Lieutenant Collins and twenty-eight soldiers and teamsters were killed, though the Indians paid a heavy price for their victory, losing as many as sixty killed and one hundred-thirty wounded.[4]

The campaign, of which Sully's 1865 expedition and the final act of the Dakota War was a part, got underway in July. While Sully marched again into the Dakota Territory, General Patrick Connor, who had won a major victory over the Shoshones at Bear River in January 1863 (killing, by his count, 224 hostiles at a cost of 21 killed and 46 wounded), commanded the Powder River Expedition, slashing with the sabers of three columns north and west into Wyoming and Montana. The right-hand column, 1,400 strong and led by Colonel Nelson Cole, marched out first from Omaha. Lt. Colonel

Samuel Walker commanded the center column of 700 trooping out from Fort Laramie. Also departing from Fort Laramie was the westernmost arm of the expedition, 500 infantrymen and cavalrymen, plus 179 Pawnee and Omaha Indian scouts, led directly by Connor.[5]

The mission of the Powder River Expedition was to find, fix, and finish off the Indian menace. All three columns found plenty of Indians, but fixing them in place in order to finish them off was an altogether more difficult endeavor. Only the left wing of the expedition managed to inflict any real punishment. The Pawnee scouts of Connor's vanguard surprised twenty-seven Cheyenne and gleefully carried their scalps back to camp as trophies of their triumph. The scouts also located an Arapaho village on the Tongue River and guided Connor with 125 soldiers and 90 Indian auxiliaries to a successful assault on the camp on August 29. The Arapaho fled the field, leaving thirty-five of their dead behind. Connor's command escaped with only seven men wounded.[6]

The other two columns were successful only in narrowly escaping total disaster. They encountered Indians in large numbers—as many as 1,000 braves at a time—in three serious battles on September 1, 5, and 8 and in numerous lesser skirmishes and harassments. But the hostiles fought as they always did—hit and run, strike and fade, refusing to stand toe-to-toe and fight it out to a decision. Cole and Walker recorded losses of thirteen killed, two missing, and five wounded in these battles. The losses among the Indians were a matter of dispute: Cole claimed a ridiculous toll of 200 to 500 braves killed or wounded, but Walker concluded more honestly, "I cannot say as we killed one."[7]

The human enemy presented problems enough for the Cole-Walker columns, but nature proved an even more formidable foe. Poorly planned and coordinated, the expedition required good weather and good fortune to have a realistic chance at success. Instead, the marching columns had only bad luck and worse weather. Scurvy swept the ranks. A searing drought weakened the expedition's horses and mules, and lowered rations because of resupply snafus made both man and beast more vulnerable to a sudden 180 degree turn in the weather that saw early northers blow in. Exhausted columns of men and mules, sweltering only days before, were suddenly shivering in icy winds. One thousand horses and mules died under the cold fire of nature's battalions.

For days the two columns wandered around lost, close to calamity. Finally, on September 24, scouts from Connor's column found the lost battalions and guided them to a rendezvous at Fort Connor, ending the Powder River Expedition in ignominy.[8]

The Last Sioux Raid into Minnesota

While Sully was gearing up for his final and most fruitless Dakota campaign in the spring of 1865, the Santees carried out their last raid on the Minnesota frontier. Compared to the cataclysm of August 1862, the attack was only a mild aftershock following a massive quake, but to the family on whom its fury fell it was all-consuming.

Led by Jack Campbell, a half-breed who nurtured his viciousness with liquor, a party of Santee renegades managed to elude the frontier guards and penetrate to the Jewett family farm near Mankato. All five members of the Jewett clan were killed, the last white noncombatant Minnesotans to die at the hands of native Minnesotans (although five U.S. soldiers were killed in the Chippewa uprising at Leech Lake thirty-three years later).[9]

Jack Campbell, drunken and straggling, was quickly rounded up by white pursuers and hung, but the other raiders escaped west into the Dakota Territory. They did not manage to avoid the white man's vengeance for long, however. It came in the form of their own kind, when the raiders stumbled onto a camp of eleven Santee scouts tracking the hostiles for the U.S. Army. Solomon Two Stars, the scouts' leader, recognized one of the raiders as the teenage son of his sister. His orders had been to take no prisoners, and he carried out his orders by personally gunning down his nephew. Fifteen of the sixteen hostiles were killed in the gunfight, while the scouts suffered not a scratch. The last raider was chased to near Fort Wadsworth (present-day Sisseton, South Dakota) and captured by soldiers. His ultimate fate is unrecorded.[10]

This last Santee raid had a broader significance than simply a final footnote in Minnesota history's most horrific chapter. For it changed the whole direction and intent of Sully's final Dakota expedition. Because the sixteen raiders were thought to have ridden out from the Devil's Lake area, part of Pope's grand strategy (that had Sully pushing west from the Missouri to erect a fort on the Powder River) was altered. There would be no grand pincer movement in concert with General Connor's Powder River Expedition. Instead, Sully would swing in a long loop through northern Dakota east of the Missouri to strike at empty air.

Both Sibley and Major General Samuel Curtis, the new commander of the Department of the Northwest, had added their voices, to which authority gave more volume, to those of the common citizens of Minnesota calling for Sully to redirect his expedition in order to eliminate the "hive of hostile Sioux" at Devil's Lake.[11] Pope had resisted the clamor initially, pointing out, with barely restrained fury, that eighteen companies of cavalry and four companies of infantry should have been more than enough to sanitize the Minnesota frontier if it had not been for a "want of vigilance" and "inefficiency (to call it no worse)" on the part of the guardians.[12]

Pope, now commanding the Division of the Missouri, considered the queasiness of his subordinates a sign of weakness. He was particularly disgusted with Sibley and his prediction of "a desolating war involving frontier settlements of Minnesota, Iowa, and Wisconsin in one common ruin."[13] Not having been a witness to the devastation of 1862 that Sibley had seen, Pope had by now, after a year or more of alarmist baying from Sibley, come to consider the victor of Wood Lake no more than the largest steer in the "stampedes" that swept Minnesota every spring and autumn. Writing to Grant on June 2, Pope proclaimed that Sibley's messages of mayhem "exhibit a panic which I hardly know how to deal with, except by asking you to send me an officer to command in Minnesota who is not subject to such uneasiness."[14]

Pope also objected to a march against Devil's Lake on the grounds that, even if the lake shore was lined with the tepees of hostile Sioux, little of lasting impact could be accomplished as long as the British in nearby Manitoba refused to allow pursuit across the border.

Those, both in and out of uniform, calling for a march on Devil's Lake finally had their way, however, when new intelligence added to the pressure of their fears to convince Pope to point Sully in a new direction. Scouts and friendly Indians reported to Pope from the upper Missouri that many of the recently hostile Teton Sioux had demonstrated a willingness to travel to Fort Rice to parley for peace with Sully. Seeing the possibility of forging peace by talking with the Tetons and tangling with the Santees, Pope gave in to the pleas of his subordinates in late May and authorized Sully to aim his column not at the Powder River but at Devil's Lake by way of Fort Rice.[15]

The Sully Campaign of 1865

Like Patrick Connor's campaign, Sully's 1865 expedition accomplished next to nothing, but unlike Connor's columns, Sully's soldiers accomplished their nothing while encountering no one, or at least no one who was overtly hostile.

Redirected and misdirected from the beginning, General Sully's expedition encountered little but frustration and failure to the end. The general's plan to commence his third march through Dakota by May 10 dissolved in the rains that turned the Iowa roads to muck and made the Missouri too fast and furious to navigate. The stockpiling of supplies for the campaign at his base in Sioux City was so slowed down because of the rainy weather that Sully's command managed only with difficulty to feed itself at its base, let alone undertake an offensive sortie into the prairies. Three boatloads of supplies intended for the expedition sank into the waters of the Missouri during the month of May. The column, composed of 840 Iowa, Minnesota, and Dakota cavalrymen, finally left Sioux City on June 7, with a long supply train manned by 200 teamsters carrying the expedition's arduously accumulated provisions in the cavalry's wake.[16]

With Sully's initial mission changed from waging war to talking peace, the column headed for Fort Rice, where 3,000 lodges full of Lakotas were said to be en route. But forcing the Plains tribesmen into serious diplomacy was often as difficult as coercing them into decisive battle, and such was the case for Sully in 1865. It was not clear which chiefs or which tribes he was supposed to talk to and what form of peace he was supposed to offer. There were two approaches to peace talks, steering Sully in somewhat contradictory diplomatic directions: the congressionally mandated method as represented by Dakota Governor Newton Edmunds involved bribing recalcitrant warriors with presents and annuities; General Pope's path toward peace, on the other hand, was a more forceful and less forgiving arrangement, giving the Indians to understand that if they kept the peace all would be well, but if they broke it, there would be no more gifts and glitter to bribe them back into proper behavior. The only favor the army was willing to offer in that case would be hard-fisted retaliation.

This straightforward and manly formula was considerably undermined by the reality of the army's relatively poor record in hunting down and killing hostiles, so the intimidation implicit in such agreements was largely absent. Pope's method also ignored the fact that the army was no more successful at protecting peaceful tribesmen from the greed and aggression of white civilians than it was at reining in the raiding instincts of young Indian braves.

Edmunds had been empowered by an act of Congress to deal with the Sioux, but Pope circumvented his authority by declaring that the Dakota Sioux were openly hostile and thus a matter to be dealt with by the military. Though Edmunds tried to influence the projected tenor of Sully's peace proposals, it was Pope's prescription for peace that primarily guided Sully as he marched toward Fort Rice.[17]

Pope's peace formula never advanced beyond the realm of the theoretical however, because of events at Fort Rice, both prior to and subsequent to Sully's arrival.

The commander at Fort Rice was Colonel Charles Dimon, the twenty-three-year-old firebrand whose career had been nurtured by Massachusetts General Benjamin F. Butler. Dimon was as energetic and self-confident as he was youthful, and it was his firm discipline and total confidence in his own infallibility that largely saw the Fort Rice garrison through an abysmal winter. His First U.S. Volunteers was made up of "galvanized Yankees," the Confederate POWs recruited to serve under federal officers on the Great

Plains. Scurvy and diarrhea had killed ten percent of the regiment during the winter months, and 206 of the ranks were on sick call in April. Harsh weather and roving Indians attacking mail carriers had all but isolated the command. But Dimon had held his garrison together. His winter stalwartness, however, blossomed into spring stubbornness in his dealings with the Sioux.[18]

With the exception of some friendly Yanktonais camped near the fort, Dimon was inclined to look on all Indians as hostile and to act toward them accordingly. Sighting a group of twenty Indians on the east side of the Missouri on March 30, Dimon dispatched a squad to pursue them. Two of the group sought refuge in the Yanktonai camp, but old Chief Two Bears betrayed them to Dimon in order to remain in the excitable colonel's favor. The captives were Santees who declared no hostile intention, but to Dimon all Santees were "malignantly hostile."[19] Confirmation of this attitude seemed to come on April 12 when 200 Santee and Yanktonai warriors galloped down on a guard patrol grazing the garrison's herd outside the fort, killed two soldiers, and absconded with sixty head of stock. That evening, in retaliation, Dimon stood the new Santee prisoners before a firing squad. The herd guard was struck again on April 26 and another major firefight flared up on June 2. Dimon's dealings with the Indians through a belligerent spring made Fort Rice a symbol of conflict and a most unlikely site for peace parleying for the Lakota as Sully approached the fort on July 13.[20]

The general's hopes for a great peace conclave were shattered when he reached the east bank of the Missouri across from Fort Rice to discover, not the 3,000 Lakota lodges he had anticipated, but less than one-tenth that number. Most of the Lakota were camped on the Knife River, fifty miles southwest of Fort Berthold, and, according to the few Indians at Fort Rice, they were wracked by bitter quarrels over the issue of peace or war. Many groups were reportedly inclined toward joining the peace palaver, but were "deathly afraid" of approaching Fort Rice and its impetuous commander.[21]

That fear was confirmed for Sully on the day of his arrival. A band of nervous and suspicious Blackfeet and Hunkpapas moving toward the fort scattered like startled quail when Colonel Dimon fired his cannon in salute to Sully, who was aboard a boat carrying him across the river to the fort. The same scene of stampede was repeated a few nights later, and more Indians took flight when rumors transformed a ration boat crossing the river into a Trojan Horse concealing soldiers intent on killing Lakota. The few chiefs remaining at Fort Rice easily convinced Sully after these incidents that a peace conference was not possible in Dimon's domain. The general agreed with the chiefs to relocate the talks to Fort Berthold, and on July 21 he resumed his march toward Devil's Lake.[22]

Sully assigned most of the blame for the week of failure and disappointment at Fort Rice to its commander. Though he initially admired Dimon's "pluck," the general quickly consigned that pluck to rashness and advised Pope that Dimon was cast too much in the mold of his over-zealous mentor, Ben Butler, to deal with Indians perched on the precipice of hostility. An "older and cooler head" was required to command a fort that had become a symbol of white intransigence to the Indians. Sully found such a commander in Lt. Colonel John Pattee of the Seventh Iowa Cavalry, an unassuming frontiersman completely in contrast to the martinet posturing of his predecessor. Dimon was sent packing on an "important mission" to the nation's capital.[23]

Sully's expectations were minimal as he pushed his column along a three-week route to Devil's Lake and back to the Missouri. He expected no repeat of Whitestone Hill or Killdeer Mountain. The Indians of the northern Dakota Territory were not about to be burned a third time by resisting or being surprised by a bulky body of U.S. regiments. At the most, the general hoped his expedition would be a convincing show of force, but he encountered no one to show his force to. It was an utterly fruitless exercise. The closest Sully came to encountering Indians were Red River half-breeds who confirmed what he expected: that those hostile Santees, who had not joined their brother Tetons and Yanktonais to the south and west, had fled north into the sanctuary of Canada. The column, after its long northeast loop, regained the Missouri opposite Fort Berthold on August 8, having accomplished only a reconnaissance mission of the Devil's Lake area in search of a suitable site for a military post that was to serve as a Dakota barrier to protect the Minnesota frontiersmen still traumatized by the events of 1862. That post was finally erected as Fort Totten in 1867, long after any lingering Indian threat to the white population of Minnesota had passed.[24]

While Sully's march to Devil's Lake had brought about only blisters and boredom, the fort they had left in their rear continued to serve as a magnet for hostilities. The general's message had reached the Lakota camps on the Knife River. The choice the runners delivered to the assembled warriors—negotiations at Fort Berthold for those who desired peace and war for the rest—had stirred up a storm. Peace seemed to be winning the day before Sitting Bull turned the tide of opinion toward war with an artful blend of rhetoric and deception. Slashing himself with a knife, the young chief, whose fame and influence was soon to eclipse all others, went from band to band claiming that his wounds had been incurred at infamous Fort Rice. He convinced many that he was among the lucky survivors to escape a massacre by the troops of Fort Rice of all those who came to the fort to offer the hand of peace to the treacherous white soldiers. Crying for vengeance, Sitting Bull attracted at least 350 warriors (other accounts claim up to 500) to his call for action and led them against Fort Rice.[25]

The situation now had the makings of that rarest of western frontier actions—an all-out assault by hostile Indians on a U.S. Army fort. Though a staple of Hollywood Westerns, the spectacle of an Indian attack on a palisade manned by soldiers was an event more common in the previous century during the Indian wars of the east and was more likely to involve red-coated musketmen than the blue uniforms of the new nation. Major Indian assaults on U.S. Army posts occurred only at Fort Defiance in 1861 during the Navajo Wars and at Fort Ridgely in 1862. There were other armed demonstrations and long-range skirmishes against military posts, but generally the Indians of the west, who rarely challenged the firepower of regimental-size army columns in the open in a set-piece battle, were not about to take on the firepower of forts with their cannons and entrenchments. Even the sieges of Fort Phil Kearny and Fort C. F. Smith during the Red Cloud War of 1866–68 were conducted as blockades and long–range skirmishes with no full-scale frontal assaults undertaken against the besieged garrisons.

Sitting Bull's war party seemed strong enough and stirred up enough to launch just such a unique assault, however. But just as the Lakota refused the whites the opportunity to repeat Whitestone Hill or Killdeer Mountain, the new American commander at Fort Rice was determined not to give the Indians a chance to reverse the results of their attack on Fort Ridgely.

Lt. Colonel John Pattee may have lacked the spit-and-polish veneer of Colonel Dimon as well as his appetite for aggressive action against the Sioux, but he did possess the frontier solder's instincts on the right way to fight Indians. Rather than wait for the hostiles to storm the fort or pin his garrison down by surrounding and blockading the post, Pattee, as soon as he spotted the Sioux gathering on the overlooking hills, deployed his troops—four companies of the First Volunteers, two companies of the Fourth Volunteers, and one company of the Sixth Iowa—outside the fort in a long skirmish line that curled around on the north, west, and south sides of the stockade.[26]

Sitting Bull's warriors closed on horseback to bow-and-arrow range of the blue line to send a rain of arrows down on the soldiers, who responded with volleys of musketry. Then Pattee's howitzers went into action, and the Lakota rapidly lost their enthusiasm for direct assault and withdrew. For three hours the Sioux kept up a long-distance duel with the outnumbered but certainly not outgunned soldiers. Pattee, certain that his superior firepower would keep the hostiles at bay, firmly held his line and kept in check his more impulsive subordinates who wanted to accept the Indians' blandishments and rush into an offensive action that might have resulted in either great victory and glory or in the same kind of ambush and massacre that befell the command of Captain Fetterman the following year.

Pattee was satisfied with the defensive victory he attained as the discouraged Sioux finally melted away. Whether Dimon would have been willing to settle for less than a glorious charge is debatable. One soldier was killed and four wounded, one of whom later died, in the defense of Fort Rice. Sioux losses are unknown but were undoubtedly heavier.[27]

Ironically, the war chief who had instigated and initiated the fight at Fort Rice proved, according to the testimony two months later of Hunkpapa participants in the battle, to have little stomach for sustained combat that day. Streaked with scarlet warpaint and wearing little but a long feathered warbonnet, Sitting Bull had thrown the fight's first punch on the north side of the fort by barreling down on two horses owned by the post trader and grazing in the river bottoms. He and six other warriors easily rounded up the pair of mounts, but then as Pattee's troopers deployed from the fort to meet the assault, Sitting Bull and another Hunkpapa led the captured stock away from the action and took no further part in the battle. After the assault on Fort Rice had failed, the Hunkpapas and Blackfeet, who had endured probably grievous losses to Pattee's cannonballs, took out their frustrations on the less-than-sterling Sitting Bull by flailing him with horsehide whips and by butchering the two horses that had seemingly been enough to satisfy his theatrically displayed thirst for vengeance. This was not to be the last time that Sitting Bull's warrior reputation would be impugned. Although his martial career was resplendent with feats of courage and boldness, it was also marred by accusations of inaction and even cowardice—not the least of which was his conduct at the Little Bighorn.[28]

The long-range exchange at Fort Rice on July 28 settled the issue for Sully's 1865 expedition. There would be no great battlefield victory, nor would there be a meaningful peace conference. The suspicious tribes along the Knife were all but certain now that Sully, if he had not been inclined toward treachery before, would now in the heat of his rage over the attack on Fort Rice be hell-bent on retaliation. Those Indians once inclined to peace now looked upon a meeting with Sully at Fort Berthold as an invitation to disaster. The general fully realized the final failure of his mission, commenting that "they are convinced that it is only a trap I have set to capture and slay them."[29]

Most of the Lakota camps withdrew to the Little Missouri River. Early the next month braves from those same camps joined the war parties harassing the columns of the Powder River Expedition.

Sully had been undecided about his next move. A thrust west of the Missouri, which, given the Indians' evasive tactics thus far, would probably be fruitless, would only add to his image of impotence and encourage those Lakota advocating continued conflict. When he heard that the Sioux had trickled away to the west, the general decided that his expedition could no longer serve a useful purpose in northern Dakota, and he directed his tired command back down the Missouri. The victories of 1863 and 1864 now seemed like distant and largely hollow memories.[30]

Eventually, a makeshift and very provisional peace was established in 1865, but it was to be a peace based much more on the Indian Bureau's concept of annuities and moderation than on Pope's and the military's concept of a peace enforced by coercion and conquest. The uneventful results of Sully's expedition and the bloody results of Connor's Powder River expedition convinced Pope that costly far-flung military efforts were bound to fail and might even cost him his job. The Indian Bureau also backed away somewhat from its reluctance to let the army play any role whatsoever in the peace process and agreed to at least allow generals to talk peace, along with civilian commissioners, to the warring tribes.

Thus the intermingled wars on the Great Plains were brought to a conclusion in the fall of 1865, pretty much along the lines of goods exchanged for promises of good behavior that Pope had so adamantly resisted before his grand strategy of 1865 had turned to dust and despair. The southern tribes, aroused to fury by the Sand Creek Massacre, agreed to the terms of the Treaty of the Little Arkansas in October. The northern Plains tribes, theoretically at least, ended their conflict that had started with the massacre in Minnesota by treaty at Fort Sully in the same month.[31]

Governor Edmunds, struggling since spring and against Pope's protests to construct a peace of reconciliation, had put together a commission consisting of himself, Superintendent of Indian Affairs Edward B. Taylor, two other civilians, and generals Samuel Curtis and Henry Sibley. They met with minor chiefs who had always been inclined toward peace. Nine separate treaties were signed with representatives from the Miniconjou, Lower Brule, Two Kettle, Blackfeet, Sans Arc, Hunkpapa, Oglala, and Upper and Lower Yanktonai. In exchange for annuity payments, the Indian signatories agreed to end their attacks on emigrant trails.[32]

The peace achieved at Fort Sully was, of course, only a pause in the hostilities between Indians and whites. Only one chief of any prominence, an elderly Miniconjou named Lone Horn, had signed his name to the Fort Sully concords.[33] Most of the real leaders of the tribes camped along the Little Missouri and the Powder rivers disdained to take any part in the peace process. The peace was hardly worth the paper it was written on, but the white commissioners deceived either themselves or, more likely, their superiors in Washington into believing that it was a first step toward a true accord. All that would be required, in their rosy view, was to await spring when the weather would permit the nonsignatory chiefs the opportunity to travel in from their winter refuges to affix their marks to the treaty papers. But their view of the temper of the absent tribes and tribal leaders proved as unrealistic as the bogus treaties they had signed.

Results of the 1865 Campaigns

The failure of Sully's 1865 Dakota expedition was, of course, just part of the larger failure of the comprehensive campaign that was to have swept the plains clean of hostile tribesmen in that first post–Civil War summer. Altogether, some 6,000 American soldiers had plodded across the plains in the summer of 1865 and had accomplished the execution of no more than 100 Indians. Another 4,000 Civil War veterans had been brought west for defensive duties. Furious at being reassigned to fight Indians and almost mutinous in their demands for immediate discharges, they deserted in droves. The months of planning, the months of marching, and the logistical logjams encountered and disentangled had resulted in fewer dead hostiles than the number accounted for by defensive troops guarding the trails and the towns during the same period.[34]

In raw numbers of dead braves, Sully could boast the most success in offensive operations across the plains from 1863–65. He spoke to the heart of the essential failure of massed conventional columns chasing an increasingly more ephemeral enemy when he proposed that a scalp bounty "would be cheaper and more effective than sending large bodies of troops, who can never be successful in hunting small bodies of Indians in their broken, mountainous country."[35]

The cost of the 1865 campaigns in the Powder River country and along the Missouri exceeded twenty million dollars,[36] but with the exception of Connor's limited victory on the Tongue, the hostiles had refused to be cornered and brought to decisive battle. They had evaded, eluded, and exasperated the heavy blue columns, and had fought only on their own terms. The 1865 expeditions had demonstrated in general that the massive scale of warfare practiced in the east by the Civil War combatants was not transferrable to the prairies.

Civil War generals such as Pope and Grenville M. Dodge (the commander of the Department of the Missouri) had dispatched not companies and battalions, but regiments and brigades against their prairie foes just as they had against the defenders of the Confederacy. The rare but glamorous examples of set-piece battles at Whitestone Hill, Killdeer Mountain, and Adobe Walls had convinced them that the Indians could be engaged and defeated in heavy, sustained combat, and they ignored the fact that those battles were preceded and succeeded by months of fruitless, uneventful campaigning that made the contests seem like solitary mountains rising abruptly from an endless plain.

In convincing themselves that Whitestone Hill and Killdeer Mountain—not the quick raid, the sudden ambush, the unexpected arrow in the sentinel's back—represented the future of Plains warfare, Pope and his kind failed to understand that the open battle that they all yearned so much for was the exception that was to become even more infrequent. Heavy columns had enjoyed what success they had won not because of the inherent superiority of the strategy, but due to the carelessness and limited experience of the Plains tribes in engaging in serious warfare with an aggressive and better armed opponent. As the 1865 operations demonstrated, the Indians had learned the lessons of Whitestone Hill and Killdeer Mountain well. They understood that the best defense against the bloated blue columns was no defense at all, but avoidance.

Where no strategic points, fortresses, or cities existed to be taken, the only target for the invading regiments had to be the nomadic enemy himself. All those nomads needed to do to avoid destruction, however, was to remain true to their way of life and warfare and take advantage of the vast reaches of a still largely unexplored countryside to disappear into. Once it became clear to the Plains hostiles that they could not contend with large numbers of American soldiers in open battle, they realized they could easily outdistance the too big and too slow pursuers, who were paralyzed by their numbers, their lack of mobility, and their dependence on a logistical system operating in an area still largely bereft of a network of supporting forts and posts.

It was to be many years before the U.S. Army came close to understanding that Indian warfare required small, fast-moving units operating from a web of frontier forts. In 1865, regardless of the sorrowful results of that summer's operations and Sully's insightful, if hard-hearted, call for a scalp bounty in place of ponderous brigades, the army was not ready for that kind of warfare. In fact, the temptation to settle the conflicts in one glorious large-scale offensive never entirely left the imagination or the planning of American frontier commanders. This remained true in spite of the fact that the post–Civil War army, shrunken in size and in resources, was never able to again mount such operations on the scale of the Plains campaigns of 1863–65.

14. The Ride
of Sam Brown

Although Sitting Bull's Hunkpapas harried Forts Buford and Stevenson on the upper Missouri during Red Cloud's war against the forts along the Bozeman Trail from 1866 to 1868, the Dakota Territory east of the Missouri remained little troubled by Indian violence after Sully's final expedition in 1865. There were alarms and incidents but no real conflict and no serious confrontation between the races as the decade waned. The Indian wars, to the overwhelming relief of the white settlers, had passed eastern Dakota by.

The old terrors and the dreaded dreams, however, lingered on. As long as there were hostiles active on the western side of the Missouri, the fears of further outbreak, the apprehension that the supposedly passive reservation Indians nearby might be incited by red recalcitrants into one last surge of savagery, remained. Rumors of raiders and the ghastly gossip of fresh atrocities swirled across the Dakota prairie like wind-borne telegrams. Almost always those rumors wilted, but a ground richly sewn with the scarlet seeds of August 1862 would continue for years to sprout new saplings of warning and near panic.

Among the more famous of the alarms to disturb the serenity of eastern Dakota was the report of an approaching Sioux war party that prompted the famous ride of Sam Brown. Whipping his mount into a full gallop, the twenty-one-year-old half-breed rode west on the night of April 15–16, 1866, from Fort Wadsworth in present-day northeastern South Dakota to spread the alarm all the way to the Elm Creek scout station in what is now Brown County. Upon realizing that the report of descending red demons was but another of a long line of frontier fantasies, Brown saddled a fresh mount and headed back east, determined to vindicate himself by preventing the panic from being relayed further from Fort Wadsworth to Fort Abercrombie on the Minnesota border.

As he galloped east, a freezing rain pelted Sam Brown. The sleet soon turned into a freak spring blizzard, but Brown rode on. Finally reaching

Fort Wadsworth with his revised report, Brown collapsed from his horse in utter exhaustion, having ridden 150 miles in fifteen agonizing hours. His legs and back had been so abused by the ordeal that paralysis set in, and Sam Brown, who lived to the age of eighty, never walked again. The false alarm that cost the young mixed-blood his mobility is still celebrated in northeastern South Dakota by an annual "Sam Brown Day."[1]

Results of the Campaigns of 1863–65

Were the results of campaigns led by Sibley and Sully in the Dakotas, which, by the relative terms of Indian warfare on the Great Plains, were mounted on a massive scale, worth the effort? Can the campaigns be called a victory in a conventional or any other sense? Did the U.S. Army win the Dakota War?

The answers depend upon the terms of the objective. Because so many men in high places, both in the army and in civilian society, expressed so many varying goals for the Dakota campaigns, the yardstick of success must be laid alongside several different dimensions. There were those who saw the Sibley/Sully expeditions in purely punitive terms. Others hoped that the outcome of the campaigns would be a permanent liberation of the Minnesota frontier from the terror of further Indian raids and a concomitant forcing of all Dakota Indians across the barrier of the Missouri River. Still other authorities envisioned Sibley and Sully marching on campaigns of conquest that would convince the Sioux that resistance against the U.S. Army was hopeless and force them to accept a lasting peace by recognizing the hegemony of the white race.

For those who looked on Sibley's and Sully's men primarily as agents of vengeance, the results of the campaigns (at least those of 1863 and 1864) must have been very gratifying. If revenge or punishment in warfare is calculated by the body count, then the expeditions of 1863 and 1864 were surely among the most successful in the history of Indian warfare in the American West. If 300 warriors really did die at Whitestone Hill, the battle site represented the greatest killing ground of red warriors west of the Mississippi, and Killdeer Mountain was exceeded in its probable toll of Indian combatants by only few battles. Taking the highest figures claimed by army commanders, as many as 700 Sioux soldiers died in the major battles and skirmishes of the 1863–1865 campaigns. Even if only half as many Sioux warriors died, it would still represent a significant punishment for the Sioux nation, exceeding both the Santee toll in the Minnesota Uprising and the Indian losses in the Great Sioux War of 1876–77, as well as, in all likelihood, the Native American toll in the Red Cloud War of 1866–68. If an eye-for-an-eye had not been strictly exacted for the white death toll of 800 in the Minnesota massacre of 1862, vengeance had clearly been served by the executions in the Dakota Territory.

The Santees, who suffered the majority of the battle deaths in 1863–65 and who had always been significantly smaller in numbers than the Tetons, never fully recovered from their casualties incurred at Whitestone Hill and Killdeer Mountain. Though Santees would continue to take part in the Sioux Wars of the next dozen years and would be present at the annihilations of Fetterman's and Custer's commands, they always represented an insignificant segment of the Sioux nation at war.[2]

The sense of victory based on the number of casualties was heightened by the disparity between the number of deaths suffered in combat by the U.S. Army compared to its Dakota enemies. Unlike many of its conflicts with the Sioux, particularly the Red Cloud War and the Great Sioux War, in which more soldiers than warriors fell in battle, the Dakota campaigns provided the army with one of its best kill ratios in all of its many Indian wars.

Of the 6,000 or so soldiers who had taken part in the three summers of campaigning across the Dakota Territory, as well as the hundreds who had garrisoned the string of military posts scattered through the territory or had escorted civilian wagon trains across the prairie, only about fifty had died in battles with the Sioux. No accurate records were kept of the number who died in garrisons or along the campaign trail from disease, accident, or other misfortune, but the total could have been twice the number of combat deaths. Close to half of the soldiers killed in action fell in a single battle—as many as twenty-two died at Whitestone Hill. (Almost half of the Indian dead of the Dakota War died on the slopes and in the ravines of Whitestone Hill.) Accepting even the lowest figure for Indian battle deaths that is plausible, about 350, would still give the U.S. Army a kill ratio of seven to one.

In comparison, in the Sioux War of 1876–77 the army lost (including civilian volunteers and Indian scouts enrolled in its ranks) over 300 killed in action, while killing probably no more than 150 to 200 Sioux and Cheyenne.[3]

Of course, in Indian warfare the toll of combatants was not always, in fact not often, the main source of statistics for violent deaths for both sides. Massacre of the unarmed and the helpless was as often the norm as battle between armed combatants—witness the 700 Minnesotans butchered in the 1862 uprising and the 200 Cheyenne slaughtered at Sand Creek two years later. But the Dakota War featured comparatively little of the atrocity so common in the history of the frontier wars. This is partially due to the general lack of noncombatant targets for the Indians—there were still relatively few white settlers in the Dakota Territory in the early 1860s. There was only one brief resurgence of significant Indian raiding on Minnesota settlements in 1863, and the main emigrant wagon trails passed further south through Nebraska. Surely no more than fifty to sixty white civilians were killed by the Sioux in the Dakotas and Minnesota between 1863 and 1865. More than one-third of the white noncombatant deaths came in a single incident, the attack in 1863 on the Mackinaw boat in the Missouri River.

Though the Indians complained of the heavy toll of their women and children at Whitestone Hill and Killdeer Mountain, the evidence does not support such claims. Sibley and particularly Sully were professional soldiers who kept a tight rein on their men and did not countenance war on innocents. In addition to their natural inclination to wage war according to the rules, the Dakota War generals had the added restraint of General Pope, and the Indian Bureau looking over their shoulders to be certain that operations were conducted against warriors and not against women and children. The Indian Bureau was, of course, more in favor of negotiations than punishment to begin with, and Pope, who insisted on hard blows before handouts, was not about to let his commanders in the field give the bureau an excuse in the form of butchered bodies of native women and children to shut down the army's retaliatory efforts and take the easy and ultimately empty route to peace through bribes and blandishments.

Sibley's forces included many civilian volunteers and militia forces from Minnesota who might have been tempted to kill any Sioux regardless of gender or age in revenge for Minnesota's terrible summer of 1862. Luckily, Sibley's brigade did not encounter Sioux noncombatants in any significant number in their three battles in the summer of 1863. Sully's forces, drawn from more veteran volunteer units of the U.S. Army and including fewer men who had witnessed the devastation in Minnesota, ran into large numbers of Sioux women and children at Whitestone Hill and Killdeer Mountain. Although a small number of unarmed Indians were killed in the confusion and crossfire at Whitestone Hill and a few more died at Killdeer Mountain, the Sioux warriors, at great cost, did a good job of placing their bodies between the soldiers' guns and their young, weak, and female. Sully's soldiers also made a concerted effort at directing their fire at the armed enemy and not at their dependents. If 300 Sioux died at Whitestone Hill, it is unlikely that more than fifty were women and children. Certainly, a considerably smaller percentage of the 150 Indian dead at Killdeer Mountain were noncombatants.

For those who defined victory as the lifting of the physical and psychological terror of the Sioux raiders from the Minnesota frontier, the Dakota campaigns also came close to fulfilling that mission. The very last pinprick raids against Minnesota settlers came in the spring of 1865. Never again would the lakes, prairies, and forests of the northern state be visited by the hatred and horror brought by Sioux warriors. The state that had endured the worst Indian massacre of any area west of the Mississippi would be only a thankful spectator as the conflict between natives and white Americans moved west across the prairies and mountains (although, ironically, Minnesota was to be the site of the last organized Indian resistance in the nineteenth century when Chippewas in the Leech Lake area briefly rebelled in 1898).[4]

Sibley's and Sully's victories did effectively create a buffer zone from eastern Dakota to the banks of the Missouri. Combined with the chain of forts erected along or near the river, the Dakota campaigns not only ended the Indian menace to Minnesota but, with minor exceptions, terminated all hostile Indian activities east of the Missouri River. Those Indians remaining in eastern Dakota remained peaceful and reconciled themselves to the dominance of the white race.

Thus, in the more limited visions of victory, the march of the U.S. Army into the Dakota Territory in 1863–65 achieved its aims.

In the grander scope of things, however, the fullest measure of triumph was not realized. Though most of the Santee and Yanktonai Sioux were convinced by the losses of Whitestone Hill and Killdeer Mountain to permanently give up the warpath, the far greater Teton wing of the Lakota-Dakota nation was far from subdued. The white invasions of Dakota seemed to the Indians to have been directed against any and all Sioux, not just against the Santees guilty of the Minnesota atrocities. The Sibley-Sully campaigns thus served to incite the Teton tribes to enter into a long-term and almost implacable resistance to the American army that ended only on the snowy field of Wounded Knee in December 1890.

Epilogue

Though the Santees were indeed stung into relative quiescence by the Dakota campaigns and were never again to present a serious challenge to the settlement of the Great Plains, the warrior spirit and war-making powers of the Teton branch of the Sioux nation were far from broken. It would be twelve more years before that spirit and those powers were snapped and thirteen years beyond that before the final flickers of Lakota resistance to the inevitable were stamped out.

The first conflict between the Teton Sioux and the U.S. government following the Civil War, the Red Cloud War of 1866–68, resulted in that rarest of events, an outright Indian victory over the U.S. Army. Led by the Oglala war chief Red Cloud, the Teton, Northern Cheyenne, and Arapaho reacted to the erection of a chain of forts along the Bozeman Trail, which ran through northern Wyoming and eastern Montana to the gold fields around Virginia City in western Montana, by blockading the army posts of forts Reno, C. F. Smith, and Phil Kearny. On December 21, 1866, Captain William J. Fetterman rode out of Fort Phil Kearny with the eighty men with whom he had boasted he could "ride through the whole Sioux nation" and instead rode only a short distance into disaster. Fetterman and his entire command were annihilated in the second deadliest battle ever fought by the U.S. Army in the Indian Wars of the West. Several months later, U.S. soldiers fared much better when the repeating rifles of a wood-cutting detail inflicted serious losses on the Sioux and Cheyenne in the Wagon Box Fight of August 2, 1867.

In the end, however, the U.S. Army, for the first and only time in the history of its 130-year conflict with the American Indians, openly acknowledged defeat by evacuating the forts along the Bozeman Trail and recognizing all of the Dakota Territory west of the Missouri River as the Great Sioux Reservation in accordance with the terms of the April and November 1868 Treaties of Fort Laramie. Red Cloud had won his war, but that victory was only a reprieve.[1]

A probing expedition by Colonel Custer's Seventh Cavalry into the

Paha Sapa (Black Hills) led to an invasion of gold prospectors digging into the sacred soil of the Indians and brought on the most famous confrontation in American history between red and white warriors. Pressure by U.S. agents upon the Lakota to sell their spiritual center brought on resistance and wholesale flight from the Great Sioux Reservation in South Dakota to join the recalcitrants in Wyoming and Montana, led by Sitting Bull and Crazy Horse, who had never accepted reservation life. When the thousands of tribesmen roaming the hunting grounds between the Yellowstone and the Powder rivers ignored a government ultimatum to return to the reservation by January 31, 1876, the U.S. Army launched a winter campaign on March 6, 1876, to enforce that order.

"Grey Eagle" Crook marched north toward the Powder River country, but his vanguard under Colonel John Reynolds was repulsed in bitter fighting and even more bitter weather at the Powder River on March 17 and the winter campaign ended in failure.

The white offensive in Montana was renewed in June 1876 with a three-pronged attack against the Lakota and Cheyenne. Crook, once again marching from the south, was once again checked, this time on Rosebud Creek on June 17. Eight days later, in arguably the most famous battle in American history (with the possible exception of Gettysburg), the vanguard of General Alfred Terry's column—Colonel Custer's Seventh Cavalry—was overwhelmed on the Little Bighorn, losing 268 killed or died of wounds (somewhat less than the highest estimate of Sioux believed killed in the Battle of Whitestone Hill).[2]

While the greatest Indian victory of all occurred in the eastern wars— when Little Turtle's native legions destroyed General Arthur St. Clair's army on the banks of the Wabash on November 4, 1791, killing 632 American soldiers[3]—the greatest victory of the western Indian tribes brought only more U.S. Army columns and renewed invasion of the Sioux territory in the fall and winter of 1876/77. Harried constantly, out of ammunition and hope, the hostile bands surrendered one by one, with Crazy Horse capitulating in May 1877 (only to be killed in September of that year while resisting arrest) and Sitting Bull fleeing to the protection of the redcoats in Canada, where he remained until July 1881.

The Ghost Dance movement, which spread across the West from the mind of Paiute medicine man Wovoka in the late 1880s, culminated in the killing of Sitting Bull at Standing Rock and the destruction of Big Foot's Miniconjou Sioux band at Wounded Knee on December 29, 1890, by the Seventh Cavalry, seeking and gaining revenge for its defeat in the Centennial Year. The last Sioux War was also the last real Indian war of the nineteenth century. The Sioux tradition of resistance was renewed in the next century when the Lakota nation supplied the site—the Pine Ridge Reservation and

Wounded Knee—and many of the fighters of the American Indian Movement's armed militancy of the early 1970s.

Though the Sioux fought three more wars against the U.S. Army between 1866 and 1890, in many ways the Minnesota Uprising and the Dakota campaigns were the greatest of the Sioux-U.S. conflicts. Certainly never again did the Sioux slay white civilians in such prodigious numbers as in the Santee explosion in Minnesota in 1862. And never again, not even in the army expedition against the Lakotas in Montana in the 1876–77 war, did so many American soldiers carry out such massive military offensives against the Sioux as did the columns of generals Sully, Sibley, and Connor for three straight years from 1863 to 1865. And, finally, never again did the U.S. Army win such overwhelming victories over the Dakota nation as the two triumphs gained, not by Custer or Crook or Miles, but by General Alfred Sully at Whitestone Hill and Killdeer Mountain.

Appendix A:
Non-hostile Fatalities

A conspicuous omission in the deadly statistics of the frontier conflicts between the races is the number of deaths suffered by either side due to disease or other noncombat causes. Men, women, and children, armed and unarmed, military and civilian, on opposing sides of the fault line of violence died from musket ball and rifle shell, from cannonball and howitzer shell, from saber and tomahawk, from lance and arrow. But most of all, in numbers far larger they died from microbes and viruses, from bacteria and cold and hunger, from sun and storm, from wind and water, from multi-legged, multifanged creatures as small as a scorpion and as big as a bear.

The American West was rich with potentially fatal dangers quite apart from the armed quarrels between red and white men. The concentration of relatively large numbers of military personnel in forts or on the march in punitive expeditions heightened the incidence and spread of contagious diseases common to the region and to the era and gave accident and misfortune more opportunities to plunder mortal flesh. The Indians also suffered from hunger caused by the soldiers' slaying and scattering of the buffalo herds and other game and from exposure to rain and cold after the blue columns had destroyed their camps.

War has always exacted a heavy toll outside combat. Even in our own century more American Doughboys died from the Spanish Flu than from German shot and shell in the trenches of World War I's Western Front. More than one out of every six servicemen whose names are engraved in the granite of the Vietnam Veterans Memorial died from noncombat causes.

The proportion of non-hostile deaths to deaths from hostile causes was even larger in the nineteenth century. Nearly two-thirds of the more than 600,000 soldiers in blue and gray who died during the Civil War were victims of disease, accident, and other causes outside combat. Only 1,733 American servicemen died in battle in the 1846–48 war with Mexico, but more than 11,000 expired because of disease.[1] The Indian Wars were no different, although because fewer military personnel were concentrated in large units at one place, the possibilities of highly communicable diseases sweeping the ranks were lessened. Still, there is no doubt that sunstroke and malaria, snakebites and dysentery, falls from horses and pneumonia, suicide and sepsis, as well as other causes not related to combat, took more lives among soldiers and tribesmen than did battle.

Calculating the number of those who died from causes other than battle, however, is extremely difficult for any Indian campaign. Summaries and final statistics common to other American wars, in which non-battle deaths were counted as closely as combat fatalities, were generally lacking in the Indian wars because the campaigns against the Native Americans were limited and regional, involving only specific units for a limited time while the rest of the army remained at a peacetime standing. Thus, casualties, other than those that could be directly attributable to the arms of hostile tribesmen, were usually ignored by authorities on the scene and by later historians. Very rarely in the histories of the Indian wars are there records of disease deaths—the 1835–42 Seminole War is a conspicuous exception, with 1,500 U.S. servicemen recorded as fatal casualties of the war, only 328 of them combat deaths.[2] To count the noncombat deaths of any particular Indian war, the researcher must usually despair of finding summaries and must laboriously search the records for the mortalities among each column and expedition sent into hostile territory and among the garrisons of each of the military posts playing a direct or supporting role in the campaign.

The Dakota War is no exception to this nearly impossible task of ascertaining noncombat deaths. Counting combat casualties is relatively easy for the Dakota War. One just adds up the figures from the official records and accounts of the battles and skirmishes fought by Sibley's and Sully's columns and the forts that supported their operations, to arrive at a total of about fifty. But the records kept by the commanders or their adjutants in field and fort are scanty, confusing, and incomplete when it comes to counting the men who died not from a lance thrust but from a mosquito bite. Sorting these numbers becomes largely a guessing game and requires many judgment calls. For example, which posts, spread out over several military departments, can be considered to have played a direct or even indirect role in a strategic and/or logistical aspect of the Dakota expeditions and which ones have to be considered outside the scope of those campaigns for the purpose of counting the casualties?

Given all these impediments to anything approaching absolute accuracy, a fair estimate of total disease and other non-hostile deaths in Sibley's and Sully's commands and in the units and military posts directly supporting those commands in the years 1863–65 would be about 100, or twice the number claimed by Santee, Yanktonai, and Teton weapons.

Appendix B:
Whitestone Hill and
Killdeer Mountain Today

I visited the major battlefields of the Dakota War in August 1989. I reached Whitestone Hill in Dickey County by traveling north on ND 281 to the tiny town of Monango, then driving west seventeen miles on a gravel road through flat crop and range land, bordered by cultivated acres ablaze with mammoth sunflowers, with the smaller variant growing wild in the roadside ditches. My wife and I passed a few farms and one abandoned site, and then the road narrowed as it approached the hill line. From this eastern approach, the hills gently swelled in their ascent, with cattle grazing on their treeless slopes carpeted with short grass. The hillsides were strewn with boulders, white, pink, and gray, and sequined with flecks of quartz.

The historic site, sixty-six acres operated by the State Historical Society, we found nicely preserved and maintained. A prominent monument stands on the highest part of the mound, with a small museum and lake to the west. To the east the monument overlooks a bowl or ravine covered with sage and short grass; that is where the Sioux camp stood concealed by a ring of small hills. The bowl, where the warriors had sung their death song and where most of the Sioux had died, is partially open to the north, with a prominent ridgeline on its south side.

The monument mound bears a section of the original tall grass that danced a century ago to the tune of the prairie winds. On the white granite monument, freckled with dots of green mold, is carved the figure of a cavalry trooper with a bugle to his lips blowing taps for the men memorialized by the twenty markers surrounding him.

The markers bear these names, with their companies and regiments:

William W. Davis   Company A, 6th Iowa
Lt. T. J. Leavitt   Company B, 6th Iowa

Avery Clark	Company C, 6th Iowa
Charles Stephens	Company C, 6th Iowa
George Killsa	Company E, 6th Iowa
Quartermaster Sgt. J. N. Rogers	Company E, 6th Iowa
W. G. Armstrong	Company F. 6th Iowa
C. M. B. Wagner	Company F, 6th Iowa
E. McCallister	Company F, 6th Iowa
Charles Uekerman	Company H, 6th Iowa
W. K. Dummett	Company H, 6th Iowa
Corporal M. N. Higgins	Company I, 6th Iowa
J. N. O. Hurley	Company K, 6th Iowa
John Mann	Company K, 6th Iowa
J. E. Van Order	Company G, 2nd Nebraska
G. W. Devenport	Company G, 2nd Nebraska
T. H. B. Packwood	Company I, 2nd Nebraska
J. E. Freeman	Company I, 2nd Nebraska
Luke Johnson	Company K, 2nd Nebraska
Sgt. H. S. Blair	Company K, 2nd Nebraska

Though many records of the battle agree that Sully lost twenty-two men killed, not twenty, the names of the other two men go unrecorded on the monument. And, of course, the names of up to 300 slain Sioux are also uncommemorated.

The scene was very bucolic that summer day 126 years after the battle. Although a grasshopper invasion of the North Dakota prairie that summer had followed the drought of 1988, the area around the site of one of the American west's fiercest battles seemed serene and tranquil. Cattle grazed at the northern open end of the killing bowl. The monument mound sloped to a barbed wire fence at its northern foot. All along the slope were scattered tiny purple, yellow, and silver-green wildflowers intermingled with long-stemmed yellow-green beaded plants. Flat farmland dominated the northern approach by which Sully's soldiers had marched. In all other directions gently rolling prairie undulated in the summer sun.

The battle site seemed fairly isolated. The town of Merricourt, five-and-a-half miles northeast of the battlefield, was largely abandoned and seemed like a ghost town. We were the only visitors at the battle site that afternoon except for a couple with their children. To people I spoke with in the area, the site was just a small state park where some obscure Indian battle had taken place. No one seemed very interested. Later that month we visited the Little Bighorn National Battlefield Park, which attracts enormous crowds. About as many Americans died at Whitestone Hill as at the Little Bighorn, but they were mostly Native Americans and none of the dead

Whitestone Hill battle monument.

were of such flamboyant character as George Armstrong Custer. History, or at least remembrance, has largely passed Whitestone Hill by.

If Whitestone Hill is little visited, it is at least nicely maintained. The site of the Killdeer Mountain battlefield, two-and-a-half miles north and six miles west of the town of Killdeer in Dunn County, is on private range-land, even more isolated, and in 1989 it was woefully neglected. We approached the battlefield from the south on a one-lane gravel road with a high range of hills sweeping across our front to the north. The hills, almost worthy of the title of low mountains, are mostly flat-topped, with a few peaks jutting here and there, timbered at their base and thinning out halfway up to bare white rock bluffs crowning the upper third. The area definitely looked well-suited to hiding hostiles and ill-suited for tactical deployment of offensive troops.

The road winds through the Diamond C Ranch gate and on past corrals and a pond (excavated by ranchers long after the battle had taken place) west to the memorial site. The site overlooks the final stage of the battle as the Sioux retreated into the nearby timbered ravines. The memorial consists of a historical marker describing the battle, a flag and a flagpole, and two memorial gravestones bearing the names of the five soldiers who died during the battle or the day after:

> Sgt. George W. Northrup   Company C, Brackett's Battalion—killed in battle
>
> Horatio N. Austin   Company D, Brackett's Battalion—killed in battle

Grave markers for George Northrup and Horatio Austin on Killdeer Mountain Battle Historic Site.

> Anton Holzgen   2nd Minnesota Cavalry—killed on guard duty
> David LaPlante   2nd Minnesota Cavalry—killed on guard duty
> Sgt. Isaac Winget   6th Iowa Cavalry—accidentally shot

The five were buried in concealed graves, the location of which is unknown.

A range of dry bare hills covered with prairie scrub, with just a few small stands of timber, stretches south of the memorial site. It was along these hills that the Sioux had erected their camp from which they were driven into the timbered ravines to the north of the memorial. On those bare hills Sully's artillery was unlimbered to shell the ravines. Thick and densely overgrown then as now, the ravines radiated out from the base of Killdeer Mountain. Sully's decision not to pursue the Sioux into the tangled ravines with his infantry but to shell them instead appears wise when one views the gnarled thickets. There can be little doubt that Sully's howitzers inflicted considerable damage on the enemy, for the shells exploding in the trees would have added natural shrapnel to the detonations. But, conversely, the thickness of the timber would have made it impossible to gauge an accurate body count.

Killdeer Mountain overlooks the battlefield in a curve from the northwest to the northeast before it peters out into rolling prairie. Most of the mountain is smooth or flat-topped, but the center section is crowned with a rock-crested bluff capped by a peaked dome rising above. Because the ravines radiating from Killdeer's base extended only part way up the mountainside, the Sioux had to break out onto bare slopes in order to escape the shelling in the timber and flee over the mountain. It was while presenting these easy targets in the clear to Sully's artillery that many of the Indian victims of the battle died.

Although the site lies at a scenic and dramatic location, we were the only visitors that hot and dry August afternoon. The nearby town that bears the name of the mountain and the battle seems much more interested in dispensing liquor to the locals than in serving as a conduit to travelers interested in frontier history. Spread along curving Highway ND 22, the town is built on a series of rolling mounds and featured in 1989 five bars on just one side of Main Street, buttressed by numerous liquor stores.

Chapter Notes

Prologue

1. *The War of the Rebellion: A Compilation of the Official Records of the Union and Confederate Armies* (hereafter cited as *O. R.*), series 1, vol. 22, part 1, Washington, D.C., 1880; Sully's report, p. 558; Wilson's Report, p. 561; House's Report, pp. 564–565.

1. The Frontier Army

1. *U.S. Statutes.* vol. 10, pp. 575–576 (Aug. 4, 1854).
2. U.S. Secretary of War, *Annual Report* (1861), pp. 115–116.
3. Richard H. Coolidge, *Statistical Report on the Sickness and Mortality in the Army of the United States* (1839–55), Senate Ex. Docs., 34th Congress, 1st Session, No. 96. Cf. also P. M. Ashburn, *A History of the Medical Department of the United States Army* (Boston, Mass., 1929), ch. 2.
4. Robert M. Utley, *Frontiersmen in Blue: The United States Army and the Indian, 1848–1865* (New York: Macmillan, 1967), p. 28.
5. Augustus Meyers, *Ten Years in the Ranks (U.S. Army),* (New York, 1914) p. 93.
6. Geoffrey Perret, *A Country Made by War* (New York: Random House, 1989) p. 141.
7. Frank Myers, *Soldiering in Dakota Among the Indians, 1863–65* (Huron, Dakota Territory: Huron Printing Co., 1888), p. 25.
8. Thomas Dunlay, *Wolves for the Blue Soldiers* (Lincoln: University of Nebraska Press, 1982), pp. 32–33. Cf. also Governor Newton Edmunds, *Official Report* (Sept. 20, 1864), p. 260.

2. The Sioux Nation

1. John C. Ewers, *Teton Dakota History and Ethnology* (National Park Service, 1938), pp. 7–8.

2. Doane Robinson, *A History of the Dakota or Sioux Indians* (Minneapolis: Ross & Haines, 1956), p. 19.

3. Ibid., p. 21.

4. John R. Swanton, *The Indian Tribes of North America,* Bureau of American Ethnology Bulletin 145 (Washington, D.C., 1952), p. 282.

5. Ewers, *Teton Dakota History and Ethnology,* pp. 7–8.

6. Utley, *Frontiersmen in Blue,* p. 114.

7. Ibid., pp. 116–117.

8. Gary C. Anderson, *Little Crow: Spokesman for the Sioux* (St. Paul: Minnesota Historical Society Press, 1986), pp. 4, 39.

9. Charles M. Oehler, *The Great Sioux Uprising* (New York: Oxford University Press, 1959), p. 17.

10. Duane Schultz, *Over the Earth I Come: The Great Sioux Uprising of 1862* (New York: St. Martin's Press, 1992), pp. 35–37.

3. Inkpaduta and the Spirit Lake Massacre

1. Joseph Wall, *Iowa: A Bicentennial History* (New York: Norton, 1978), pp. 62–64.

2. Ibid.

3. Robinson, *History of the Dakota or Sioux Indians,* pp. 342–344.

4. Ibid., pp. 344–346.

5. Ibid., p. 235. Cf. also Wall, *Iowa: A Bicentennial History,* p. 62.

6. Curtis Harnack, "Prelude to Massacre," *The Iowan,* vol. 4 (February/March, 1956), pp. 36–39.

7. Ibid.

8. Abigail Gardner (as told to L. P. Lee), *History of the Spirit Lake Massacre* (New Britain, Conn., 1857), pp. 64–83. Cf. also Wall, *Iowa: A Bicentennial History,* pp. 62–64.

9. Robinson, *History of the Dakota or Sioux Indians,* pp. 237–240; and Gardner, *History of the Spirit Lake Massacre,* pp. 96–102.

10. Wall, *Iowa: A Bicentennial History,* p. 64.

11. Gardner, *History of the Spirit Lake Massacre,* pp. 174–176.

12. Ibid, pp. 193–194, 217–219, 241.

13. Ibid., pp. 287–289.

14. Ibid., p. 292.

4. Little Crow and the Minnesota Massacre

1. Gary C. Anderson and Alan R. Woolworth, eds., *Through Dakota Eyes: Narrative Accounts of the Minnesota Indian War of 1862* (St. Paul: Minnesota Historical Society Press, 1988), p. 39. Cf. also William W. Folwell, *A History of Minnesota* (St. Paul: Minnesota Historical Society Press, 1924), vol. 2, pp. 415–416.

2. Willoughby M. Babcock, "Minnesota's Indian War," *Minnesota History*, vol. 38, no. 3 (September 1962), p. 115.

3. Anderson and Woolworth, *Through Dakota Eyes*, pp. 40–42. Cf. also Oehler, *The Great Sioux Uprising*, pp. 31–34.

4. Folwell, *A History of Minnesota*, vol. 1, pp. 266–304, 352–354.

5. Ibid.

6. Roy W. Meyer, *History of the Santee Sioux: United States Indian Policy on Trial* (Lincoln: University of Nebraska Press, 1980), pp. 109–110.

7. House, Executive Document, No. 68, 38th Congress, 1st Session, p. 26.

8. Kenneth Carley, ed., "Chief Big Eagle's Story," *Minnesota History*, vol. 38, no. 3 (September 1962), p. 130.

9. Folwell, *History of Minnesota*, vol. 2, p. 232.

10. Carley, "Chief Big Eagle's Story," p. 130.

11. House, Executive Document, No. 68, p. 29; Stephen R. Riggs, *Tah-Koo Wah-Kan, or the Gospel among the Dakotas* (Boston, 1869), p. 330.

12. Joint Committee on the Conduct of War, "Report of Maj. General John Pope," *Supplemental Report of the Joint Committee on the Conduct of the War, 1865*, vol. 2, p. 198.

13. *Report of the Secretary of the Interior, 1862*, pp. 174–177, 227–231, 236–237.

14. *Minnesota in the Civil and Indian Wars, 1861–1865*, vol. 2, *Official Reports and Correspondence* (St. Paul, Minnesota, 1893), pp. 5, 245–248.

15. Carley, "Chief Big Eagle's Story," p. 134.

16. *Minnesota in the Civil and Indian Wars*, vol. 2, pp. 166–170.

17. Ibid., pp. 171–173, 183–186.

18. Ibid., pp. 203–208.

19. Carley, "Chief Big Eagle's Story," p. 135.

20. Stephen R. Riggs, *Mary and I: Forty Years with the Sioux* (Chicago, 1880), p. 139.

21. Senate Miscellaneous Document, no. 241, pp. 81–82.

22. *Minnesota in the Civil and Indian Wars*, vol. 2, pp. 187–189.

23. Abner M. English, "Dakota's First Soldiers: History of the First Dakota Cavalry, 1862–1865." *South Dakota Historical Collections*, vol. 9 (1918), pp. 253–255.

24. *Minnesota in the Civil and Indian Wars*, vol. 2, pp. 257–260.

25. *O. R.*, series 1, vol. 13, p. 597.

26. Ibid.

27. Robert H. Jones, *The Civil War in the Northwest* (Norman, Oklahoma: University of Oklahoma Press, 1960), p. 6.

28. *Minnesota in the Civil and Indian Wars*, vol. 2, Pope to Halleck correspondence, pp. 232–237.

29. Ibid.

30. Jones, *The Civil War in the Northwest*, p. 3.

31. T. Harry Williams, *Lincoln and His Generals* (New York: Grosset & Dunlap, 1952), pp. 50–53.

32. Jones, *The Civil War in the Northwest*, p. 7.

33. Ibid.

34. Ibid., p. 11.

35. Ibid., pp. 13–14.

36. Oehler, *The Great Sioux Uprising*, p. 140.

37. Nathaniel West, *The Ancestry, Life, and Times of Henry Hastings Sibley* (St. Paul, Minnesota, 1889), p. 47.

38. Schultz, *Over the Earth I Come*, p. 89.

39. Ibid.

40. Ibid.

41. Ibid., p. 90.

42. Ibid.

43. Ibid.

44. Mark M. Boatner, *The Civil War Dictionary* (New York: David McKay, 1988), p. 759.

45. Anderson and Woolworth, *Through Dakota Eyes*, p. 195.

46. Ibid., pp. 196–197.

47. Schultz, *Over the Earth I Come*, pp. 205–207.

48. *Minnesota in the Civil and Indian Wars*, vol. 2, pp. 212–223.

49. *St. Paul Press*, Sept. 6, 1862.

50. Kenneth Carley, "The Sioux Campaign of 1862: Sibley's Letters to His Wife," *Minnesota History*, no. 38 (September 1962), pp. 102–107. Cf. also *Minnesota in the Civil and Indian Wars*, vol. 2, pp. 227–229, 234–237.

51. West, *Ancestry, Life, and Times of Henry Hastings Sibley*, p. 264.

52. *Minnesota in the Civil and Indian Wars*, vol. 2, pp. 244–247.

53. Ibid. Cf. also Folwell, *History of Minnesota*, vol. 2, p. 182.

54. West, *Ancestry, Life, and Times of Henry Hastings Sibley*, p. 471.

55. Anderson and Woolworth, *Through Dakota Eyes*, p. 224.

56. David A. Nichols, *Lincoln and the Indians* (Columbia, Missouri: University of Missouri Press, 1978), p. 141.

57. Sarah F. Wakefield, *Six Weeks in the Sioux Tepees (Little Crow's Camp): A Narrative of Indian Captivity* (Shakopee, Minnesota, 1864), pp. 53–59.

58. Charles S. Bryant, *A History of the Great Massacre by the Sioux Indians in Minnesota, Including the Personal Narratives of Many Who Escaped* (Cincinnati, 1864), p. 475.

59. Schultz, *Over the Earth I Come*, pp. 279–280.

60. Anderson and Woolworth, *Through Dark Eyes*, p. 261.

61. Isaac V. D. Heard, *History of the Sioux War and Massacre of 1862* (New York, 1864), p. 295.

62. Meyer, *History of the Santee Sioux*, p. 143.

63. Richard N. Ellis, *General Pope and U.S. Indian Policy* (Albuquerque: University of New Mexico Press, 1970), pp. 16–17.

5. The Death of Little Crow

1. Folwell, *History of Minnesota*, vol. 2, pp. 283–284.

2. Anderson, *Little Crow*, pp. 170–176.

3. Ibid.

4. Anderson and Woolworth, *Through Dakota Eyes,* p. 280.

5. Ibid.

6. Schultz, *Over the Earth I Come,* p. 273.

7. West, *Ancestry, Life, and Times of Henry Hastings Sibley,* p. 333.

8. Folwell, *History of Minnesota,* vol. 2, pp. 449–450.

9. Kenneth Carley, *The Sioux Uprising of 1862* (St. Paul: Minnesota Historical Society, 1976), p. 75.

10. Minnesota Historical Society.

11. Ibid. Cf. also Joseph P. Peters, comp. "Indian Battles and Skirmishes on the American Frontier," *Adjutant General's Chronological List* (New York, 1966).

12. Meyer, *History of the Santee Sioux,* p. 120; and Minnesota Historical Society.

6. The Raiding Season, 1863

1. *O. R.,* series 1, vol. 22, part 2, p. 123. Cf. also Minnesota in the Civil and Indian Wars, vol. 2, pp. 292–294.

2. Ibid., vol. 1, p. 353; vol. 2, p. 296.

3. Ibid., vol. 1, p. 387.

4. Ibid., vol. 1, pp. 417, 457, 520. Cf. also *Adjutant General's report,* Executive Document, 1863, pp. 339–341.

5. Ibid., pp. 342–345.

6. *St. Paul Press,* June 13, 1863, and July 3, 1863.

7. *Minnesota in the Civil and Indian Wars,* vol. 2, p. 294.

8. *Adjutant General's Report,* Executive Document, 1863, pp. 192–198, 223–226.

9. *St. Paul Press,* June 23, 1863, June 26, 1863, and July 12, 1863. Cf. also *O. R.,* series 1, vol. 22, part 2, pp. 493–495.

10. Ibid., pp. 371, 384, 494, 498.

11. "Charles Nash Narrative of Hatch's Independent Battalion of Cavalry," *Minnesota in the Civil and Indian Wars,* vol. 1, Regimental Histories, pp. 595–598. *O. R.,* series 1, vol. 22, part 2, p. 569.

12. "Nash Narrative," *Minnesota in the Civil and Indian Wars,* vol. 1, pp. 598, 601. *O. R.,* vol. 34, part 2, p. 29.

13. "Nash Narrative," *Minnesota in the Civil and Indian Wars,* vol. 1, p. 600.

14. William Dole, *Report of Commissioner of Indian Affairs,* 1863, p. 157.

15. Ibid., p. 152.

16. Ibid., p. 153.

17. Henry Reed and S. N. Latta, *Reports of Indian Agents to the Commissioner of Indian Affairs,* June 11, 1863, p. 169.

18. Ibid., August 16, 1863 and August 27, 1863, pp. 170–172.

19. Ibid.

20. Dole, *Report,* pp. 153–154, 157–158.

21. Ibid., p. 152–153.

22. *Minnesota in the Civil and Indian Wars,* vol. 2, p. 353.

7. Into Dakota

1. Geraldine Bean, "General Alfred Sully and the Northwest Indian Expedition," *North Dakota History*, vol. 33, no. 3 (Summer 1966), p. 241.
2. *O. R.*, series 1, vol. 13, Pope's letter to Halleck, p. 755.
3. *O. R.*, vol. 22, part 1, Pope's letter to Halleck, p. 110.
4. Bean, "General Alfred Sully," p. 246.
5. Dole, *Report*, p. 270.
6. *O. R.*, vol. 22, part 1, pp. 176, 287.
7. Ibid., p. 288 and Bean, "General Alfred Sully," p. 246.
8. Ibid., p. 247.
9. Ibid.
10. Col. M. T. Thomas, "General Alfred Sully's Expedition of 1864," *Montana Historical Collections*, vol. 2 (1896), p. 152.
11. J. H. Drips, *Three Years Among the Indians in Dakota* (Kimball, South Dakota, 1894—reprint New York: Sol Lewis, 1974), p. 132.
12. *O. R.*, vol. 22, part 1, pp. 349–350, 406.
13. *O. R.*, vol. 22, part 1, Pope's letter to Halleck, pp. 304–305.

8. The Sibley Brigade

1. Sisseton and Wahpeton Claim Case Record, Defendant's Brief and Argument, Minnesota Historical Society, pp. 10, 12.
2. *O. R.*, series 1, vol. 22, part 2, p. 116.
3. Ibid., Halleck's letter to Pope, p. 403.
4. Ibid., pp. 403–406.
5. *St. Paul Press*, June 20, 1863. Cf. also West, *Ancestry, Life, and Times of Henry Hastings Sibley*, p. 304.
6. Clement Lounsberry, *Early History of North Dakota* (Washington D.C., 1919), p. 293.
7. *St. Paul Press*, July 7 and 10, 1863. Cf. also *Central Republican* (Faribault), June 10 and 17, July 8 and 15, 1863. *O. R.*, series 1, vol. 22, part 2, pp. 119, 380–381.
8. "First Regiment of Mounted Rangers," in *Minnesota in the Civil and Indian Wars*, vol. 1, pp. 520–521.
9. West, *Ancestry, Life, and Times of Henry Hastings Sibley*, pp. 304–307.
10. *O. R.*, series 1, vol. 22, part 2, Sibley's letter to Acting Assistant Adjutant-General J. F. Meline, pp. 907–908.
11. Louis Pfaller, "The Peace Mission of 1863–64," *North Dakota History*, vol. 37 (Fall 1970), pp. 300–301.
12. *O. R.*, series 1, vol. 22, part 1, Report of Col. W. Crooks, 6th Minnesota Infantry, Aug. 5, 1863, pp. 361–364.
13. Capt. John W. Burnham, "Sibley's Expedition of 1863," *The Record* (Fargo), June 1896, pp. 2–5.
14. *O. R.*, series 1, vol. 22, part 1, Sibley's Report, Aug. 7, 1863, pp. 352–353.

15. Jared W. Daniels, "General Sibley's Campaign, 1863," Daniels Papers, Minnesota Historical Society, pp. 1–4.

16. Ibid. Cf. also A. L. Van Osdel, "The Sibley Expedition," Monthly South Dakotan, October 1899, pp. 97–100.

17. "G. Merrill Dwelle Narrative of the Third Battery of Light Artillery," in *Minnesota in the Civil and Indian Wars*, vol. 1, p. 671.

18. *O. R.*, series 1, vol. 22, part 1, Reports of Col. W. Marshall, 7th Minnesota Infantry, July 25, 1863, and Aug. 5, 1863, pp. 364–370.

19. "First Regiment of Mounted Rangers," in *Minnesota in the Civil and Indian Wars*, vol. 1, p. 521.

20. *O. R.*, series 1, vol. 22, part 1, Marshall Report, p. 370.

21. Ibid., Report of Col. S. McPhail, 1st Minnesota Mounted Rangers, Aug. 5, 1863, p. 359.

22. Ibid., pp. 359–360.

23. "First Regiment of Mounted Rangers," p. 521.

24. Burnham, "Sibley's Expedition of 1863."

25. *O. R.*, series 1, vol. 22, part 1, Marshall Report, pp. 364–366.

26. Ibid.

27. Pfaller, "The Peace Mission of 1863–64," p. 301.

28. Burnham, "Sibley's Expedition of 1863."

29. Van Osdel, "The Sibley Expedition," pp. 97–100. Cf. also *O. R.*, series 1, vol. 22, part 1, Reports of Sibley and Crooks, pp. 354–355, 362, 366.

30. *O. R.*, series 1, vol. 22, part 1, Report of Col. James H. Baker, 10th Minnesota Infantry, August 5, 1863, pp. 907–909.

31. West, *Ancestry, Life, and Times of Henry Hastings Sibley*, p. 314.

32. *O. R.*, series 1, vol. 22, part 1, Reports of Sibley and Baker, pp. 355–356, 907–909.

33. Burnham, "Sibley's Expedition of 1863."

34. Ibid. Cf. also Lounsberry, *Early History of North Dakota*, p. 291.

35. *O. R.*, series 1, vol. 22, part 1, Sept. 2, 1863, Sibley's letter to Acting Assistant Adjutant-General J. F. Meline, pp. 909–910.

36. Ibid., Sibley Report, pp. 356–357.

37. Ibid., Crooks Report, p. 364.

38. Ibid., Sibley Report, pp. 356–357.

39. Ibid., Crooks Report, p. 364.

40. Daniels, "General Sibley's Campaign, 1863," p. 9.

41. Lounsberry, *Early History of North Dakota*, p. 293.

42. *O. R.*, ibid., Marshall's Report, Aug. 5, 1863, p. 370.

43. Dana Wright, "Military Trails in Dakota," *North Dakota History*, vol. 13, no. 3 (July 1946), p. 106.

44. *O. R.*, ibid., Sibley Report, p. 357.

45. West, *Ancestry, Life and Times of Henry Hastings Sibley*, pp. 315, 317.

46. *O. R.*, ibid., Sibley Report, p. 356.

47. Ibid., Sibley's letter to Pope, p. 912.

48. West, *Ancestry, Life, and Times of Henry Hastings Sibley*, pp. 309, 311.

49. *O. R.*, ibid., McPhail Report, p. 360.

50. Daniels, "General Sibley's Campaign, 1863," p. 7.

51. *O. R.,* ibid., Sibley Report, p. 357. *O. R.,* ibid., Sibley's letter to Meline, p. 910.

52. Ibid., pp. 909–910.

53. "William Houlton Narrative of the 8th Minnesota Infantry," in *Minnesota in the Civil and Indian Wars,* vol. 1, p. 387.

54. Lounsberry, *Early History of North Dakota,* p. 292.

55. *O. R.,* ibid., Sibley's letter to Meline, pp. 909–910.

56. Lounsberry, *Early History of North Dakota,* p. 292.

57. Ibid.

58. *O.R.,* ibid., Sibley's letter to Meline, pp. 908–909.

59. Ibid., pp. 907–911. Cf. also West, *Ancestry, Life, and Times of Henry Hastings Sibley,* pp. 322–326.

60. *O. R.,* ibid., Sibley Report, pp. 357–358.

61. Ibid.

62. *O. R.,* ibid., Pope's letter to Sibley, p. 497.

63. Meyer, *History of the Santee Sioux,* pp. 133–136.

9. The Battle of Whitestone Hill

1. Boatner, *The Civil War Dictionary,* p. 818.

2. Ibid.

3. Langdon Sully, *No Tears for the General: A Biography of Alfred Sully* (Palo Alto, Cal.: American West Publishing, 1974), pp. 63–70.

4. Ibid., pp. 147–160. Cf. also Stewart Sifakis, *Who Was Who in the Civil War* (New York: Facts on File Publications, 1988), p. 634.

5. D. Alexander Brown, *The Galvanized Yankees* (Urbana Ill.: University of Illinois Press, 1963) p. 102.

6. Sully, *No Tears for the General,* pp. 214–215.

7. Sifakis, *Who Was Who in the Civil War,* p. 634.

8. Lounsberry, *Early History of North Dakota,* p. 294. *Soldier and Brave* (National Park Service, 1973), p. 17. *O. R.,* ibid., pp. 349–350, 406.

9. Drips, *Three Years Among the Indians in Dakota,* p. 7.

10. Alvin M. Josephy, *The Civil War in the American West* (New York: Knopf, 1991), p. 141.

11. *Weekly Dakotan* (Yankton), Oct. 31, 1863.

12. House, *Executive Document,* no. 1 (Serial 1182), 38th Congress, 1st Session, p. 442.

13. "Official Correspondence Pertaining to the War of the Outbreak, 1862–1865," (hereafter cited as Official Correspondence), *South Dakota Historical Collections,* vol. 8 (1916), p. 334.

14. *Weekly Dakotan* (Yankton), Aug. 25, 1863.

15. *O. R.,* ibid., Pope's letter to Sully, p. 434.

16. Ibid.

17. Ibid., Pope's letter to Halleck, p. 463.

18. Ibid., Pope's letter to Sully, pp. 496-497.

19. Ibid.

20. Pvt. Milton Spencer, "The Letters of Private Milton Spencer, 1862–65: A Soldier's View of Military Life on the Northern Plains," *North Dakota History* (Fall 1970), p. 249.

21. House, *Executive Document*, no. 1 (Serial 1184), "Expedition of Brig. General Sully Against the Northwest Indians," 38th Congress, 1st Session, pp. 495–500.

22. *O. R.*, ibid., Sully Report, Sept. 11, 1863, pp. 555–556.

23. Ibid., p. 556.

24. Ibid., p. 557. Cf. also Lounsberry, *Early History of North Dakota*, p. 294.

25. Ibid., Sully Report, p. 557.

26. Ibid., Report of Maj. A. E. House, 6th Iowa Cavalry, Sept. 3, 1863, p. 564.

27. Ibid., Sully Report, p. 558.

28. Ibid.

29. Lounsberry, *Early History of North Dakota*, p. 294.

30. *O. R.*, ibid., House Report, p. 564.

31. *O. R.*, ibid., Sully Report, p. 558.

32. *O. R.*, ibid., Report of Col. Robert W. Furnas, 2nd Nebraska Cavalry, Sept. 6, 1863, pp. 565–568.

33. Ibid., House Report, p. 564.

34. Spencer, "The Letters of Private Milton Spencer," p. 251.

35. *O. R.*, ibid., Report of Col. David S. Wilson, 6th Iowa Cavalry, Sept. 3, 1863, pp. 561–564.

36. Ibid., House Report, pp. 564–565.

37. Ibid., Furnas Report, p. 567.

38. Ibid., Sully Report, p. 558.

39. Ibid., p. 559.

40. Ibid.

41. Spencer, "The Letters of Private Milton Spencer," p. 251.

42. Ibid.

43. Ibid., p. 252.

44. *O. R.*, ibid., Wilson Report, p. 564.

45. Ibid., Sully Report, p. 559.

46. Ibid., Furnas Report, p. 568.

47. Lounsberry, *Early History of North Dakota*, p. 295.

48. Drips, *Three Years Among the Indians in Dakota*, pp. 45–46.

49. *O. R.*, ibid., Sully Report, p. 560.

50. *O. R.*, ibid., part 2, p. 608.

51. Ibid., part 1, Sully Report, p. 559. Cf. also Ibid., Report of Lt. Charles W. Hall, 2nd Nebraska Cavalry, Sept. 6, 1863, p. 611.

52. Ibid., Sully Report, p. 559.

53. Ibid., pp. 559–560.

54. Ibid., p. 560.

55. Ibid., House Report, p. 565. Cf. also Ibid., Furnas Report, p. 568.

56. Ibid., Sully Report, p. 560.

57. Ibid., p. 561.

58. "Letter to Joseph R. Brown," Samuel J. Brown Papers, Nov. 13, 1863.

59. Lounsberry, *Early History of North Dakota*, p. 295.

60. Spencer, "The Letters of Private Milton Spencer," pp. 245–246.

61. *O. R.*, ibid., Sully Report, p. 560.

62. Steven Hoekman, "The History of Fort Sully," *South Dakota Historical Collections*, vol. 16 (1952), p. 231.

63. *Weekly Dakotan* (Yankton), Sept. 30, 1863.

64. *O. R.*, ibid., Pope's letter to Sully, p. 608.

65. "Report of the Commissioner of Indian Affairs," 38th Congress, 1st Session, House Executive Document, No. 1 (Serial 1182), p. 270.

66. Ibid., p. 271.

67. Ibid., p. 281.

68. "Report of the Commissioner of Indian Affairs," 38th Congress, 2nd Session, House Executive Document, No. 1 (Serial 1220), p. 403.

69. Newton Edmunds, "Report to the Commissioner of Indian Affairs," Sept. 20, 1864, p. 259.

70. Ibid., p. 260.

71. Ibid.

72. William P. Dole, "Report of the Commissioner of Indian Affairs," Nov. 15, 1964, p. 28.

73. Frederick T. Wilson, "Old Fort Pierre and Its Neighbors," *South Dakota Historical Collections*, vol. 1 (1902), p. 304.

10. The Battle of Killdeer Mountain

1. Richard N. Ellis, "Civilians, the Army, and the Indian Problem on the Northern Plains, 1862–1866," *North Dakota History*, vol. 37, no. 1 (Winter 1970), pp. 24–25.

2. *O. R.*, ibid., p. 633.

3. Spencer, "The Letters of Private Milton Spencer," p. 258.

4. *Minnesota in the Civil and Indian Wars*, vol. 2, p. 387.

5. *O. R.*, ibid., pp. 69, 152.

6. Ibid., pp. 607, 622–625.

7. "Houlton Narrative," *Minnesota in the Civil and Indian Wars*, vol. 1, p. 387.

8. *O. R.*, series 3, vol. 3, p. 791.

9. *Minnesota in the Civil and Indian Wars*, vol. 2, pp. 388, 451, 752. Cf. also David L. Kingsbury, "Sully's Expedition Against the Sioux in 1864," in *Minnesota Historical Collections*, vol. 8 (1898), pp. 451–452.

10. Ibid. Cf. also Jones, *The Civil War in the Northwest*, p. 87.

11. Ibid., p. 88.

12. *O. R.*, series 1, vol. 34, part 2, p. 289. Cf. also Louis Pfaller, "Sully's Expedition of 1864, featuring the Killdeer Mountain and Badlands Battles," in *North Dakota History*, vol. 31, no. 1 (January 1964), p. 29.

13. Ibid., pp. 32–33.

14. English, "Dakota's First Soldiers," *South Dakota Historical Collections,* vol. 9, 1918, p. 278.

15. Robinson, *History of the Dakota or Sioux Indians,* pp. 330, 345.

16. Lounsberry, *Early History of North Dakota,* p. 296.

17. Dole, Report 1864, pp. 276–283.

18. Pfaller, "Sully's Expedition of 1864," pp. 35–36.

19. *O. R.,* series 1, vol. 41, part 2, p. 228.

20. Thomas E. Cooper, "The Tom Holmes Expedition," *Montana Historical Society,* p. 3.

21. *O. R.,* ibid., Report of Col. Robert N. McLaren, 2nd Minnesota Cavalry, July 29, 1864, pp. 172–173.

22. Ibid., Report of Brig. General Alfred E. Sully, July 31, 1864, p. 141.

23. Ibid., p. 142. Cf. also Ibid., Report of Maj. General John Pope (to Gen. Halleck), Nov. 3, 1864, p. 135.

24. Walter S. Campbell (Stanley Vestal, pseudonym) Collection, "Interviews with White Bull, et. al.," University of Oklahoma Library, Box 105, notebook 24, pp. 1–6.

25. John Pattee, "Dakota Campaigns," *South Dakota Historical Collections,* vol. 5 (1910), p. 306.

26. John H. Strong Diary, Minnesota Historical Society, July 28, 1864.

27. J. E. Robinson Letter, Minnesota Historical Society, Oct. 11, 1864.

28. Edward Eggleston, "The Kit Carson of the Northwest," *Minnesota History,* vol. 33, p. 281.

29. *O. R.,* ibid., Sully Report, p. 143.

30. Ibid., Pope to Halleck, p. 135.

31. Campbell Collection, "Interviews with White Bull," pp. 1–6.

32. Pattee, "Dakota Campaigns," p. 308.

33. Ibid. *O. R.,* ibid., McLaren Report, p. 173.

34. Pattee, "Dakota Campaigns," pp. 308–309. Folwell, *History of Minnesota,* pp. 297–298.

35. Pattee, "Dakota Campaigns," p. 309.

36. Myers, *Soldiering in Dakota Among the Indians, 1863–65,* p. 18.

37. "Isaac Botsford Narrative of Brackett's Battalion of Cavalry," in *Minnesota in the Civil and Indian Wars,* vol. 1, p. 581.

38. *Minnesota History,* vol. 19, Minnesota Historical Collections, p. 390.

39. "Botsford Narrative," in *Minnesota in the Civil and Indian Wars,* vol. 1, p. 582. Cf. also Ibid., vol. 2, p. 390.

40. *O. R.,* ibid., Sully Report, p. 143.

41. Campbell Collection, "Interviews with White Bull," pp. 1–5.

42. Ibid.

43. Official Correspondence, pp. 375, 388.

44. Myers, *Soldiering in Dakota Among the Indians, 1863–65,* p. 20.

45. Pfaller, "Sully's Expedition of 1864," p. 51.

46. *Minnesota in the Civil and Indian Wars,* vol. 2, p. 673.

47. Myers, *Soldiering in Dakota Among the Indians, 1863–65,* p. 21.

48. Kingsbury, "Sully's Expedition Against the Sioux in 1864," p. 456.

49. Official Correspondence, pp. 364, 389.

50. George Doud Diary, Minnesota Historical Society, July 30, 1864. Ebenezer Rice Diary, Minnesota Historical Society, July 30, 1864.

51. *Minnesota in the Civil and Indian Wars*, vol. 2, p. 546.

52. James Atkinson Diary, North Dakota Historical Society, July 30, 1864. Doud Diary, July 29, 1864.

53. Strong Diary, Aug. 2, 1864.

54. Official Correspondence, p. 334.

55. *O. R.*, ibid., Sully Report, p. 143. Ibid., Pope to Halleck, p. 135.

11. The Battle of the Badlands

1. "Narrative of the 2nd Minnesota Cavalry," in *Minnesota in the Civil and Indian Wars*, vol. 1, p. 545.

2. *O. R.*, ibid., Sully Report, p. 144.

3. Nicholas Hilger, "General Alfred Sully's Expedition of 1864," *Montana Historical Society*, vol. 2 (1896), p. 317.

4. Official Correspondence, p. 314. "Harlan P. Bruch Narrative," *Frontier Scout*, Fort Union, Aug. 17, 1864.

5. Pfaller, "Sully's Expedition of 1864," p. 57.

6. "Narrative of the 2nd Minnesota Cavalry," in *Minnesota in the Civil and Indian Wars*, p. 545.

7. *O. R.*, ibid., Sully Report, p. 145. English, "Dakota's First Soldiers," p. 285.

8. Pattee, "Dakota Campaigns," p. 312.

9. George T. Campbell Papers, 1888, Minnesota Historical Society, p. 23.

10. Pattee, "Dakota Campaigns," p. 312. *Minnesota in the Civil and Indian Wars*, vol. 2, p. 674.

11. Ibid., p. 392.

12. Ibid.

13. *O. R.*, ibid., Sully Report, p. 146.

14. Hilger, "Sully's Expedition of 1864," p. 318.

15. Myers, *Soldiering in Dakota Among the Indians, 1862–65*, p. 25.

16. Pattee, "Dakota Campaigns," p. 313.

17. Hilger, "Sully's Expedition of 1864," p. 319.

18. Myers, *Soldiering in Dakota Among the Indians, 1862–65*, p. 27. *O. R.*, ibid., Sully Report, p. 146.

19. Ibid.

20. Campbell Collection, "Interviews with White Bull," pp. 6–10.

21. *O. R.*, ibid., Report of Col. M. T. Thomas, pp. 167–170.

22. Ibid., Sully Report, p. 147.

23. Ibid.

24. Ibid., Thomas Report, p. 170. Cf. also *Minnesota in the Civil and Indian Wars*, vol. 2, p. 393.

25. Hilger, "Sully's Expedition of 1864," p. 319.

26. Gilbert Benedict Diary, Minnesota Historical Society, Aug. 11, 1864.

27. "Houlton Narrative," in *Minnesota in the Civil and Indian Wars,* vol. 1, p. 393.

28. Pfaller, "Sully's Expedition of 1864," p. 68.

29. Doud Diary, Aug. 12, 1864.
Myers, *Soldiering in Dakota Among the Indians, 1862–65,* p. 32.

30. Rice Diary, Aug. 14, 1864. Strong Diary, Aug. 15, 1864.

31. *Minnesota in the Civil and Indian Wars,* vol. 2, p. 548.

32. *Frontier Scout,* Fort Union, Aug. 17, 1864.

33. Atkinson Diary, Aug. 18, 1864.

34. *O. R.,* ibid., Sully Report, p. 149.

35. Ibid., Pope to Halleck, p. 136.

36. English, "Dakota's First Soldiers," p. 292.

37. Ibid., p. 293. Myers, *Soldiering in Dakota Among the Indians, 1862–65,* p. 35.

12. The Siege of Fort Dilts

1. Atkinson Diary, Aug. 31, 1864.

2. Doud Diary, Sept. 2, 1864.

3. *Minnesota in the Civil and Indian Wars,* vol. 2, p. 549.

4. Pattee, "Dakota Campaigns," pp. 316–317.

5. Official Correspondence, p. 328.

6. Pattee, "Dakota Campaigns," p. 317.

7. Official Correspondence, p. 330.

8. Campbell, "Interviews with White Bull," Box 105, Notebook 8.

9. "Expeditions of Capt. Jas. L. Fisk to the Gold Mines of Idaho and Montana, 1864–1866," *North Dakota Historical Collections* 2 (1908) pp. 421–440. Cf. also Lounsberry, *Early History of North Dakota,* p. 304.

10. Ibid., Ray Mattison, ed., "The Fisk Expedition of 1864: The Diary of William L. Larned," *North Dakota History* 36 (Summer 1969) pp. 227–238.

11. Lounsberry, *Early History of North Dakota,* p. 305.

12. *O. R.,* ibid., Sully Report, p. 149.

13. Fanny Kelly, *My Captivity Among the Sioux Indians* (New York: Corinth Books, 1962), pp. 274–278.

14. *O. R.,* ibid., Report of Col. Daniel J. Dill, Oct. 4, 1864, pp. 795–796. Lounsberry, *Early History of North Dakota,* p. 305.

15. "Narrative of the 2nd Minnesota Cavalry," in *Minnesota in the Civil and Indian Wars,* pp. 550–551.

16. "Botsford Narrative of Brackett's Battalion," in *Minnesota in the Civil and Indian Wars,* p. 583.

17. Pattee, "Dakota Campaigns," pp. 318–319.

18. *O. R.,* Ibid., Reports of Sibley, Pope, and Sully, pp. 39, 135, 153.

19. Utley, *Frontiersmen in Blue,* p. 280.

20. *O. R.*, ibid., vol. 48, part 1, pp. 208–209.

21. Ibid., vol. 41, part 1, Pope to Halleck, p. 136.

22. Pell to Sully, Oct. 26, 1864, U.S. Army Records, Department of the Northwest, entry 3446, Box 2, 1864, National Archives and Records Administration.

23. Doane Robinson, "The Rescue of Francis Kelly," in *South Dakota Historical Collections* 4 (1908), pp. 109–117.

24. Campbell, "Interviews with White Bull," Box 106, Notebook 53.

25. *O. R.*, ibid., Pope to Halleck, Oct. 6, 1864, p. 131.

26. Ibid., Pope to Halleck, Nov. 3, 1864, p. 138.

27. Ibid., p. 139.

13. The Last Dakota Campaign

1. *O. R.*, ibid., Reports of Col. Christopher (Kit) Carson, Dec. 4 and Dec. 15, 1864, pp. 939–943.

2. Utley, *Frontiersmen in Blue,* pp. 293–296. Josephy, *The Civil War in the American West*, pp. 308-311.

3. Paul I. Wellman, *The Indian Wars of the West* (New York: Doubleday, 1947), pp. 75–76.

4. Utley, *Frontiersmen in Blue,* pp. 319–322.

5. Ibid., pp. 324–325.

6. Leroy and Ann Hafen, eds., *Powder River Campaigns and Sawyers Expedition of 1865* (Glendale, Calif.: Arthur H. Clarke & Co., 1961), pp. 46–48.

7. Utley, *Frontiersmen in Blue,* p. 332.

8. Ibid., pp. 329–330.

9. Robinson, *History of the Dakota or Sioux Indians,* p. 336.

10. Ibid.

11. *O. R.*, ibid., vol 48, part 1, p. 391.

12. Ibid., pp. 413–414.

13. Ibid., p. 731.

14. Ibid.

15. Utley, *Frontiersmen in Blue,* p. 323.

16. *O. R.*, ibid., vol. 48, part 2, pp. 162, 617–618.

17. Utley, *Frontiersmen in Blue,* p. 333.

18. *O. R.,* ibid., pp. 208–209.

19. Ibid., pp. 434–435.

20. Brown, *The Galvanized Yankees,* pp. 89–90.

21. *O. R.*, ibid., part 2, Sully's Reports to Pope, July 14–20, 1865, pp. 1080, 1084–1085.

22. Ibid., pp. 1090–1091, 1109–1110.

23. Ibid., pp. 851–852.

24. Ibid., Sully's Reports of July 31 and Aug. 8, 1865, pp. 1136–1138, 1172–1174.

25. Ibid., Sully's Report of Aug. 8, 1865, pp. 1172–1174. Cf. also Pattee, "Dakota Campaigns," pp. 339–341.

26. Ibid. *Frontier Scout,* Fort Rice, Aug. 3, 1865.

27. Brown, *The Galvanized Yankees,* pp. 104–107. Also: Pattee, "Dakota Campaigns," pp. 339–341.

28. *Frontier Scout,* Oct. 12, 1865.

29. *O. R.,* ibid., Sully's Reports of Aug. 8 and Aug. 13, 1865, pp. 1172–1174, 1181–1182.

30. Ibid., Sully's Report of Aug. 13, 1865, pp. 1181–1182.

31. Annual Report of the Commissioner of Indian Affairs, (1865), pp. 168–176.

32. Charles J. Kappler, comp., *Indian Affairs: Laws and Treaties,* 2 vols. (Washington, D.C., 1904), pp. 883–887, 896–908.

33. George Hyde, *Red Cloud's Folk: A History of the Oglala Sioux Indians* (Norman, Okla.: University of Oklahoma Press, 1957), pp. 135–139.

34. *O. R.,* ibid., part 1, Report of Maj. General Grenville Dodge, Nov. 1, 1865, pp. 335–366.

35. Annual Report of the Commissioner of Indian Affairs (1865), p. 211.

36. House Executive Document No. 5, 39th Congress, 2nd Session.

14. The Ride of Sam Brown

1. Edna LaMoore Waldo, *Dakota: An Informal Study of Territorial Days* (Caldwell, Idaho, 1936), pp. 284–298. Kingsbury, *History of Dakota Territory,* p. 466.

2. Robinson, *History of the Dakota or Sioux Indians,* p. 349.

3. Joseph Peters, "Indian Battles and Skirmishes on the American Frontier," Adjutant General's Chronological List (New York, 1966).

4. Ibid.

Epilogue

1. Robert Utley, *Frontier Regulars: The United States Army and the Indian, 1866–1890* (New York: Macmillan, 1973) pp. 93–107, 121–125.

2. John S. Gray, *Centennial Campaign: The Sioux War of 1876* (Norman, Okla.: University of Oklahoma Press, 1988), p. 287.

3. Wiley Sword, *President Washington's Indian War: The Struggle for the Old Northwest, 1790–1795* (Norman, Okla.: University of Oklahoma Press, 1985), p. 195.

Appendix A

1. Senate Executive Document No. 36, 30th Congress, 1st Session, pp. 6–7.

2. John Mahon, *History of the Second Seminole War, 1835–1842* (Gainesville, Fla.: University of Florida Press, 1967), p. 328.

Bibliography

Books

Adams, Alexander. *Sitting Bull*. New York: Putnam, 1973.

Anderson, Gary C. *Little Crow: Spokesman for the Sioux*. St. Paul: Minnesota Historical Society Press, 1986.

_____, and Alan R. Woolworth, eds. *Through Dakota Eyes: Narrative Accounts of the Minnesota Indian War of 1862*. St. Paul: Minnesota Historical Society Press, 1988.

Andrist, Ralph K. *The Long Death: the Last Days of the Plains Indians*. New York: Macmillan, 1967.

Athearn, Robert G. *Forts of the Upper Missouri*. Englewood Cliffs, New Jersey: Prentice-Hall, 1967.

Boatner, Mark M. *The Civil War Dictionary*. New York: David McKay, 1988.

Brown, D. Alexander. *The Galvanized Yankees*. Urbana, Illinois: University of Illinois Press, 1963.

Bryant, Charles S. *A History of the Great Massacre by the Sioux Indians in Minnesota*. Cincinnati: Rickey & Carroll, 1864.

Carley, Kenneth. *The Sioux Uprising of 1862*. St. Paul: Minnesota Historical Society Press, 1976.

Drips, J. H. *Three Years Among the Indians in Dakota*. New York: Sol Lewis, 1974.

Dunlay, Thomas W. *Wolves for the Blue Soldiers*. Lincoln: University of Nebraska Press, 1982.

Ellis, Richard N. *General Pope and U.S. Indian Policy*. Albuquerque: University of New Mexico Press, 1970.

Ewers, John C. *Teton Dakota History and Ethnology*. Washington D.C.: National Park Service, 1938.

Folwell, William W. *A History of Minnesota*, 2 vols. St. Paul: Minnesota Historical Society Press, 1924.

Fridley, Russell W., Leota M. Kellett, and June D. Holmquist, eds. *Charles E. Flandrau and the Defense of New Ulm*. New Ulm, Minnesota: Brown county Historical Society, 1962.

Fritz, Henry E. *The Movement for Indian Assimilation, 1860–1890*. Philadelphia: University of Pennsylvania Press, 1963.

Gardner, Abigail (as told to L. P. Lee), *History of the Spirit Lake Massacre*. New Britain, Conn., 1857.

Gray, John S. *Centennial Campaign: The Sioux War of 1876*. Norman, Oklahoma: University of Oklahoma Press, 1988.

Hafen, Leroy, and Ann Hafen, eds. *Powder River Campaigns and Sawyers Expedition of 1865*. Glendale, California: Arthur H. Clarke & Co., 1961.

Hamilton, James M. *From Wilderness to Statehood: A History of Montana, 1805–1900*. Portland, Oregon: Binfords and Mort, 1957.

Heard, Isaac V. D. *History of the Sioux War and Massacre of 1862 and 1863*. New York: Harper and Brothers, 1864.

Hyde, George E. *Red Cloud's Folk: A History of the Oglala Sioux Indians*. Norman, Oklahoma: University of Oklahoma Press, 1957.

Jones, Robert H. *The Civil War in the Northwest*. Norman, Oklahoma: University of Oklahoma Press, 1960.

Josephy, Alvin M. *The Civil War in the American West*. New York: Knopf, 1991.

Kelly, Fanny. *My Captivity Among the Sioux Indians*. New York: Corinth Books, 1962.

Kingsbury, George W. *History of Dakota Territory*. Chicago: S. J. Clarke, 1915.

Lamar, Howard R. *Dakota Territory, 1861–1899: A Study of Frontier Politics*. New Haven, Conn.: Yale University Press, 1956.

Lounsberry, Col. Clement A. *Early History of North Dakota*. Washington D.C.: Liberty Press, 1919.

Mahon, John. *History of the Second Seminole War, 1835–1842*. Gainesville, Florida: University of Florida Press, 1967.

McConkey, Harriet E. *Dakota War Whoop: Indian Massacre and War in Minnesota, 1862–63*. Minneapolis: Ross & Haines, 1970.

Meyer, Roy W. *History of the Santee Sioux: U.S. Indian Policy on Trial*. Lincoln: University of Nebraska Press, 1980.

Meyers, Augustus. *Ten Years in the Ranks, U.S. Army*. New York, 1914.

Myers, Frank. *Soldiering in Dakota Among the Indians in 1863–65*. Huron, Dakota Territory: Huron Printing Co., 1888.

National Park Service. *Soldier and Brave*. New York: Harper & Rowe, 1963.

Nelson, Bruce. *Land of the Dacotahs*. Minneapolis: University of Minnesota Press, 1950.

Nichols, David A. *Lincoln and the Indians*. Columbia, Missouri: University of Missouri Press, 1978.

Oehler, Charles M. *The Great Sioux Uprising*. New York: Oxford University Press, 1959.

Perret, Geoffrey. *A Country Made by War*. New York: Random House, 1989.

Riggs, Stephen R. *Mary and I: Forty Years with the Sioux*. Chicago, 1880.

_____. *Tah-Koo Wah-Kan; or, The Gospel Among the Dakotas*. Boston: Congregational Publishing Society, 1869.

Robinson, Doane. *A History of the Dakota or Sioux Indians*. Minneapolis: Ross & Haines, 1956.

Robinson, Elwyn B. *History of North Dakota*. Lincoln: University of Nebraska Press, 1966.

Sanford, Paul. *Sioux Arrows and Bullets*. San Antonio: Naylor, 1969.

Schultz, Duane. *Over the Earth I Come: The Great Sioux Uprising of 1862.* New York: St. Martins, 1992.

Schutz, Wallace, and Walter Trenerry. *Abandoned by Lincoln: The Military Biography of General John Pope.* Urbana, Illinois: University of Illinois Press, 1990.

Sifakis, Stewart. *Who Was Who in the Civil War.* New York: Facts on File Publications, 1988.

Steele, Matthew F. *American Campaigns*, 2 vols. Harrisburg, Pennsylvania: Military Service Publishing, 1949.

Sully, Landon. *No Tears for the General: A Biography of Alfred Sully.* Palo Alto, California: American West Publishing, 1974.

Sunder, John E. *The Fur Trade on the Upper Missouri, 1840–1865.* Norman, Oklahoma: University of Oklahoma Press, 1965.

Sword, Wiley. *President Washington's Indian War: The Struggle for the Old Northwest, 1790–1795.* Norman, Oklahoma: University of Oklahoma Press, 1985.

Teakle, Thomas. *The Spirit Lake Massacre.* Iowa City, Iowa, 1918.

Utley, Robert M. *Frontier Regulars: The United States Army and the Indian, 1866–1890.* New York: Macmillan, 1973.

_____. *Frontiersmen in Blue: The United States Army and the Indian, 1848–1865.* New York: Macmillan, 1967.

_____. *The Lance and the Shield: The Life and Times of Sitting Bull.* New York: Henry Holt, 1993.

Wakefield, Sarah F. *Six Weeks in the Sioux Tepees (Little Crow's Camp): A Narrative of Indian Captivity.* Shakopee, Minnesota, 1864.

Waldman, Carl. *Atlas of the North American Indian.* New York: Facts on File Publications, 1985.

Waldo, Edna LaMoore. *Dakota: An Informal Study of Territorial Days.* Caldwell, Idaho: Caxton Printers, 1936.

Wall, Joseph F. *Iowa: A Bicentennial History.* New York: Norton, 1978.

Wellman, Paul I. *The Indian Wars of the West.* Garden City, New York: Doubleday, 1947.

West, Nathaniel. *The Ancestry, Life, and Times of Henry Hastings Sibley.* St. Paul: Pioneer Press, 1889.

Williams, T. Harry. *Lincoln and His Generals.* New York: Grosset & Dunlap, 1952.

Articles

Babcock, Willoughby M. "Minnesota's Indian War." *Minnesota History*, vol. 38, no. 3 (September 1962).

Barsness, John, and William Dickinson. "The Sully Expedition of 1864." *Montana: The Magazine of Western History*, no. 16 (July 1966).

Bean, Geraldine. "General Alfred Sully and the Northwest Indian Expedition." *North Dakota History*, vol. 33, no. 3 (Summer 1966).

Buell, Salmon A. "Judge Flandrau in the Defense of New Ulm During the Sioux Outbreak of 1862." *Minnesota Historical Society*, vol. 10 (1900).

Carley, Kenneth, ed. "Chief Big Eagle's Story." *Minnesota History*, vol. 38, no. 3 (September 1962).

_____. "The Sioux Campaign of 1862: Sibley's Letters to His Wife." *Minnesota History*, vol. 38, no. 3 (September 1962).

Collins, Loren W. "The Expedition Against the Sioux Indians in 1863, under General Henry H. Sibley." *Glimpses of the Nation's Struggle*, (1901).

Cooper, Thomas E. "The Tom Holmes Expedition." *Montana Historical Society*.

Eggleston, Edward. "The Kit Carson of the Northwest." *Minnesota History*, vol. 33 (1957).

Ellis, Richard N. "Civilians, the Army, and the Indian Problem on the Northern Plains, 1862–1866." *North Dakota History*, vol. 37, no. 1 (Winter 1970).

English, Abner M. "Dakota's First Soldiers: History of the First Dakota Cavalry, 1862–1865." *South Dakota Historical Collections*, vol. 9 (1918).

"Expeditions of Captain James L. Fisk to the Gold Mines of Idaho and Montana, 1864–66." *North Dakota Historical Collections*, no. 2 (1908).

Gerber, Max. "The Steamboat and the Indian on the Upper Missouri." *South Dakota History*, vol. 4, no. 2 (Spring 1977).

Harlan, Edgar R. "Hostile Raid into Davis County, Iowa." *Annals of Iowa*, no. 13 (July 1922).

Harnack, Curtis. "Prelude to Massacre." *The Iowan*, vol. 4 (February/March 1956).

Hedren, Paul L. "On Duty at Fort Ridgely, Minnesota, 1853–1867." *South Dakota History*, vol. 7, no. 2 (Spring 1977).

Hilger, Nicholas. "General Alfred Sully's Expedition of 1864." *Montana Historical Society*, vol. 2 (1896).

Hoekman, Steven. "The History of Fort Sully." *South Dakota Historical Collections*, vol. 24 (1952).

"Iowa Troops in the Sully Campaigns." *Iowa Journal of History and Politics*, vol. 23, no. 3 (July 1922).

Jacobson, Clair. "A History of the Yanktonai and Hunkpatina Sioux." *North Dakota History*, vol. 47, no. 1 (Winter 1980).

Johnson, Roy P. "The Siege of Fort Abercrombie." *North Dakota History*, vol. 24, no. 1 (January 1957).

Kingsbury, David L. "Sully's Expedition Against the Sioux in 1864." *Minnesota Historical Collections*, vol. 8 (1898).

Lass, William E. "The Removal from Minnesota of the Sioux and Winnebago Indians." *Minnesota History* (December 1963).

Lingle, Ray W. "The Northwest Indian Expedition." *North Dakota History*, vol. 24, no. 4 (October 1957).

Mattison, Ray H., ed. "The Fisk Expedition of 1864: The Diary of William L. Larned." *North Dakota History*, vol. 36 (Summer 1969).

_____. "Fort Rice: North Dakota's first Missouri River Military Post." *North Dakota History*, vol. 20 (1953).

McKenzie, John H., and Giguere Owisime. "Capture of Little Six and Grey Iron in 1864." *Minnesota Historical Society* (February 1867).

"The Northwest Indian Expedition: The Sully Trial (1864) from the Little Missouri River to the Yellowstone River." *North Dakota History*, vol. 24 (October 1957).

Pfaller, Louis. "The Peace Mission of 1863–64." *North Dakota History*, vol. 37 (Fall 1970).

_____. "Sully's Expedition of 1864, Featuring the Killdeer Mountain and Badlands Battles." *North Dakota History*, vol. 31, no. 1 (January 1964).

Raymond, L. K. "Trip Over the Plains of Dakota in 1865." *North Dakota Historical Society Quarterly*, vol. 2, no. 3 (1928).

Robinson, Doane. "The Rescue of Francis Kelly." South Dakota Historical Collections, vol. 4 (1908).

Shambaugh, Benjamin F., ed. "Iowa Troops in the Sully Campaigns." *Iowa Journal of History*, vol. 20, no. 3 (July 1922).

"The Sibley Expedition." *Monthly South Dakotan* (October 1899).

"Sibley's Expedition of 1863." *The Record* (Fargo, June 1896).

"The Sibley Expedition." *Sisseton Courier* (September 30, 1992).

Steelye, W. E. "Early Military Experiences in Dakota." *North Dakota Historical Collections*, vol. 3 (1910).

"Story of Solomon Two Stars." *Monthly South Dakotan* (November 1900).

Trenerry, Walter N. "The Shooting of Little Crow: Heroism or Murder?" *Minnesota History* (September 1962).

Thomas, Col. M. T. "General Alfred Sully's Expedition of 1864: Battle with the Combined Tribes of Sioux Indians Among the Bad Lands of the Little Missouri." *Montana Historical Collections*, vol. 2 (1896).

Van Osdel, A. L. "The Sibley Expedition." *Monthly South Dakotan*, October 1899.

Ward, Dr. Joseph. "Life of Governor Newton Edmunds." *Monthly South Dakotan* (June 1898).

Welty, Raymond L. "The Frontier Army on the Missouri River, 1860–1870." *North Dakota Historical Society Quarterly*, vol. 2 (1928).

Wilson, Frederick T. "Old Fort Pierre and Its Neighbors." *South Dakota Historical Collections*, vol. 1 (1902).

Wright, Dana. "Military Trails in Dakota: The Fort Totten-Abercrombie Trail." *North Dakota History*, vol. 13, no. 3 (July 1946).

_____. "The Sibley Trail in North Dakota." *North Dakota Historical Society Quarterly*, vol. 1, no. 3 (1927).

Newspapers

Central Republican. Faribault, Minnesota, 1863.

Frontier Scout. Fort Rice, Dakota Territory.

St. Paul Pioneer. St. Paul, Minnesota.

St. Paul Press. St. Paul, Minnesota.

Weekly Dakotian. Yankton, Dakota Territory.

Diaries, Memoirs, Letters, etc.

André, Father Alexis, letters, St. Boniface Diocesan Archives.

Atkinson, James B., diary, North Dakota Historical Society.

Benedict, Gilbert (emigrant in the "Idaho Train"), diary, Montana Historical Society.

Brown, Samuel J., Brown Papers, Minnesota Historical Society.

Burnham, Captain J .W. (sergeant in 6th Minnesota Infantry), "Sibley's Expedition of 1863," memoirs, The Record (June 1896).

Campbell, George T. (8th Minnesota Infantry), Campbell Papers, Minnesota Historical Society.

Campbell, S. S. "Diary of S.S. Campbell of the 1864 Campaign." Fargo Forum, 1915.

Campbell, Walter S. (pseudonym, Stanley Vestal), "Interviews with White Bull," *Collections of Stanley Vestal*, University of Oklahoma, Boxes 105–106.

Daniels, Jared W. "General Sibley's Campaign, 1863." Daniels Papers, Minnesota Historical Society.

Doud, George W. (8th Minnesota Infantry), diary, Minnesota Historical Society.

Hagadorn, Henry, Jr., diary, North Dakota Historical Society Quarterly (November 1930).

King, James T., ed. "The Civil War of Private Morton." *North Dakota History*, no. 35 (Winter 1968).

King, J. R. "A Synopsis of the Origins and Movements of the Sully Indian Expedition in the Summer of 1863." Box 33, Folder 1, *Orin G. Libby Collections*, North Dakota Historical Society.

Marshall, Col. William R. "Journal of the Military Expedition Against the Sioux Indians from Camp Pope in the Summer of 1863 under the command of Brig. General Henry Hastings Sibley." Manuscript Division, Minnesota Historical Society.

_____. "Narrative of the 1863 Campaign." *St. Paul Press* (August 15, 1863).

Mooers, Sgt. Calvin (Hatch's Battalion), diary, Minnesota Historical Society.

Morton, Pvt. Thomas (7th Minnesota Infantry), letters, *North Dakota Historical Collections*.

Pattee, John. "Dakota Campaigns." *South Dakota Historical Collections*, vol. 5 (1910).

Paxson, Lewis C., diary, *North Dakota Historical Collections*, vol. 4, no. 2.

Rice, Ebenezer, diary, Minnesota Historical Society.

Robinson, J. E., letters, Minnesota Historical Society.

Sibley, Henry Hastings "Reminiscences, Historical and Personal." *Minnesota Historical Collections*, vol. 1 (1870).

_____. Sibley Papers, Minnesota Historical Society.

Spencer, Pvt. Milton "The Letters of Pvt. Milton Spencer, 1862–65: A Soldier's View of Military Life on the Northern Plains." *North Dakota History* (Fall 1970).

Strong, John H., diary, Minnesota Historical Society.

Sully, Alfred E. *Sully Papers*, Box 2, Folder 54, Beinicke Library, Yale University.

Wall, Oscar H., diary, *Roy P. Johnson Collection*, File 2, Minnesota Historical Society.

Williams, J. Fletcher, ed., "Memoir of General Henry H. Sibley." *Minnesota Historical Collections*, vol. 6 (1894).

Government Documents

Adjutant General's Report, Executive Document, 1863.

Annual Reports of the Commissioner of Indian Affairs, 1862–65.

Annual Reports of the Secretary of the Interior, 1862–65.

Annual Reports of the Secretary of War, 1861–65.

Ashburn, P.M. A History of the Medical Department of the United States Army. Boston, Mass., 1929.

Coolidge, Richard H. Statistical Report on the Sickness and Mortality in the Army of the United States (1839–55), Senate Executive Document, 34th Congress, 1st Session, No. 96.

Heitman, Francis B. *Historical Register and Dictionary of the United States Army, 1789–1903.* House Executive Document, 57th Congress, 2nd Session, No. 446, 1902–03.

Kappler, Charles J., comp. *Indian Affairs: Laws and Treaties.* 2 vols. Washington D.C., 1904.

Minnesota Board of Commissioners. *Minnesota in the Civil and Indian Wars, 1861–65*, vol. 1, *Regimental Histories.* St. Paul: Pioneer Press, 1893.

_____. *Minnesota in the Civil and Indian Wars, 1861–65*, vol. 2, *Official Reports and Correspondence,* St. Paul: Pioneer Press, 1893.

Miscellaneous House and Senate Executive Documents.

"Official Correspondence Pertaining to the War of the Outbreak, 1862–1865." *South Dakota Historical Collections*, vol. 8 (1916).

Peters, Joseph P., comp. "Indian Battles and Skirmishes on the American Frontier." *Adjutant General's Chronological List.* New York, 1966.

"Report of Governor Newton Edmunds." Dakota Superintendent, September 20, 1864.

"Reports of Henry Reed and S. N. Latta." U.S. Indian agents, June 11, 1863, August 16, 1863, August 27, 1863.

"Report of the Joint Committee Investigating the Condition of the Indian Tribes." Senate Executive Document, 39th Congress, 2nd Session, no. 156 (Serial 1279), 1865–66.

"Report of Maj. General John Pope." *Supplemental Report of the Joint Commission on the Conduct of the War,* vol. 2, 1865.

Sisseton and Wahpeton Claim Case Record, Defendants' Brief and Arguments, Minnesota Historical Society.

Sully, Alfred. "Expedition of Brig. General Sully Against the Northwest Indians." House Executive Document, 38th Congress, 1st Session, no. 1 (Serial 1184), 1863–64.

"Suppression of Indian Hostilities." House Executive Document, 39th Congress, 2nd Session, vol. 5, no. 5 (Serial 1287), 1866.

Swanton, John R. *The Indian Tribes of North America.* Bureau of American Ethnology Bulletin 145, Washington D.C., 1952.

U.S. Senate Records of Sioux War Trials of 1862. Record Group 46, National Archives, Washington D.C.

U.S. Statutes. Vol. 10, 1854.

U.S. War Department. *The War of the Rebellion: A Compilation of the Official Records of the Union and Confederate Armies.* Series 1, vols. 13, 22, 34, 41, 48, Washington D.C., 1880–1901.

"Wagon Road from Niobara to Virginia City." House Executive Document, 39th Congress, 1st Session, vol. 8, no. 58 (Serial 1256), 1866.

Index